Learning to Teach Grammar

by Simon Haines

Picture credits:
55:4; 71 Shutterstock (Here), New York; **179; 212** © Glynn Thomas; **139: 3, 5; 140: 1** Shutterstock (ahmad agung wijayanto), New York; **21.1** Shutterstock (Anna Om), New York; **21.2** Shutterstock (MPH Photos), New York; **22.1** Shutterstock (Ilan Derech), New York; **22.2** Shutterstock (PRASHANT VAIDYA), New York; **30** Shutterstock (Framework Wonderland), New York; **31** Shutterstock (Milles Vector Studio), New York; **37** Alamy (Granger, NYC), Abingdon, UK; **42** Shutterstock (Everett Historical), New York; **49.1** Getty Images (Jacobs Stock Photography), München; **87: 3; 106: 7** Shutterstock (Andrey_Popov), New York; **139: 2, 4; 140: 2** Shutterstock (Julia Khimich), New York; **194: 1, 3** Shutterstock (Isuaneye), New York; **172: 7; 177: 5** Shutterstock (Koldunova Anna), New York; **172: 6; 177: 4** Shutterstock (Shvaygert Ekaterina), New York; **172: 5; 177: 3** Shutterstock (Sharomka), New York; **172: 4; 177: 2** Shutterstock (Maxx-Studio), New York; **172: 3; 177: 1** Shutterstock (udra11), New York; **172: 2; 176: 2** Shutterstock (AsexuaL), New York; **172: 1;176: 1** Shutterstock (MarcelClemens), New York; **194: 2, 4** Shutterstock (Stephen Marques), New York; **178: 1; 183** Shutterstock (Picsfive), New York; **49.2** Shutterstock (Dusan Milenkovic), New York; **49.3** Getty Images (AndreyPopov), München; **55.1** Getty Images (mmac72), München; **55.2** Shutterstock (Silvia Pascual), New York; **55.3** Getty Images (Marc Bruxelle), München; **58.2** Shutterstock (Pixel Embargo), New York; **58.3** Shutterstock (mhatzapa), New York; **70.1** Bruce Dale/National Geographic Creative; **70.2** Shutterstock (PaulWong), New York; **80** Shutterstock (fizkes), New York; **87.1** Shutterstock (SpeedKingz), New York; **87.2** Shutterstock (Alexandru Nika), New York; **87.4** Getty Images (franckreporter), München; **87.5** Shutterstock (Africa Studio), New York; **88.1** Shutterstock (Artsplav), New York; **88.2** Shutterstock (PK Studio), New York; **88.3** Shutterstock (sirtravelalot), New York; **88.4** Shutterstock (Rawpixel.com), New York; **88.5** Shutterstock (Alexander Raths), New York; **88.6** 123RF.com (Volodymyr Melnyk), Nidderau; **90** Ingram Image, London; **98** Shutterstock (Marco Brockmann), New York; **106.1** Getty Images (Dave & Les Jacobs), München; **106.2** Shutterstock (Jaguar PS), New York; **106.3** Shutterstock (Luis Molinero), New York; **106.4** Shutterstock (pathdoc), New York; **106.5** Getty Images (SolStock), München; **106.6** Getty Images (Dougal Waters), München; **106.8** Shutterstock (Mega Pixel), New York; **107.9** Shutterstock (bejo), New York; **117** Shutterstock (Mascha Tace), New York; **122.1** Shutterstock (bmphotographer), New York; **122.2** Shutterstock (IrenaV), New York; **122.3** Shutterstock (Richie Chan), New York; **122.4** Shutterstock (Nicholas Grey), New York; **122.5** Shutterstock (S.Borisov), New York; **122.6** Shutterstock (Martin M303), New York; **122.7** Shutterstock (titipongpwl), New York; **122.8** Shutterstock (Pius Lee), New York; **122.9** Shutterstock (Rajdeep Matharu), New York; **122.10** Shutterstock (byvalet), New York; **122.11** Shutterstock (trevor kittelty), New York; **122.12** Shutterstock (Viacheslav Lopatin), New York; **122.13** Shutterstock (E. O.), New York; **122.14** Shutterstock (Hung Chung Chih), New York; **122.15** Shutterstock (photo.ua), New York; **122.16** Shutterstock (David Ionut), New York; **122.17** Shutterstock (Ilonde van), New York; **122.18** Shutterstock (f11photo), New York; **122.19** Shutterstock (sdecoret), New York; **122.20** Shutterstock (Christian Draghici), New York; **123** Shutterstock (Best Vector Elements), New York; **132.1** Shutterstock (Africa Studio), New York; **132.2** Shutterstock (Victoria 1), New York; **133.1** Shutterstock (IR Stone), New York; **133.2** Shutterstock (Norbert9), New York; **134.1** Shutterstock (Serg Zastavkin), New York; **134.2** Shutterstock (GuoZhongHua), New York; **139.1** Shutterstock (Olivier Le Moal), New York; **140.3** Shutterstock (johavel), New York; **154.1** Shutterstock (Rawpixel.com), New York; **154.2** Shutterstock (Africa Studio), New York; **159.1** Shutterstock (Denis Makarenko), New York; **159.2** Shutterstock (Kathy Hutchins), New York; **159.3** Shutterstock (David Peterlin), New York; **159.4** Shutterstock (Shaun Jeffers), New York; **159.5** Shutterstock (Tinseltown), New York; **159.6** Shutterstock (Tinseltown), New York; **159.7** Shutterstock (Leonard Zhukovsky), New York; **159.8** Shutterstock (Andrea Raffin), New York; **160** Shutterstock (Katarinanh), New York; **162.2** Shutterstock (KatarinaF), New York; **168.1** Shutterstock (Jeremy Bentham), New York; **168.2** Shutterstock (Pete Burana), New York; **168.3** Shutterstock (Dino Osmic), New York; **178.2** Shutterstock (tovovan), New York; **181** @Glen Baxter; **181** @Glen Baxter; **185.1** Shutterstock (NadineVeresk), New York; **186.1** CartoonStock.com (Burns, Shannon), Bath; **186.2** CartoonStock.com (Madden, Chris), Bath; **186.3** CartoonStock.com (Bucella, Marty), Bath; **186.4** CartoonStock.com (Baloo -Rex May-), Bath; **187, 197** Shutterstock (springsky), New York; **189** Shutterstock (Air Art), New York; **190** Shutterstock (Cheryl Casey), New York; **195** Shutterstock (ideyweb), New York; **196.1** Shutterstock (aijaphoto), New York; **5; 58: 1** Ingram Image, London

Download the free DELTA Augmented app onto your device

Open the app and select the cover.

Start picture recognition and scan the **first page** of this book.

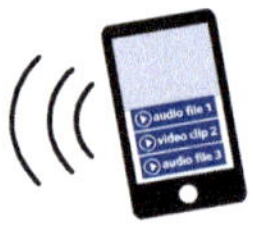

Download the digital material and use it now or save it for later.

1st edition 1 5 4 3 2 1 | 2024 23 22 21 20

The last figure shown denotes the year of impression.

Delta Publishing, 2020
www.deltapublishing.co.uk

Editor: Astrid Proctor, Stuttgart, Germany
Cover: Andreas Drabarek, Stuttgart, Germany
Layout: Greta Gröttrup, Hamburg
Illustrations: Greta Gröttrup, Hamburg
Printing and binding: Elanders GmbH, Anton-Schmidt-Str. 15, 71332 Waiblingen, Deutschland

ISBN 978-3-12-501628-6

Contents

I Introduction 4

II The Grammar 16

01 Talking about now – The present 16

02 Looking back – The past 32

03 Linking the present and the past – The present perfect 44

04 Looking forward – The future 58

05 Shades of meaning – Modal verbs 72

06 What if? – Conditionals 90

07 Who does what? – The passive 108

08 People, places, things and abstract ideas – Nouns 124

09 Describing people, things and actions – Adjectives and adverbs . 142

10 Making connections – Connecting sentences 162

III Consolidation 178

IV Glossaries 198
- Grammar / Vocabulary
- Methodology

V Key to the consolidation exercises 212

Introduction

I have taught the grammar element on initial teacher training courses for many years. Colleagues often wonder how I am able to go on teaching the same thing year after year. My answer is simple: *I don't do the same thing year after year*. This is for two important reasons. Firstly, no two groups of trainees are the same, so like any thinking teacher, what I teach is related to the level, experience and personalities of the people I'm teaching as well as to the course syllabus. Secondly, following each course, I ask trainees for any comments or suggestions they may have on how my programme could be improved. The end result of these two factors is that every course I teach is different.

Having said that, there have been noticeable similarities between groups over the years. Most significantly from my point of view is that many trainees, especially native speakers of English, have feelings of inadequacy when it comes to their knowledge of the grammar itself. Because of this, the prospect of their teaching grammar fills them with feelings which range from mild insecurity to downright terror. Underlying these feeling is the common misconception that teaching grammar is the main or even the only element in an English language syllabus for speakers of other languages. They are often completely unaware of the importance of other elements such as functions of language, vocabulary, register, discourse and the development of skills.

In order to discover something about a new group of trainee's attitudes, I ask them a very simple question: *How do you feel about English grammar?* The answers to this question are revealing …

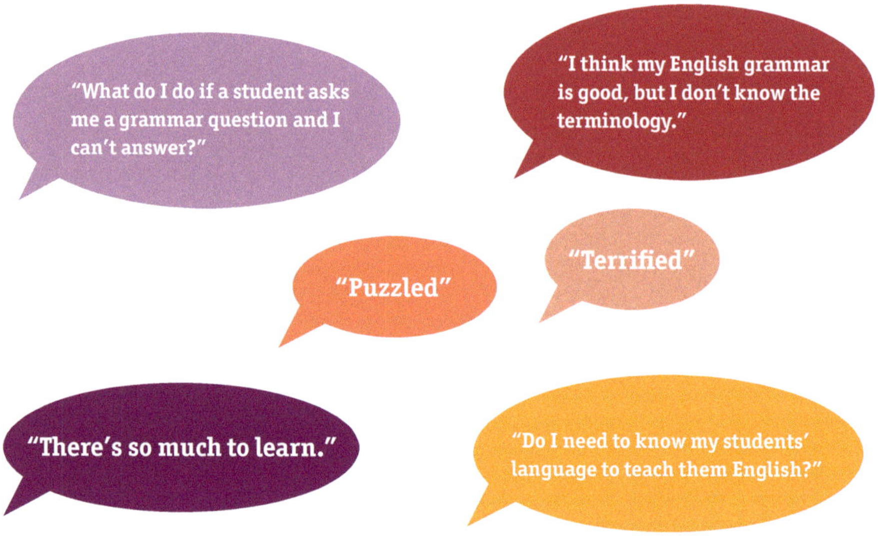

> **"Grammar is the greatest joy in life, don't you find?"**
>
> (Lemony Snicket)

I should perhaps point out that these answers were all given by trainees who were native speakers of English. Many non-native speakers who have learnt English as a second or foreign language are more knowledgeable about the grammar itself, but rarely more confident about teaching it for the first time.

I tell trainees that my ambition on the course is to teach them to love grammar and not to be afraid of teaching it. While I have had some notable successes, I can't pretend there haven't been failures.

My top tips

for easing troubled trainees' fears about grammar

1 There's more to language than just grammar

Mastering grammar is only one element of learning a language. There are many others, including functions, register, skills, vocabulary, pronunciation. These elements combine with grammar to enable students to understand spoken and written English and to communicate effectively in the language.

2 Don't be obsessed with terminology

By obsessing, trainees are in danger of losing sight of the end goal of language teaching – to help students to *use language*. It is quite possible to teach and learn a language without using any grammatical terminology at all. I give them the example of a 17-year old Danish student I once taught. She was by far the most fluent and accurate student in one of my advanced groups, but after a pre-exam revision class she stayed behind when the others had gone and asked somewhat sheepishly *Do I need to know words like verb, noun or present continuous for the exam? I don't know what they mean.* She had become a fluent speaker and writer of English without having come across any terminology. This, after all, is how most of us become fluent and accurate users of our own first language.

3 You don't need to know everything

Most teachers don't know the answers to all the questions students might ask. If you don't know the answer to a question, don't pretend by giving an answer you're not sure about. Offer to find out the answer and get back to the student. The key is to be familiar with the basics and to know where to find information that you're not sure of. In addition to a coursebook you may be using with your students, there are dozens of grammar reference books at a variety of levels and with a variety of emphases.

4 Practice trumps exposition

It is important to resist the temptation to spend too long *explaining* grammar. For some students understanding rules is interesting, but most prefer to spend time *practising* using language. Many teachers now doubt the link between the understanding of a grammatical rule and the ability of students to apply that rule in their use of language, particularly speech. Remember your main aim is to teach the language not talk about the language. With this in mind, avoid spending too much class time answering one student's question which might be of little or no interest to the rest of the class. Instead, try always to put the emphasis on language use.

Here's an extreme example of this problem from an intermediate level class of mine: It was five minutes before lunch and one of my students asked: *Please could you go through the differences between the past tenses in English?* While it was very tempting simply to answer *No,* I assured the student that we would be revising past tenses the following week and that this would probably take us several lessons.

5 Students will continue to make mistakes

"I've been going over the present simple for two weeks now and some of my students still forget to put the -s on the he and she forms." It may be hard to accept this, but just because you have taught something, it doesn't mean that students will automatically be able to use it correctly. Don't be surprised if students continue making mistakes even after you've taught something several times. What makes the difference is students being exposed to and being given the chance to practise using the grammar in question.

6 Authentic, personalized contexts are the way to go

Grammar should be presented to students in ways which make sense to them. This may be through contexts or via themes where the target language occurs naturally. Where possible this should be of personal interest to students themselves or of some relevance to them and their lives. For example, if you are teaching the use of the present simple to talk about daily routines, get students to practise using this form in relation to their own personal, domestic situation.

What is *Learning to Teach Grammar*?

Who is this book for?

It is mainly for teachers in training and recently qualified teachers, but may also be of use to teachers looking for ideas or for anyone who doesn't feel comfortable teaching grammar. The main aim is to help you not be afraid of teaching grammar, and to realize that, with the right preparation, it can be fun.

What are you going to get out of the book?

Familiarity with some of the main elements of English grammar and the confidence to present grammar to students in a way which is effective and means something to them. Following each grammar section, there will be suggestions for suitable natural contexts in which this grammar can be presented and practised.

Don't expect the book to be a comprehensive grammar reference. Most sections focus on specific aspects of the verb tense system simply because this forms the backbone of most coursebook syllabuses you are likely to teach from.

Each section presents an area of grammar in as simple and straightforward a way as possible; not every facet of each point or every exception to rules are listed or examined. Examples are consistently used to illustrate rules or patterns presented. Terminology is used and there is a glossary of terms, but, as suggested earlier, terminology should be seen as a useful shorthand not the be-all and end-all of teaching English. Don't think that simply knowing the terminology will enable you to teach grammar successfully.

How does the book work?

This book comprises an introduction, ten grammar units and a glossary of terms.

Each of the 10 units of grammar consists of the following four sections (all examples here are taken from Unit 3 *Linking the present and the past* (page 44) – the first three sections illustrate the grammar point's form and use, while the final section focuses on the teaching of the grammar point.

How to recognize it presents initial examples in context of the grammar point of the unit and asks readers to think about its use and meaning. Realizing that one does in fact recognize a particular grammar form and is able to notice its structures and uses and understand why we use it the way we do is a first step in shaking off the fear of teaching grammar.

How to recognize it

Look at the cartoon and choose the verb forms in 1-4 which sound more natural in this context. Consider why.

How to use it gives details of the form itself – a brief overview of the basic rules, as it were.

How to use it

	present perfect simple *= have / has + past participle*	**present perfect continuous** *= have been / has been + present participle*
affirmative (+)	*I / You / We / They* ***have worked*** *hard today.* *He / She* ***has worked*** *hard today.*	*I / You / We / They* ***have been playing*** *tennis.* *He / She* ***has been playing*** *tennis.*
negative (-)	*I / You / We / They* ***haven't worked*** *hard today.* *He / She* ***hasn't worked*** *hard today.*	*I / You / We / They* ***haven't been playing*** *tennis.* *He / She* ***hasn't been playing*** *tennis.*
question (?)	***Have*** *I / you / we / they* ***worked*** *hard today?* ***Has*** *he / she* ***worked*** *hard today?*	***Have*** *I / you / we / they* ***been playing*** *tennis?* ***Has*** *he / she* ***been playing*** *tennis?*

When to use it lists some of the common uses of the grammar point and suggests possible teaching contexts and themes related to these uses.

When to use it

Present perfect simple / continuous	Possible teaching contexts / themes, with examples
to refer to completed past actions without specifying a time	**Making arrangements to go on holiday to a new place / see a particular film etc.** *Shall we go to Greece? — No,* ***I've already been*** *there.* *How about Egypt? — Yes, ok,* ***I've never been*** *there.* **Talking about superlatives** *What's the most expensive thing* ***you've ever bought****?* *What the funniest film* ***you've ever seen****?*

The **simple form** is used to refer to **actions.** The continuous form emphasizes the **duration of the action.** In many but not all instances the continuous form refers to recent and short-lived events or actions.

Some of the ideas listed in this section are further developed in the **Suggested classroom activities section** (see below) or may even form part of the **sample lesson plan** (see right) for this unit. In such cases there will be a cross reference.

to refer to past happenings which have an effect on the present	**Recent local, national and international news stories with continuing repercussions** ***It's been raining*** *non-stop for the last 24 hours causing widespread flooding.* ***There's been*** *an explosion in the city centre. Three people* ***have died*** *and many others* ***have been injured****.* **Your life in the last year** *How* ***have you earned / spent*** *your money?* ***Have you taken up*** *any new hobbies or sports?*

See lesson plan 3.

At this point, most chapters include a **Good to know** section in which related grammar points are noted. In Unit 3, for example, the focus is on time adverbs typically used with present perfect simple and continuous verbs, for example *already, never, just, yet* etc.

Good to know

How to teach it is a section in three parts:

- **Practical matters** are general notes on specific issues related to the grammar point of the chapter: when the best time is to introduce the form, points to emphasize when teaching it, how best to distinguish between various tenses when teaching them etc.
- **What to watch out for** lists some of the problems or difficulties learners may have when learning the grammar point: typical mistakes learners make, first language interference, potential pitfalls etc.
- **Suggestions for classroom activities** lists ten possible classroom activities for presenting and practising the grammar point of the chapter. These are free standing activities rather than whole lesson plans, though some are further developed and are more detailed than others.

3 Topic Interesting experiences
Language Present perfect simple vs past simple
Activities Learners interview each other about interesting things they've done (in their lives) and then find out more information. Sample conversation:

A *So tell me the most interesting place* ***you've been to****?*
B ***I've been*** *to Brazil.*
A *Cool, when* ***did you go*** *to Brazil?*
B ***I went*** *there in 2016.*
A *How* ***did you get*** *there?*
B ***I flew.***

Each activity includes the headings **Topic, Language, Activities**. Some activities may be included as part of the sample lesson plan related to the chapter.

For each of the 10 units of grammar there is also a sample lesson plan as well as worksheets.

Lesson plans

Each grammar unit has a related lesson plan which presents and practises the grammar point of the unit. Different commonly used grammar lesson structures are illustrated by these plans (see page 14 for more details). These include:

- Presentation → Practice → Production (**PPP**)
- Engage → Study → Activate (**ESA**)
- Test → Teach → Test (**TTT**)
- Authentic → Restricted → Clarifying (**ARC**)
- Pre → While → Post (for skills lessons which include a focus on grammar)

These plans are primarily given as examples of lesson types and are not aimed at specific levels of learners. Neither is a length of time specified for these lessons. There are circumstances in which these plans could be used in real classes, but teachers should be prepared to adapt and re-order materials and activities to suit the level, interests and prior knowledge of their learners.

Worksheets

There are two copiable worksheets for each grammar unit:

- a **sample worksheet** (e.g. WS 3.1) that can be used in conjunction with the lesson plan related to that unit. This is clearly aimed at learners. The **key** to activities on these worksheets can be found in the lesson plans.
- a **consolidation worksheet** (e.g. WS 3 C) that provides extra back-up activities for teachers themselves. Most of these sections include short authentic texts incorporating the grammar point. The consolidation worksheets are provided en bloc together from page 178. The **key** to activities on these worksheets can be found from page 212.
- If teachers decide to use these consolidation activities with their own classes, they may need to adapt them to make them more appropriate to students' age, level or interests.

Digital material

Some of the worksheets include listening comprehensions. The audio tracks are available for download via the DELTA Augmented app (available for iOS and Android) for free. Simply scan the title page of this book to download or stream the tracks. You will also find all the photos used as examples in the grammar units there. For more information see page 2.

Teaching grammar

The challenges

In relation to your function as teacher

- *overcoming lack of knowledge*
- *overcoming lack of confidence*

In relation to students' needs

- *contextualizing and personalizing the language in ways that mean something to students*
- *presenting new grammar in interesting, enjoyable, non-threatening ways*
- *stressing the functional value – the practical usefulness – of grammatical structures*
- *providing realistic useful practice activities in which new language is used for clear and specific purposes*
- *achieving the dual aim of accuracy and fluency – usually via controlled and freer practice activities*

Initial considerations

Before you start, consider these points!

Learner backgrounds: What problems are your learners likely to experience in relation to a particular point of grammar? When learning English, learners may experience particular problems caused by "first language interference". This means they assume that English is similar to their own language and thereby make errors. For example some languages do not have articles *(a/an, the)*. Teaching these learners when to use which article – definite or indefinite – can be very tricky because this is not an issue in their own language. Typically, students with such first languages simply do not use articles at all.

Existing knowledge: What do your learners already know? Do all the learners in the class have the same level of knowledge?

Objectives: Why are your learners learning a language? It could be for everyday use, for example as a tourist, because they are hoping to work in an English-speaking situation, for a specific type of work, for an exam or just for interest.

Scope: What do learners need to know? This will depend on why they are learning.

The FAQs

"How is language broken down for teaching purposes?"

The traditional and most common way of breaking language down for teaching purposes is by **word class**. Nouns, verbs, adjectives etc. are word classes. Each class can be further broken down, for example:

- **nouns** *can be singular or plural; countable or uncountable*
- **verbs** *can be simple or continuous; transitive or intransitive*; *active or passive*
- **adjectives** can be *basic, comparative* or *superlative; gradable* or *ungradable*

However the other way of organizing language sometimes used by course designers and teachers is by **function**. This approach breaks language down according to the particular purposes for which it is being used. So we may teach the language used to ask for or give advice, to talk about past experiences etc.

Syllabuses which take functions into account usually also teach the grammar needed to realize these functions. For example:

Function	Exponents	Related grammar
Giving advice	*If I were you, I'd take up a new sport.*	Second conditional structures
	You should do more exercise.	Modal verbs + base form
Talking about experiences	*I've climbed Mount Everest twice.* *I climbed Mount Everest last in 2017.*	Contrast between present perfect and past simple verb forms

These are sometimes called "integrated syllabuses" and may also incorporate a systematic approach to teaching lexis (vocabulary).

"What grammar point are you aiming to teach in a particular lesson?"

This apparently simple question can be difficult to answer. The syllabus you are using as a teacher may provide you with a straightforward answer (for example, *present simple*), but the next question might be *Which parts of the present simple?* The affirmative form, the negative form, the Wh-question form, the Yes/No question form.

"How much do your learners need to know?"

You could say that in the long term your learners need to know everything, but teaching all parts of a particular verb form might take many lessons. The way of answering this question is to focus on the word *need*. There are some points of grammar that most students don't actually **need** to know at all in relation to their future situations. The most satisfactory answer to this question would probably be *It depends on why learners are learning the language and what they are going to use it for.* For example, it could be argued that learners do not need to know *will* when used to refer to typical, routine behaviour. For example: *Most weekdays I'll get up at 6.00 and leave home at 7.00. I'll get home around 8.00pm, have something to eat and then I'll go straight to bed.* Yet this is a very common structure among native speakers of English often used instead of the present simple. So maybe we *should* be teaching it.

"When do we use the structure in English?"

It is important that when we present a new grammar point or structure to learners, that structure is seen in a realistic situation. This may be via an audio recording, a film clip, a reading text or a teacher-led conversation. It should be clear that the structure is being used naturally in the situation. For example, take the structure *used to* which is commonly used to talk about past routines and habits that no longer occur. A realistic situation in which *used to* could be presented is a conversation in which adults reminisce about their childhood:

A *What did you use to do after school?*
B *As soon as I got home, I used to have a snack and then watch telly.*
A *I used to do my homework before I watched telly.*
C *I didn't use to watch telly at all during the week. I was only allowed to watch it at the weekends.*

"What can go wrong when teaching this structure?"

Certain problems are predictable when teaching a particular structure to certain students. The problem may relate to difficulties intrinsic to the point of grammar itself; for example getting over the difference in meaning and use of *must* and *have to* to talk about obligation. Or it may relate to differences between English and a learner's first language; for example the difference in use between the present perfect in English and the *passé composé* in French. In these cases, the teacher can be ready for the difficulties which may arise, but there are other things that can go wrong without warning. In monolingual classes such problems may be common to most or all students, whereas in multilingual classes problems are more difficult to predict.

"How can you avoid these problems?"

If problems can be predicted by teachers, they can prepare strategies to deal with them. Here are a few:

- Make sure you have lots of examples of the structure in everyday use. Use these examples where possible to get students to work out a pattern or rule for themselves. Avoid the temptation to resort to technical explanations using grammatical terminology. This approach may work for a small number of students but can also compound the problem.
- Sometimes simply exposing students to grammatically correct language in natural contexts and then getting them to use that language for themselves, correcting them as needed will prevent the problem from arising in the first place.

"Who are you teaching the structure to?"

The age, level, previous language learning experience and general educational background of learners may affect how and what you teach. In many instances, the school will have chosen a coursebook or syllabus which incorporates the language they wish their students to learn. The syllabus or coursebook for school students may be chosen by a government education department in the case of state education systems, or by the staff of private schools catering for adults. In situations where you as a teacher can choose what to teach, it is possible to devise a grammar syllabus which suits your particular students.

"Why are you teaching the structure?"

This is a question many teachers and probably their learners ask themselves as they work through their English course. The true answer may well be "because it's there in the coursebook". What teachers would like to be able to say is "because this structure is an element of language you will need in order to be able to communicate effectively in English" It is often difficult to see how any specific language structure will be needed in the future, and this is why classroom activities should involve using new structures in meaningful contexts, that is contexts which resemble real life as closely as possible. This is the rationale underlying integrated language syllabuses in which grammatical structures are presented in functional or situational settings.

How can grammar be taught?

This is a huge question and one which has absorbed teachers and academics for decades if not centuries. When I myself learnt French and German in the 1950s and 1960s in a British secondary school, the so-called **Grammar-Translation** approach ruled the day. I learnt about French and German grammar and proved this by translating from English into French or German and vice versa. Much classroom time was spent reading and writing, but almost no attention was devoted to speaking, the commonest form of everyday communication. I knew how to construct the subjunctive form of French verbs, but when I tried to buy a train ticket at Gare du Nord in Paris on my first visit to France, I couldn't make myself understood. A few years later, when I first started teaching, the **Audio-lingual / Audio-visual** approach was in vogue. It had been decided that pupils should be able to speak – yes speak! – language that sounded natural and was grammatically accurate, so a large proportion of classroom time was spent on oral drills – getting pupils to look at pictures or watch filmclips and repeat phrases related to them. Many secondary schools had language laboratories where students sat with headphones on repeating what they heard to improve their pronunciation or doing mindless, meaningless drills to prove they could manipulate a structure correctly. Sadly, though, little attention was paid to when and why this language could be used in real-life situations.

Around the late 1970s and early 1980s, these two methods more or less disappeared as various versions of the **Communicative approach** took over. Teachers realized that most of their learners wanted, in fact needed, to be able to use the language in its spoken and written forms. This realization has meant that for the last 40 years or so there has been a general consensus about the main purpose of teaching and learning languages. Although there are different ways in which the communicative approach has been interpreted and practised, this consensus continues to dominate and has also led to broad agreement about the place of grammar in language teaching. This has affected syllabus design, coursebooks and teacher training. Because functional language is now considered as important as grammar, the two are frequently integrated. It is rare to find a point of grammar being taught simply because it is there, without attention being paid to how and when it is used for communicative purposes. For example, the two future verb forms, *will* and *going to* are often taught as a contrasting pair of structures in the context of predictions and intentions. Teaching a verb form out of context would now seem pointless. The practical objective of this twin focus on form (grammar) and meaning (function) is to develop both grammatical accuracy and communicative fluency in learners.

In recent years, the **Lexical approach** has appeared. This advocates the idea that vocabulary could be the organizing principle underpinning a language teaching syllabus. This would involve basing a teaching programme on high-frequency vocabulary, idioms, collocations and chunks of formulaic language. So far, however, this approach has not led to the widespread use of systematically organized teaching material.

A related and logical development of the joint focus on form and meaning is the importance of introducing new language in the context of topics or themes which engage learners' interest. We have finally realized that very few students are interested in a language and its rules for their own sake, but we have a good chance of gaining learners' interest by choosing a topic which interests them and then finding ways to personalize the topic in some way so that it is relevant to learners' own lives.

Lesson structures

The general agreement on what is an appropriate approach to language teaching has brought with it a number of commonly used lesson structures. Adaptations of these structures often form the basis of teaching sequences in published coursebook materials as well as in individual lessons designed by teachers themselves. Significantly each of these methodologies divides lessons into three parts where ...

- the first part introduces new language or checks what learners already know

- the second part studies or clarifies the target language
- the third part provides learners with practice in using the target language correctly and appropriately, firstly in a controlled way and then more freely.

Here are some of the more commonly used lesson structures (there is a sample lesson based on these three-part lesson structures, for each unit of grammar in the book):

PPP **Presentation → Practice → Production** (e.g. lesson plan in Unit 4)

- ▶ **Presentation** is the stage at which a new target grammar point is presented to learners.
- ▶ **Practice** is the stage during which learners use the target language in a controlled way, maybe via oral or written drills.
- ▶ **Production** is a freer practice stage in which learners are given opportunities to use the target language in a more natural way. This might be a role play or a game which allows or encourages the use of the target language without forcing it and sometimes in a different context.

ARC **Authentic → Restricted → Clarifying** (e.g. lesson plan in Unit 7)

Rather than prescribing a sequence of stages, this system classifies activities according to their purpose:

- ▶ **Authentic** – activities in which language is used for realistic purposes. This could be a speaking activity which includes the target language, or learners listening to part of a radio programme.
- ▶ **Restricted** – activities in which learners practise the target language in a controlled way.
- ▶ **Clarifying** – activities which help students become aware of and understand patterns or rules underlying the target language.

ESA **Engage → Study → Activate** (e.g. lesson plan in Unit 8)

- ▶ **Engage** is the stage in which the target language is introduced in a way which captures learners' interest. Interesting topics may be chosen as the vehicle to contextualize the grammar.
- ▶ **Study** is the stage which focuses more overtly on the form and pattern of the target language and provides an initial controlled activity.
- ▶ **Activate** is the stage during which learners are given opportunities to use the target language in a less controlled and more meaningful context.

TTT **Test → Teach → Test** (e.g. lesson plan in Unit 5)

- ▶ **Test (1)** is the stage in which the teacher can find out, via a practical task, how well learners are able to use a specific language point.
- ▶ **Teach** in which the teacher teaches the language which students need to perform the task more effectively.
- ▶ **Test (2)** contains the original or a similar task and the teacher checks students' improvement.

This method is particularly appropriate with mixed ability groups of learners with different past learning experiences.

Unit 1 - Talking about now

How to recognize it

Which of the phrases in blue in this telephone conversation sound unnatural? What would you say instead?

The phrases in blue are either in the **present simple** or the **present continuous** form. The **simple** form usually relates to **permanent states or habitual actions** while the continuous form usually refers to more **temporary activities**.

How to use it

*only third person subjects need the 'third person s', e.g. he, she, it, Mohammed, the book etc.!

	present simple = *base form*	present continuous = *am / is / are + -ing form*
affirmative (+)	*I / You / We / They **speak** German.* *He / She **speaks*** German.*	*I **am watching** TV.* *You / We / They **are watching** TV.* *He / She **is watching** TV.*
negative (-)	*I / You / We / They **don't speak** German.* *He / She **doesn't speak** German.*	***I'm not watching** TV.* *You / We / They **aren't watching** TV.* *He / She **isn't watching** TV.*
question (?)	***Do** you / we / they **speak** German?* ***Does** he / she **speak** German?*	***Am** I **watching** TV?* ***Are** you / we / they **watching** TV?* ***Is** he / she **watching** TV?*

When to use it

Present simple uses	Possible teaching contexts / themes, with examples
to refer to scientific facts or general truths	**A talk or an article about space, the environment, animals etc.** *The sun **is** our nearest star and **provides** us with light and heat. It also **gives** out dangerous ultraviolet light which **causes** sunburn.* *Blue whales **have** huge mouths and their throats **expand** like a balloon when they **fill** their mouths with water. They **eat** tiny shrimp-like creatures called krill.*
to refer to routine activities or habits	**Daily home routines** *At seven o'clock, I **get up** and **have** a shower.* **Good and bad habits** *I **eat** too much junk food, but I **exercise** every day.* **Calendar of seasonal events** *We **give** each other birthday presents but we **don't send** cards.*
to make an action sound immediate, and make a past activity sound as if it's happening now	**Sports commentaries** *Messi **shoots** and **scores**. The crowd **goes** wild.* **Diaries** *We **leave** very early to avoid the traffic and **arrive** 2 hours early for our flight. We **spend** the time planning the rest of the day.*

Present continuous uses	Possible teaching contexts / themes, with examples
to refer to temporary activities happening right now	**Student phoning home to talk to family** *A **I'm cooking** lunch. What's everyone there doing?* *B **Dad's looking after** the children and I'm watching TV.* *A And Mum?* *B **She's working** today – it isn't a public holiday here.* **Looking at photographs** *A Who's that?* *B That's my sister.* *A **What's she doing** there?* *B I think **she's trying** to chat up that guy!*
to refer to ongoing actions happening around now	**Catching up with an old friend** *A **What are you doing** these days?* *B **I'm working** in the city.* *A So **you're commuting** every day?* *B Yes, I am, unfortunately.*
for too frequent behaviour	**Showing annoyance** ***I'm always losing** my keys.* ***You're always correcting** my mistakes. Just stop it!*

Contrast between present simple and present continuous	Possible teaching contexts / themes, with examples
contrasting routines with unusual or exceptional situations	**Everyday life vs holiday** *Normally **I get up** at 6.30 in the morning – but **I'm staying** in bed much longer this week. It's great!* **Being a student: university life vs home life** ***I always keep** in touch with my old friends, but here **I'm making** lots of new friends from all over the world.*

Good to know

Frequency adverbs used with present simple verbs

To express how often we do routine actions, we use frequency adverbs with present simple verbs. These can be represented as approximate percentage figures:

never (0%)	*I **never** eat meat.*
rarely / hardly ever (1%-10%)	*She **hardly ever / rarely** has a headache.*
occasionally (11%-20%)	*We **occasionally** go out to eat.*
sometimes (21%-40%)	*They **sometimes** have arguments.*
often (41%-70%)	*He **often** phones his mother.*
usually (71%-99%)	*I **usually** wake up at 6.30.*
always (100%)	*Do you **always** go to bed late?*

What to watch out for

The example sentences above show the most common position of frequency adverbs in sentences, but some can be placed in other positions.

***Occasionally**, we go out to eat. / We go out to eat **occasionally**.*
***Sometimes** they have arguments. / They have arguments **sometimes**.*
***Usually** I wake up at 6.30. / I wake up at 6.30 **usually**.*

Using the present simple and the present continuous for future events
Confusingly for some learners, both forms can be used in the context of **future events** or **plans**. The **present simple** can refer to a future timetabled or scheduled event:
*Next weekend, Manchester City **host** Huddersfield Town and **visit** Chelsea the following weekend.*

The **present continuous** can also refer to a future arrangement:
***I'm meeting** Jade at the theatre tomorrow evening.*
There is more information about these uses in Unit 4 **Looking forward** (page 58).

How to teach it

Practical matters

There is no generally accepted correct order of introducing these two present forms to learners, though many coursebooks start with the simple form. This is partly due to convention – we've always done this – but also because it is a form which may be immediately useful to learners in real-life situations. For example, when we meet someone for the first time, our conversations are likely to include questions like these: *Where do you come from? / Where do you live? / What do you do?* etc. Conversations involving the present continuous relating to activities taking place at the moment of speaking are less frequent. In fact in some instances the first use of the present continuous form taught is to refer to future arrangements.
Generally speaking learners will have more difficulty learning when to *use* each of the present tenses than in *understanding* them. These are the main difficulties some learners might have:

- Some languages have only one present form. This means that learners have to learn the difference between the simple and continuous and understand when each form is used.
- The use of auxiliary verbs in the formation of English verb forms. In the case of the present simple, this only applies to question and negative forms (***Do** you drink coffee? / I **don't** like tea.)*. In the case of the present continuous, however, all forms are affected (***Is** he sleeping? No, he **is** not sleeping / He'**s** watching TV.)*.
- The need to add an ***-s*** to the ***he / she / it*** form of the present simple. This is tricky for two reasons: the ***he / she / it*** form is the only form which is different from the infinitive form. And the addition of *-**s*** to words often makes them plural.
  This only applies to the affirmative form *(he drink**s**)*; the auxiliary verb **does** in the negative and question forms is followed by the base form of the verb: *He **doesn't drink** coffee. / **Does he drink** coffee?* (NOT *He doesn't ~~**drinks**~~ coffee. / Does he ~~**drinks**~~ coffee?)*
- An added complication with the *he / she / it* verb forms is that there are three different possible <u>endings</u>:

+s for the vast majority of verbs, e.g. *speak, wait, cough, put, flap, like, love, make, hate, see*	*speak – speak**s***
+es for verbs ending on-ch, -s, -sh, -z or –x, e.g. *watch, pass, rush, buzz, box* and for the verbs *go* and *do*	*watch – watch**es*** *go – go**es***
y → ies in the case of verbs ending on –y, we remove the –y and replace it with –ies, e.g. *carry, try, marry, hurry, fly*	*carry – carr**ies***

- In addition the final s can also be pronounced differently depending on the final sound of the infinitive:

[s] in the case of verbs ending in an unvoiced consonant, e.g. *speak, wait, cough, put, flap, like, make*	*speak – speak**s*** [spi:ks]
[z] for verbs ending on a vowel sound, e.g. *go, do, see, know, carry, fly* or a voiced consonant, e.g. *live, save, smile, mutter, hug, run*	*go – go**es*** [gəʊz] *live – live**s*** [lɪvz]
[ɪz] for verbs ending on the sounds [s], [z], [ʃ], [tʃ], [dʒ], [ks], e.g. *pass, buzz, rush, watch, judge, box*	*watch – watch**es*** ['wɒtʃɪz]

What to watch out for

- Even quite advanced learners frequently forget to add the *-s* to the *he / she / it* forms of the present simple. Teachers may blame themselves for not teaching this properly, but this is rarely the case. It simply takes time for this oddity of English to become automatic for learners.

- Learners may need to be reminded to use **contracted** rather than full verb forms in everyday spoken English.
  I'm reading** a book about earthquakes.* NOT ~~I am reading***~~ *a book about earthquakes.*
  Contracted forms are used for affirmative and negative sentences but not questions. These are the contracted forms:
  I'm - I'm not; you're – you aren't; he's – he isn't; she's – she isn't; it's – it isn't; we're – we aren't; they're – they aren't

- Learners may need to be reminded not to use present continuous verbs to describe conditions rather than actions. For example:

  My sister has** brown eyes and black hair.* NOT ~~My sister is having***~~ *brown eyes and black hair.*

  BUT *my sister **is having** a shower* is correct because here the verb *have* describes an action.

  Other verbs which are rarely used in the continuous forms because they describe conditions are: *prefer / want / like / know.*

  It may not be helpful at this stage to introduce learners to the potentially confusing terms *stative* and *dynamic* to describe these two groups of verbs.

Suggestions for classroom activities

1 Topic What on earth is going on?
Language Present continuous
Activities Learners ask and answer questions about strange or unusual photos or film scenes
What's happening? / What do you think is going on? / What are these people doing? Etc.

2 Topic Do you ever?
Language Present simple and frequency adverbs
Activities 1. Present learners with a list of questions related to things that people do.
Learners work through the list themselves, answering with one word, a single frequency adverb:
never / hardly ever / sometimes / occasionally

Do you ever…
…buy flowers for someone?
…go late-night shopping?
…talk to strangers on buses, trains or planes?
…give money to poor people in the street?
…vote in elections?

2. Learners then compare their answers with a partner, using their frequency adverb in full sentences. Interesting conversations may arise as a result of differences between learners' ideas. Encourage such fluency activities.

3 Topic Guess my job
Language Present continuous: questions with affirmative and negative answers
Activities Learners each think of a job and mime a routine action that a person with this job does. Other learners have to guess the job by asking questions first about the actions and then directly about the job. E.g.

A mimes someone moving a cleaning cloth around
B Are you cleaning something?
A Yes, I am.
C Are you cleaning windows?
A No, I'm not.
D Are you cleaning furniture?
A No, I'm not.
E Are you cleaning someone's car.
A Yes, I am.
F Are you a car cleaner?
A Yes, I am.

4 Topic Catching up with an old friend
Language Present simple and continuous affirmative and question forms
Activities Role play this situation. Learners could use current truthful information.

A Imagine you are meeting your friend B for the first time in 5 years. Ask questions about his / her life now. E.g.
How are you? / Where are you living / working? / How are your family? / Are you still living in xxx?

B You bump into your friend A for the first time in 5 years. Answer his / her questions about your life now.

A Suggest you meet up. Ask your friend what he / she likes to do. Ask questions like these:
Do you like swimming? / Do you play tennis? etc.

5 Topic What we do in my country / in my family
Language Present simple
Activities 1. Show a photo of a celebration to introduce the topic, e.g. Day of the Dead, dragon race, Chinese New Year, Holi etc.
In Mexico they celebrate the Day of the Dead. / In Nepal and India they celebrate Holi.

2. Ask learners what special days they celebrate.

3. Hand out a list of special days or events to learners and ask them to compare answers in pairs.
If they are from different countries, learners can discuss national differences.
What do people in your country do at weekends?
How do you celebrate New Year in your country?
Do you do anything special at Christmas in your country?
Do you have special May Day / Midsummer festivals?
What do you do for Mardi Gras?

If learners are from the same country, they could discuss how their families celebrate special occasions.
What does your family do at New year?
How do you celebrate birthdays in your family? etc.

6 Topic Am I unique?
Language Present simple: questions and answers
Activities Whole class mingle
1. Ask learners to make a list of three unusual things about themselves:
- something about themselves: *I am one of triplets.*
- something they have: *I have ten pairs of trainers.*
- something they do: *I collect Coke cans.*

2. Learners then go round the class and try to find out if these unusual things make them unique. They ask and answers questions like these:

Are you one of triplets?	*Yes, I am / No, I'm not, I'm an only child.*
Do you have ten pairs of trainers?	*Yes, I do. / No, I don't. I have 15 pairs.*
Do you collect Coke cans?	*Yes, I do. / No, I don't but I collect baseball caps.*

3. Learners can report any interesting results of the mingle back to class.

7 Topic Interviews for a job
Language Present simple and continuous – all forms
Activities 1. Start by asking learners about any interviews they have had. What sort of questions do job applicants have to answer. (If they've never had an interview, they should use their imagination.)

2. After a short initial discussion, ask learners to write some questions they could ask or be asked at a job interview. These could be e.g.

Questions about character and personality
What are your strengths and weaknesses?
How do you react in an emergency?
How do other people describe you?
What makes you laugh?
What makes you angry?
How do you get to know people you have just met?
Questions about current situation
Where are you working now?
What are you currently working on?
How much are they paying you?
Questions about the new job
Why do you want this job?
Why do you think you are suitable for the job?
What attracts you to the job?

3. Learners now work in pairs interviewing each other in turn. Interviewers can decide if the applicant is good enough to get the job. As the teacher, you can tell the learners what the job is, or you can ask them to decide on the job themselves.

8 Topic Game: Who am I?
Language Present simple and continuous – all forms
Activities Each learner has a sticky label with the name of a well-known person stuck to their back. They must not see the name on the label. They mingle and ask other learners questions to try to work out who they are. You could limit the number of questions they can ask before they guess the name. E.g. Learner A has the name **Michelle Obama** on their back:

A *Am I a man?*
B *No, you're not.*
A *Am I alive?*
C *Yes, you are.*
A *Where do I live?*
D *You live in the USA.*
A *What is my job?*
E *You are a lawyer and you write books.*
A *Am I married?*
F *Yes, you are.* etc.

9 Topic Families
Language Present simple and continuous – all forms
Activities 1. Ask learners to think about other members of their families.

2. They then work in pairs asking and answering questions about what their family members do at different times of the day and what they're probably doing now. Suggest learners add words and phrases like *I think / probably / almost certainly* etc. Sample conversation:

A *Who are you thinking about?*
B *My dad.*
A *What do you think he's doing right now?*
B *He's almost certainly travelling to work. He drives to work every day.*
A *Where does he work?*
B *He normally works in Paris, but this week he's working in Berlin.*

10 Topic Current trends and changes
Language Present continuous
Activities 1. Learners discuss changes that are currently taking place in their country. They could focus on things which are changing gradually over time, for example ***marriage, work patterns, education*** or issues of topical interest like ***climate change / health problems.***

2. After a few minutes ask learners to focus their discussion on two specific trends and make a few notes.

3. Learners then write an email to a friend in another country describing the trends they have been discussing. They should use mainly present continuous verbs but other forms may also be appropriate. Example beginning:
The pace of change in my country ***is getting*** *faster and faster. People* ***are getting*** *more worried about climate change and environmental damage. Many people still* ***do not believe*** *that this is a real problem, but other people* ***are taking*** *it very seriously. Some* ***are driving*** *less frequently, and some* ***are buying*** *electric cars even though these* ***are*** *still quite expensive.*

Make a note of your own ideas for teaching the present tenses!

Lesson plan 1

Lesson profile

Description	Pre-While-Post: A lesson based on a listening comprehension
Topic	Occupations and activities
Grammar point	present simple and present continuous
Aims	To revise and clarify the uses of present simple and continuous forms.
Material	Audio file (available via Delta Augmented app) Track 1 WS 1.1 *Current affairs: The environment* WS 1.2 *Audio script: Interview with Penny Ashworth*

PRE: 1

Warmer: Speaking activity using video prompt

T Show a video clip of a TV news or current affairs programme and ask the class

Do you watch news or documentary programmes on TV?
What current issues do you find most interesting?

Elicit a few answers, then ask learners to talk in pairs or groups about the news programmes they watch.

Have a short round up, asking for a few opinions. Is there any agreement among learners about which programmes they watch and what issues they find most interesting?

L Learners tell each other about programmes they watch and what issues they find most interesting.

2

Pre-listening: Pre-teaching vocabulary

T Check learners' understanding of these items of vocabulary used in the audio recording:

prominent / environmentalist / pollution / public transport / population / exchange / charging points

Perhaps with questions like these:
If someone is prominent are they well-known or unknown?
Is an environmentalist someone who studies the natural world or works to make money?
Is pollution good or bad for the environment?
Which of these are examples of public transport: cars and bicycles or buses and trains?

L Learners discuss the questions before giving answers.

Does population refer to the number of people who live in a place or to whether somebody is well-liked?
If I exchange something, do I keep it or get a different one?
What kind of fuel does a car use if it needs a charging point?

---

3 WHILE

Listening comprehension: gist questions

Audio file (track 01)
WS 1.1 Tasks 1, 2 and 3

T Hand out worksheet 1.1. Ask learners to read questions 1 and 2 in Task 1. Play the recording for the first time and ask learners to discuss their answers in pairs. Check / Elicit answers.

L Learners read the questions and listen to the recording, then they discuss the answers to both questions in pairs.

Key:
1. She has a busy life. She is involved in many activities: teaching, writing and doing research.
2. Optimistic: government people are finally taking the subject seriously.

Now ask learners to read the 7 questions in Task 2 and think of possible answers.

Play the recording for the second time and allow learners 4-5 minutes to come up with answers.
Check / Elicit answers.

Learners read the questions in Task 2 and consider possible answers. After listening to the recording again, they come up with the answers.

Key
1. the environment: causes and effect of air pollution in big cities
2. the effects of air pollution on people's everyday lives and health
3. their children's health
4. more people are using public transport than driving their own cars
5. the population is increasing
6. it's increasing but not enough
7. they're expensive and there are not enough charging points

Now ask learners to discuss the questions in Task 3. This could be pairwork, group work or take the form of a class discussion.

4

Grammar focus – form and use of both verb forms

T Lead up to the grammar focus of the lesson. Ask questions such as:

1. Give examples of Penny's routine activities.
2. Give examples of Penny's current activities.
3. How are the verbs we use for routine activities and current activities different?

L Learners answer the questions and give examples.
Key:
1. she teaches / writes books
2. she is travelling round the country / she is talking to people
3. routine activities = simple one word verbs / current activities = two word verbs consisting of is / are (etc.) + -ing form

T Hand out the audio script (WS 1.2) and ask learners to circle all present simple verbs and underline the present continuous verbs.

Check answers.

L Learners find all examples of both forms in the text.

Key:
Presenter
Hi everyone. My guest this evening is the prominent environmentalist, Penny Ashworth. Penny is probably best known for her interest in the causes and effects of air pollution in our big cities. She **teaches** and **does research** at Oxford University and **writes** books and newspaper articles. She also **makes** TV and radio programmes. Welcome Penny. Penny, what are you working on at the moment?
Penny Ashworth
Hello Mike. **It's good** to be here. Well, in addition to my normal teaching commitments, I'm doing long-term research into the effects of air pollution on people's everyday lives and especially the health of those who live or work in city centres so I'm travelling round the country talking to people.
Presenter
What are you finding?
Penny Ashworth
Well, **it's clear** that many people **I speak** to **are** very anxious, especially about their children's health. **I'm afraid** to say that levels of air pollution **are** still high even though more people are using public transport rather than driving their own cars. Part of the problem is that the population of many cities is increasing year by year.
Presenter
What is the solution to this problem?
Penny Ashworth
There **are** many things we can all do to improve the situation. **It's true** that more people are walking or cycling to and from work, but this **needs** to increase. And more people are exchanging their petrol or diesel cars for electric vehicles. At the moment, though, these **are** still very expensive and there **are** not enough charging points. Basically **I'm not** too unhappy about the future because at last, the government and ordinary people are taking the subject seriously.

5

Grammar practice – writing activity (identifying the tenses)

WS 1.2 Task 1

6

Grammar practice – formulating the main uses of both tenses

WS 1.2 Task 2

T Write some example verbs from the text in two columns on the board, e.g.

L Learners tell each other about programmes they watch and what issues they find most interesting.

present simple	**present continuous**
teaches	What are you working on?
does research	I'm doing research
writes books	I'm travelling
makes TV and radio programmes	I'm talking
live	people are using / driving
work	is increasing
	are walking
	are cycling
	are exchanging

Ask concept questions, e.g.
1. Which column describes regular activities or routine behaviour?
2. Which column describes activities happening around now?
3. Which verbs describe activities which are more temporary?

Learners answer the questions and write the answers on their worksheet:

1. present simple column
2. present continuous
3. present continuous

Check learners understand how these two tenses are formed. If necessary, illustrate it on the board.

POST: 7

Role play: interview situation

T Learners work in pairs: one is the interviewer and the other the interviewee. They ask and answer questions about their everyday lives and their jobs. (If learners do not have jobs, ask them to imagine one.) Allow learners a few minutes to prepare their roles and make a few notes first.

Learner A:
You are the interviewer. Ask Learner B questions about their daily routines at home and at work. Then ask him / her about current activities.
Learner B:
Answer A's questions about your life and work.

Monitor and if necessary correct learners' use of present verb forms. Make a note of any recurring mistakes to go over with the class later.

L Learners decide who will be the interviewer and who will be the interviewee in each pair. Each partner prepares their role first.

T Ask learners to write a short description of their school life or job in 80-100 words. E.g. it could be an email to a friend in another country. Ask a few of them if they would like to read out their texts in class.

L Students write a short description of their life or work using the target language.

8

Homework / Follow-up - writing activity

Adapt the lesson plan to your liking: found a better text for a listening comprehension? Make a note of it here!

Current affairs: The environment

Task 1

You're going to listen to an interview. First, read the following questions.

1. Do you think Penny Ashworth has a busy life or not? Why do you think this?

2. Is Penny optimistic or pessimistic about the future? Why do you think this?

Listen to the interview and then discuss the answers with a partner.

Task 2

Read the following questions and then listen to the interview again. Discuss the answers with your partner.

1. What is Penny Ashworth's main professional interest?

2. What is she studying at the moment?

3. What are the people she meets most worried about?

4. What change in people's travelling habits does Penny mention?

5. Why is this change not solving the problem?

6. What does Penny say about the trend for people to walk or cycle to work?

7. What two factors may be discouraging people from buying electric cars?

Task 3

Discuss these questions related to what Penny Ashworth says.

1. How should we encourage people not to use their cars in cities?

2. What could be done to reduce the growth in the population of large cities?

3. Do you think the suggestions for action that Penny Ashworth suggests are radical enough?

4. Do you think that Extinction Rebellion and similar environmental movements have a better idea of what needs to be done?

ISBN 978-3-12-501628-6

Audio script: Interview with Penny Ashworth

Task 1

This is the script of the recording you just listened to. Circle all present simple verbs and underline all present continuous verbs.

Presenter
Hi everyone. My guest this evening is the prominent environmentalist, Penny Ashworth. Penny is probably best known for her interest in the causes and effects of air pollution in our big cities. She teaches and does research at Oxford University and writes books and newspaper articles. She also makes TV and radio programmes. Welcome Penny. Penny, what are you working on at the moment?

Penny Ashworth
Hello Mike. It's good to be here. Well, in addition to my normal teaching commitments, I'm doing long-term research into the effects of air pollution on people's everyday lives and especially the health of those who live or work in city centres so I'm travelling round the country talking to people.

Presenter
What are you finding?

Penny Ashworth
Well, it's clear that many people I speak to are very anxious, especially about their children's health. I'm afraid to say that levels of air pollution are still high even though more people are using public transport rather than driving their own cars. Part of the problem is that the population of many cities is increasing year by year.

Presenter
What is the solution to this problem?

Penny Ashworth
There are many things we can all do to improve the situation. It's true that more people are walking or cycling to and from work, but this needs to increase. And more people exchanging their petrol or diesel cars for electric vehicles. At the moment, though, these are still very expensive and there are not enough charging points. Basically I'm not too unhappy about the future because at last, the government and ordinary people are taking the subject seriously.

Task 2

We use two verb forms to talk about the present: the ***present simple*** *and the* ***present continuous****.*
Answer the following questions and add some examples from the text.

a. Which form describes regular activities or routine behaviour? ....

e.g. ....

b. Which form describes activities happening around now? ....

e.g. ....

c. Which form describes activities which are more temporary? ....

e.g. ....

ISBN 978-3-12-501628-6

Unit 2 – Looking back

How to recognize it

Once upon a time …

Ben shares a flat with Will and Burt the dog. Usually the mornings are fairly peaceful. What happened this morning? Tell a microstory in three (or at the most four) sentences based on the cartoon. Notice which tenses you use.

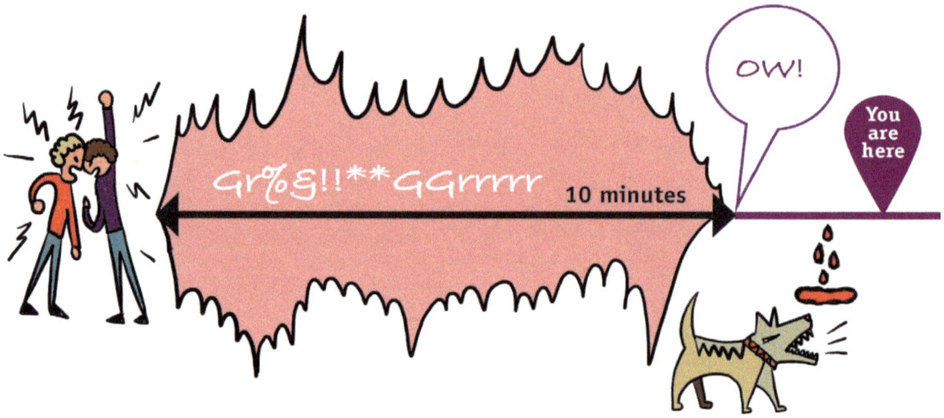

You'll probably have noticed that there are two chief verb forms used to refer to actions which happened in the past: the **past simple** and **past perfect**. Both have simple and continuous forms. Your microstory probably reads something like this:

Ben and Will **were arguing**. They **had been squabbling** for 10 minutes when Will **yelled** loudly. Burt **had bitten** him. As a result Will's leg **was bleeding** profusely.

How to use it

	past simple = *past tense* form	**past continuous** = *was / were + -ing* form
affirmative [+]	*I / You / She / We … **passed** the test.*	*I / She **was walking** home.* *You / We / They **were cycling**.*
negative [-]	*I / You / She / We …* **didn't pass** *the test.*	*I / She **wasn't cycling** home.* ***You / We / They weren't walking.***
question [?]	***Did** I / you / she / we … **pass** the test?*	***Was** I / she **walking** home?* ***Were** you / we / they **cycling**?*

	past perfect = *had* + past participle	past perfect continuous = *had been* + *-ing* form
affirmative [+]	*I / You / She / We … **had passed** the test.*	*I / You / She / We … **had been walking** home.*
negative [-]	*I / You / She / We … **hadn't passed** the test.*	*I / You / She / We … **hadn't been walking** home.*
question [?]	***Had** I / you / she / we … **passed** the test?*	*Had I / you / she / we … **been walking** home?*

When to use it

Past simple	Possible teaching contexts / themes, with examples
for completed past actions which took place once or more than once	**What I did yesterday / at the weekend etc.** *I **got up** really early and **went** for a run with my sister.* **Biography / autobiography** *I **grew up** in the south of France where my parents **owned** a farm and a small shop.* *I always **skipped** breakfast when I was a student because I **slept** late.* **News stories / Fiction / History** *The hurricane **made** landfall at 4 a.m. on Sunday and **destroyed** more than 100 homes.* *At the last moment, just before the soldiers **grabbed** her, Ruby **ducked** backwards, **spun** on the spot and **ran** faster than she had ever run in her life.*

Past continuous	Possible teaching contexts / themes, with examples
for actions that took place over a period of time in the past (these actions might have been interrupted by another, usually shorter event)	**Journeys** *We **were driving** through the tunnel when we heard a loud explosion.* **Interview: personal history** *Q What **were** you **doing** this time last year?* *A I **was working** part-time as a waiter.* *Q Where **were** you **living**?* *A I **was staying** with my parents' at the time.* **Making excuses** *Sorry, I didn't hear you. I **was working** in the garden. I **was listening** to music on my phone.*
to set the scene or describe the atmosphere in a story	**Fiction / accounts** *The snow **was falling** thick and fast, obscuring his vision.*

See lesson plan 2.

Past perfect simple and continuous	Possible teaching contexts / themes, with examples
to provide background information about a past action. This includes drawing attention to a sequence of events in the past.	**Looking back over a period of time** *By the time I was 7 I'**d flown** all over the world and **visited** ten different countries. I'**d been travelling** with my parents almost since the day I was born.* **News stories / Fiction / History** *When Napoleon arrived in St Helena on 15th October 1815, **he had** been at sea for 10 weeks. **He'd been expecting** to be sent to America.* **Discovering a crime / break-in** *When we opened our front door, we couldn't believe the mess. Someone **had climbed** through a broken window. They **had** obviously **been searching** for something. They'**d emptied** all our drawers and cupboards.*

Add your own ideas for possible teaching contexts here!

Good to know

Talking about **habits** and **actions** that took place **routinely** in the **past**? The auxiliary verb **used to** is an alternative to the past simple:

	used to = *used to + infinitive*
affirmative [+]	*(As children) We **used to go** on holiday to Guernsey.*
negative [-]	*I **never used to like** flying (when I was younger).* *I **didn't use to like** flying (when I was younger).*
question [?]	***Did** you **use to like** flying?*

In questions and negatives with ‚did', the correct form is *use to* (without the final –d), although many native speakers use *used* in all instances in writing.

used to + infinitive can be used	**Possible teaching contexts / themes, with examples**
for habitual actions that have now stopped	**Family and childhood customs** *We **used to go** camping during the summer holidays.* **Bad habits** *I **used to bite** my nails, but thank goodness I managed to stop.*
in situations / conditions that have changed	**Before and after: describing how a place has changed.** *Before they built the bypass, traffic **used to drive** through the town. There **used to be** congestion everywhere.* **Describing a person when they were younger (using a photo)** *Look! Mike **used to have** really long hair. And he **used to be** so thin.*

What to watch out for

The correct pronunciation → [ju:st] rather than [ju:zd]
Learners often use ***used to*** for an action which still happens (they may be mixing it up with *be used to + -ing form*!):
*I **used to** work late at night.* **vs** *I**'m used to working** late at night.*

Would + infinitive can also be used to refer to habits or typical behaviour in the past:
*After school **I'd run** home, **get** changed and go out and play football with my friends.*

However, it can't be used to refer to past conditions or states. You can't say:
Mike ~~would have~~ really long hair. → *Mike **had / used to have** really long hair.*

*This sequence might take several lessons over a number of weeks.

How to teach it

Practical matters

A crucial point to make is that you should NOT try to introduce all four past verbs at the same time. The only time you might do this would be a revision lesson when you knew your learners were thoroughly familiar with all the forms.

A practical sequence*, covering the four past tenses might be as follows. (All four stages in the sequence would be in the context of simple-to-follow narratives.)

1 The simple past
I ***woke*** *up at 3.30 this morning. Everything* ***was*** *quiet, but then I heard a noise I* ***didn't recognize. Was*** *it a burglar?*

2 Contrast between the simple past and the past continuous
My phone ***rang****, I* ***looked*** *at the screen and saw my girlfriend's number. So I* ***pressed*** *REPLY. Unfortunately, I* ***wasn't looking*** *where I* ***was going*** *and* ***walked*** *into a lamp post.*

3 The contrast between the simple past and the past perfect simple
When the police ***arrived*** *the party* ***had finished*** *and everyone* ***had gone*** *home. Nevertheless, the officer* ***took out*** *his notebook and started asking me questions. He* ***wanted*** *to know if any strangers* ***had gatecrashed*** *the party.*

4 Contrast between the simple past, the past perfect simple and the past perfect continuous
When our bus finally ***arrived, we'd been waiting*** *for over an hour. The driver* ***apologized*** *profusely. The bus* ***had*** *hit a sheep that* ***was crossing*** *the road on the moors. They* ***had had*** *to stop and report the incident to the police.*

Some learners may find it hard to understand when to use which past tense. If this is the case you might consider using **timelines** to illustrate the relationship between the tenses. But beware, not all learners find timelines helpful!

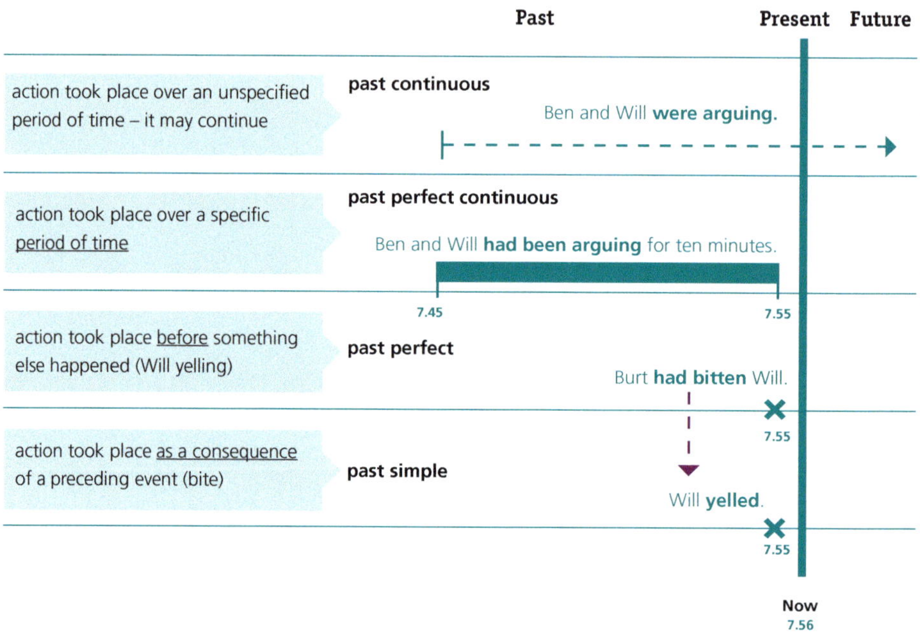

Another method that may help to clarify the time relationships between the tenses is to play a short film sequence, then to ask learners a series of questions:

1. *What happened first?*
2. *Then what happened?*
3. *What was X doing when Y came in?*
4. *What had Y been doing before she came in. etc.*

Use a film clip 2-3 minutes long and play it with the sound turned off. Silent films like Laurel and Hardy or Charlie Chaplin which are full of action work well for this purpose.

Personalized practice activities work well for all lessons involving verbs. At the beginning of lessons as "warmers" or "engage activities", and at the end as "free practice" or "activate" tasks, ask learners to tell each other about past events they remember well. Examples:

- *My first day at school or in a job*
- *My last holiday*
- *My worst journey*
- *A wonderful dream or a nightmare*

If tasks are aimed at improving learners' fluency, they should be oral activities. A follow-up writing task could be used to consolidate this oral work.

What to watch out for

- Learners may not be aware of whether verbs are regular or irregular and this may lead to incorrect past participle forms when forming the past perfect simple. Make sure learners know where they can check whether verbs are irregular or not.
- In the case of regular verbs the past participle is the same as the past simple:
  *He **watched** the film. / He **had watched** the film.*
- Some learners may use the past simple when the past perfect is preferable. They may have forgotten that this form exists or may not think the distinction matters. It should be pointed out that using a past perfect form helps to make clear the sequence of past actions.
- Learners may not understand the sometimes subtle difference between the simple and the continuous forms of the past perfect. Make this clear with examples:

  ***We'd waited** for five hours at the airport.* = the emphasis is on the fact that the wait is over

  ***We'd been waiting** for five hours at the airport.* = the emphasis is on the length of the wait
- Learners need to remember that affirmative forms of past continuous verbs cannot be contracted (NOT ~~She's~~ walking home. → *She was walking home.*)
- Learners may have difficulty distinguishing in speech between the past simple and (contracted forms of the) past perfect of regular verbs: *He talked. / He'd talked.*
- The negative and question forms of *used to* are written without the final **–d**.
  *What did you **use to** do in the evenings? / I didn't **use to** like watching football.*
  (Many native speakers use **used** to for all forms in writing – so this may become standard in the future.)
- Learners may confuse *used to do* with *be used to doing*. Example:
  *I **used to get** up early.* This refers to a habit which is no longer true.
  *I **am used to getting** up early.* This refers to a current action you are accustomed to.

See lesson plan 2

Suggestions for classroom activities

1 Topic Bad journeys
Language Contrast between past simple and past continuous
Activities Learners talk about journeys that went wrong.

2 Topic Comparing life when grandparents / parents were young and now
Language Past simple, *used to* and *would*
Activities 1. Learners talk about families
When my grandparents were young hardly anyone had a car, now some people have several cars. People used to walk to school and work. Now most people go by car or train.

2. A speaking activity could be followed by a writing task: an email or letter describing what life was like in your town or country 20-30 years ago.

3 Topic Childhood memories, e.g. My first day at school
Language All past tenses
Activities Learners find out how their lives as children were similar and different.

4 Topic The history of my village / town / city
Language All past tenses
Activities Learners find out information from older family members and research online.

5 Topic In the news
Language All past tenses
Activities Research and discuss important local, national and international events.

6 Topic What I was like
Language All past tenses, *used to* and *would*
Activities 1. Learners compare photos of themselves and others at different ages.

2. In pairs or groups learners compare photos of themselves as children (e.g.) and now. They tell each other about the photos and how they have changed since then, e.g.

I used to have blond hair but it's much darker now.
I would always go home with my best friend on Fridays after school.
I used to love horseriding but then I fell off and broke my leg. I don't ride any more.

7 Topic Famous people and their achievements – biographies
Language All past tenses
Activities Learners find out about people of national and international fame / importance and present their findings to the rest of their class. They can speak from notes.

8 Topic Stories (fact and fiction)
Language All past tenses
Activities 1. Learners decide on their favourite book or film.

2. Working with a partner they exchange their stories and re-tell the main plot.

3. This could also take the form of a class quiz: each student decides on a

book or film the others in class are likely to know or at least have heard of. They take it in turns to retell the main plot and the others have to guess. The person who guesses the correct book or film title quickest, wins the point.

9 Topic Confessions. For example: *My first lie / Something I took from someone else*
Language All past tenses
Activities Learners interview each other to find out what partners did that was wrong when they were younger.

10 Topic Microstories (Complete stories in exactly 50 words)
Language All past tenses
Activity 1. Give or show learners random photos of unusual or funny things.

2. Ask them to write a microstory (this can be done as homework) that explains the photo.

3. In class they exchange their stories and ask each other questions to find out more.

4. Alternatively, give students a few random words (e.g. *Valentine's Day, pothole, nurse, unexpected* etc.) and ask them to write a microstory that contains all of them or as many as possible.

Add your own ideas on teaching the past tenses!

Lesson plan 2

Lesson profile

Description	Engage ➞ Study ➞ Activate (See Introduction)
Topic	Journeys
Grammar point	Contrast between past simple and past continuous
Aims	To revise and clarify differences in use between the past simple and past continuous forms.
Material	WS 2.1 *A fateful journey*

ENGAGE

Photo-based speaking activity

WS 2.1 Task 1

T Show students a photo of the Titanic sinking. Ask them to discuss in pairs / small groups what they know about this event.

Don't correct grammar at this point.
Perhaps ask supplementary questions, e.g.
Where was the ship sailing to?
How many people died?
…

L Learners discuss what they know about the Titanic, e.g.
The Titanic was a passenger ship.
It sank in the Atlantic ocean.
…

Learners exchange information they came up with during their discussion, e.g.
The ship was sailing across the Atlantic.
Hundreds of people died.
It hit an iceberg.

STUDY 1

Reading / listening compre-hension

WS 2.1 Task 2

T Ask students to read a text / listen to a recording about the Titanic (e.g. WS 2.1). Ask them to mark / note down information they find interesting or surprising. Elicit answers and make a note of any verb errors.

You might ask learners to read / listen again with specific questions, e.g.
How many people died?
What were the people doing when the Titanic hit the iceberg?

L Learners read the text on WS 2.1 / listen to the recording.

Learners give answers.

STUDY 2

Grammar focus

Display the past simple and past continuous in table form on the board and ask learners to add the missing forms:

Learners look at the table and discuss in pairs which forms are missing and report back.

past simple	past continuous
(+) It sank.	*.......................*
(-)	*They weren't sleeping.*
(?) Did ....?	*.......................?*

Ask concept questions to check learners understand the difference in meaning between the two forms, e.g.
The Titanic sank while it was sailing across the Atlantic.
Which action happened suddenly?
Which action continued for some time?

past simple	past continuous
(+) It sank.	They were sleeping.
(-) It didn't sink.	They weren't sleeping.
(?) Did it sink?	Were they sleeping?

Learners give answers to show understanding.
The Titanic sank.
It was sailing across the Atlantic.

STUDY 3

Grammar practice

WS 2.1 Task 3

T Ask students to choose the correct verb forms in a text (e.g. WS 2.1 task 2). Students work on their own first and then compare with a partner. If they disagree, they should argue for their choice of answer.

Repeat concept questions to establish that learners understand the differences between the two tenses.

L Learners choose the right form in each case.

On 10 April 1912 the Titanic **(1)** left / was leaving Southampton for her first Atlantic crossing to New York. The passengers **(2)** enjoyed / were enjoying sailing on this incredibly modern ship. Then on 14 April, the captain **(3)** received / was receiving messages from other ships. After the second iceberg warning the ship **(4)** changed / was changing course. At the time of the collision, the ship's band **(5)** played / was playing and many of the passengers **(6)** slept / were sleeping in their cabins.

ACTIVATE

Speaking about own experiences

T Ask students to talk about a bad journey they have experienced in pairs / small groups.

Monitor, checking that students are on topic. Listen for but do not correct their use of past verb forms while they are in discussion.

Ask additional questions to encourage the students to speak, e.g.
Which mountains was he driving through?
Did he repair the car himself?

Finally draw attention to any common errors, e.g. incorrect forms:
Jorge's car ~~was breaking down~~ → broke down while he ~~drove~~ → was driving through the mountains.

L In pairs / small groups learners take turns to tell each other about their bad journeys.

Learners share what their partners have told them, e.g.
Jorge was driving through the Alps.

No, he called for help.

ISBN 978-3-12-501628-6

A fateful journey

Task 1

Look at the photo, and discuss these questions in pairs.

1. What is the name of the ship?
2. When did this take place?
3. What caused the accident?

Task 2

Read this short text and then answer the two questions below.

1. Were the answers you gave to the questions in Task 1 correct?

2. What do you find surprising or particularly interesting about this story?

The temperature was falling rapidly as the Titanic sailed silently across the North Atlantic. 25-year-old sailor Frederick Fleet was keeping an eye on weather conditions and checking the ship's progress. After some time he saw a small dark shadow in the distance. Fleet phoned the ship's officers to warn them that there was an iceberg ahead. The ship slowed but it was too late to avoid the iceberg and as the Titanic brushed past it tons of ice fell on to the deck but the ship continued on its way.

Hugh Woolner, who survived the accident said: "We were playing cards and drinking cocktails in the first class lounge when we realized that the ship was slowing down. Suddenly the whole room twisted and we all went up on deck to see what was happening."

In one of the lower cabins, Dickinson Bishop, another passenger, was reading a book when he felt the bump. He woke his wife who was sleeping and they went up on deck to find out what was happening. "Go back to your cabins," said one of the crew. "There is nothing to worry about."

The collision, which took place on April 14 1912, lasted only ten seconds. The iceberg ripped a 100-metre hole in the luxury liner. In just a few hours the Titanic sank to the bottom of the Atlantic. That night, 1,522 passengers and crew drowned or froze to death. Only 492 survived.

Task 3

Choose the correct verbs in this short text.

On 10 April 1912 the Titanic (1) **left / was leaving** Southampton for her first Atlantic crossing to New York. The passengers (2) **enjoyed / were enjoying** sailing on this incredibly modern ship. Then on 14 April, the captain (3) **received / was receiving** messages from other ships. After the second iceberg warning the ship (4) **changed / was changing** course. At the time of the collision, the ship's band (5) **played / was playing** and many of the passengers (6) **slept / were sleeping** in their cabins.

Find out 3 more facts about the Titanic and share them with your partner.

ISBN 978-3-12-501628-6

Add your notes here!

Unit 3 – Linking the present and the past

How to recognize it

Look at the cartoon and choose the verb forms in 1-4 which sound more natural in this context. Consider why.

Although **present perfect** verbs are sometimes thought to refer to the past, their main use is to establish a **link of some kind between the past and the present** and to focus on the result of past events or actions now. The **present perfect simple** stresses the fact of an action, the **present perfect continuous** emphasizes the duration of an action.

How to use it

	present perfect simple *= have / has + past participle*	**present perfect continuous** *= have been / has been + present participle*
affirmative (+)	*I / You / We / They **have worked** hard today.* *He / She **has worked** hard today.*	*I / You / We / They **have been playing** tennis.* *He / She **has been playing** tennis.*
negative (-)	*I / You / We / They **haven't worked** hard today.* *He / She **hasn't worked** hard today.*	*I / You / We / They **haven't been playing** tennis.* *He / She **hasn't been playing** tennis.*
question (?)	***Have** I / you / we / they **worked** hard today?* ***Has** he / she **worked** hard today?*	***Have** I / you / we / they **been playing** tennis?* ***Has** he / she **been playing** tennis?*

When to use it

Present perfect simple / continuous	Possible teaching contexts / themes, with examples
to refer to completed past actions without specifying a time	**Making arrangements to go on holiday to a new place / see a particular film etc.** *Shall we go to Greece? — No,* ***I've already been*** *there.* *How about Egypt? — Yes, ok,* ***I've never been*** *there.*
	Talking about superlatives *What's the most expensive thing* ***you've ever bought****?* *What the funniest film* ***you've ever seen****?*
	Recent discoveries **They've found** an ancient palace in the middle of the jungle.
	Reporting gossip / rumours about famous people **Have you heard,** X and Y **have just divorced**. According to friends, **they've been meeting** in secret.
	Achievements / things you're proud of ***I've run*** *a marathon.* ***I've got*** *into my first choice university.*
to refer to past happenings which have an effect on the present	**Recent local, national and international news stories with continuing repercussions** ***It's been raining*** *non-stop for the last 24 hours causing widespread flooding.* ***There's been*** *an explosion in the city centre. Three people* ***have died*** *and many others* ***have been injured****.*
	Your life in the last year *How* ***have you earned / spent*** *your money?* ***Have you taken up*** *any new hobbies or sports?* ***What haven't you done*** *that you would still like to do?*
	Explaining a photo or a situation *Q Why is she laughing / crying?* *A Someone* ***has told*** *her a joke. /* ***She's just read*** *a sad story.*
to refer to a continuous situation or a repeated activity that takes place over a period of time up to and including the present	**Personal history / biography — saying how long you have done / been doing something** *My grandmother* ***has lived*** *in the same house all her life.* ***I've been learning*** *Chinese for three years.* ***He's been working*** *at the post office since he left school.* ***I've been going*** *to the gym three times a week recently.* *She* ***hasn't passed*** *her driving test yet.*
	Catching up with someone you haven't seen for some time *Hi!* ***What have you been doing****? —* ***I've been living and working*** *in Rome for the last three months.*

Present perfect simple	Possible teaching contexts / themes, with examples
to refer to a state (not an action) which continues up to the present	**Talking about history** *The church* ***has stood*** *on this hill overlooking our village for 900 years.* *There* ***has been*** *a mall here since 2017.*

The **simple form** is used to refer to **actions.** The continuous form emphasizes the **duration of the action.** In many but not all instances the continuous form refers to recent and short-lived events or actions.

See lesson plan 3.

Good to know

Time adverbs used with the present perfect simple

In order to emphasize that we are referring to a time up to and including the present moment, we may use these time adverbs with present perfect simple verbs:

already – at some indeterminate time before now	*I've **already** told you twice not to do that.*
never – not once until now	*She's **never** flown before.*
ever – at any point in your life	*Have you **ever** seen a ghost?*
just – very recently	*He's **just** spoken to her.*
yet – at any time up until now	*Have you found a new job **yet**?*
so far – up to the present	*I've only invited three friends **so far**.*

What to watch out for

Knowing where to position adverbs in sentences can be problematic, as it is possible for them to be used **at the beginning** of a clause (front or initial position), **before the main verb** or between an auxiliary and the main verb (mid position) or **at the end** of a clause (end position).

Is it possible to change the position of the adverbs in the sample sentences above? Complete the table below.

front position	adverb + clause	
mid position	aux vb + adverb + main vb	
end position	clause + adverb	

Time adverbs used with the present perfect continuous

Adverbs of time that express or emphasize duration in some way are used primarily with the present perfect continuous, e.g.

To refer to a period of time:	
for hours / **all night** / **all day** / **for years** etc.	*I've been waiting here **for hours** / **all night**.*
how long	***How long** have you two been seeing each other?*
To refer to a point in time in the past:	
since	*I've been waiting here **since** three o'clock.*

How to teach it

Practical matters

The present perfect form is one of the most difficult for learners of some nationalities to understand and use correctly. This may be because the equivalent form in their own language is used in the way the simple past is used in English. This is likely to result in learners saying things like
I've been to the cinema last week. instead of *I went to the cinema last week.*
It is, of course, quite possible to say *I've been to the cinema **this** week* because the current week is not yet over.
One of the ways of conveying the essential concept of the present perfect is to point out that **the present perfect always relates to the present in some way**. It is used when we are looking back at the past from the present.

Here are some examples with their relevance to the present pointed out.

Example	Present relevance
Ouch, I've cut my thumb!	This has happened very recently. The thumb hurts and it may be bleeding.
I've been to Brazil.	At some point up until the present. I have memories of my visit.
I've haven't been to Argentina yet.	So far in my life. But I would like to go / plan to go one day.
She's lived there since her mother died.	She still lives there now.
I've been working here far too long.	I'm still working here.
There's been an explosion at the fireworks factory. Several people have been injured.	This is a current news story of the kind you'd hear as breaking news. You'd expect to hear more details.
I've spent all morning making phone calls.	The morning in question is **this** morning. I've been doing this all morning (and not much else) and have only recently stopped.

- In the classroom, stress the point that when using the present perfect we do not refer to an exact time.
- The distinction between the simple and continuous forms can also cause problems for learners. The facts conveyed by the two forms can be the same. In both the sentences below, the car is now cleaner than it was before:
  I've cleaned my car. | *I've been cleaning my car.*

  In the first sentence, the emphasis is more on the fact that **the action is complete**. In the second the emphasis is on the **duration** of the same action. The second sentence may also mean that the speaker hasn't finished cleaning the car yet.

- You could also point out to learners that the continuous form is often used in conversational language in expressions like these:

  I've been hoping I'd see you soon. / I've been wondering what to buy James for his birthday? / We've been thinking a lot about you since you left.

- Expect to revisit these difficulties from time to time!

What to watch out for

- As with the past perfect formation, learners may not know which verbs have irregular past participle forms and produce mistakes like this:
  ***He's ~~telled~~** his friends what happened.*

- Knowing when to use the present perfect rather than the past simple:
  ***I waited** here for twenty minutes, then I went home.* – refers to a past action now over.
  ***I've waited** here for twenty minutes.* – the speaker is still waiting.

- Learners may mishear or mispronounce contracted forms. For example
  ***I've found** the keys I lost*. can be confused with ***I found** the keys I lost.*

- Learners may use the present continuous instead of the present perfect continuous because of the influence of their first language. For example they may say:
  *I'm playing the guitar for three years. instead of **I've been playing** the guitar for three years.*

- Not being sure about when it is appropriate to use the continuous rather than simple form of this verb. It is more common to use the continuous form with certain verbs (e.g. those that describe wants and likes), e.g.
  ***I've been wondering** what happened.* rather than *I've wondered.*
  ***He's been hoping** you'd call him.* rather than *He's hoped.*

Suggestions for classroom activities

1 Topic What's happened / been happening?
Language Present perfect simple and continuous
Activities Learners ask and answer questions about photos:
What's (just) happened? / What's been happening?

2 Topic Your last week / month / year
Language Present perfect simple: questions, affirmatives, negatives
Activities Learners interview each other with questions such as these:
Who have you met? / What interesting places have you visited? / Who have you made friends with? / What's the most unusual thing you've eaten? / What's the rudest thing anyone has said to you? / What haven't you done that you wanted to do?

3 Topic Interesting experiences
Language Present perfect simple vs past simple
Activities Learners interview each other about interesting things they've done (in their lives) and then find out more information. Sample conversation:
A So tell me the most interesting place ***you've been to****?*
B ***I've been*** *to Brazil.*
A Cool, when ***did you go*** *to Brazil?*
B ***I went*** *there in 2016.*
A How ***did you get*** *there?*
B ***I flew.***

4 Topic Making excuses / giving explanations
Language Present perfect simple and continuous
Activities Role play a situation, e.g.
Situation 1
A You've been waiting for your friend for two and a half hours. You are furious. Demand an explanation.
B You arranged to meet a friend at 7 pm tonight. You arrive at 9.30. Make believable excuses.
Situation 2
A You bump into an old school friend you haven't seen for years. Find out as much as you can about your friend's life since you last met.
B You meet someone who was a friend when you were at primary school. Your life hasn't been very interesting since then, so make up some facts to impress your friend.

5 Topic Job applications
Language Present perfect simple and continuous
Activities Discussion in pairs / small groups
A company has received application forms for a job and is now considering which of the candidates is most suitable. Learners read the brief job description and consider two application forms listing experience etc. This could lead to a discussion like this:
A Sam is well qualified but ***he hasn't had*** *much experience of working with young children.*
B How about Jenny? ***She's been working*** *in school for the past seven years.*
A Yes, but ***she has only worked*** *with older children.*
etc.

See lesson plan 3.

6 Topic Guessing what's happened
Language Present perfect simple and continuous. Question and answers.
Activities Learners work in small groups and take turns to make facial expressions to show feelings such as happiness, sadness, surprise, anger, excitement. Others in the group try to guess why they feel like this. Examples:

A ***Have you failed** an exam?* *B No,* ***I haven't.***
A ***Has** your cat **died**?* *B No,* ***it hasn't.***
A ***Have you lost** something valuable?* *BYes,* ***I have. I've lost** my phone!*

7 Topic Books and films
Language Present perfect simple
Activities Each learner makes a list of 5 books they've enjoyed reading and 5 films they've enjoyed. Then they ask other students whether they have read any of the same books or seen any of the same films.

A ***Have you read** Harry Potter and The Philosopher's Stone?*
B ***No, I haven't**. **Have you read** To Kill a Mockingbird?*
A Yes, ***I have**.*

Hopefully when learners discover a book they've both read or a film they've both seen, they will want to discuss what they thought about the book or the film. Done in this way, this activity leads learners from a controlled practice exercise to a freer fluency activity.

8 Topic Your bucket list
Language Present perfect with *never / yet*
Activities Learners write a list of some of the things they haven't done but would like to do in the future, e.g.
ride a horse / see a Shakespeare play in London / drive a lorry / visit New York / sail across the Atlantic / …
In pairs students ask each other about the things on their list, making conversations like this:

A ***Have you ever** ridden a horse?*
B Yes, ***I have**, but it was very uncomfortable.*
or
A ***I've never seen** a Shakespeare play in London.* ***Have you**?*
B No, ***I haven't**.*

etc. This activity could also lead to spontaneous conversations between learners.

9 Topic Miming actions / activities
Language Present perfect continuous
Activities Learners mime an activity and ask others "What have I been doing?". Example:
Learner A mimes looking for something.

A ***What have I been doing**?*
B ***Have you been looking** for something?*
A Yes, ***I have**.*
B ***Have you been looking** for your cat?*
A No, ***I haven't**.*
B ***Have you been looking** for your keys?*
A Yes, ***I have**.*

10 Topic A getting-to-know-you activity
Language Present simple / Present perfect simple and continuous / Question words
Activities This is a good activity which learners can do to find out more about each

other.
Working in pairs they should ask and answer questions like this:

A Where do you live? B In Church street.
A ***How long have you been living*** there? B Two years. Where do you work?
A At the animal clinic. I'm a vet. B How long have you been working at the animal clinic? …

Other questions:
How long have you been learning English?
How long have you been going out with your boyfriend / girlfriend?

How would you teach the present perfect? What activities might appeal to your students?

Lesson plan 3

Lesson profile

Description	A lesson based on a reading text which incorporates examples of the target language
Topic	Recent news
Grammar point	present perfect simple and continuous and past simple
Aims	To revise and clarify the uses of present perfect simple and continuous forms and clarify the differences between these two forms.
Material	WS 3.1 *Recent news*

1

Warmer: Speaking activity using picture prompts

WS 3.1 Task 1

T Show photos or video clips of three situations, e.g. heatwave, heavy snow, volcanic eruption and ask
Have you experienced any of these situations?

Elicit a few answers, then ask learners to talk in pairs or groups about their experiences and what they can see in the photos.
Draw attention to each picture in turn and ask these questions:
What is happening now?
What has happened?

Focus on the content of the photos. There is no need to correct errors in verb forms at this stage.

L Learners tell each other about their experiences of the conditions in the photos.

Learners answer questions in present continuous and present perfect simple.

2

Pre-reading: Pre-teaching vocabulary

T Check learners' understanding of these items of vocabulary used in the three news reports (in Task 2):

crops / dormant / erupt / explosion / hospital admission / mountainous / road maintenance

Perhaps with questions like these:
Who looks after crops: mechanics or farmers?
If a volcano is dormant, is it dangerous or not?
…

L Learners discuss the questions before giving answers.

T Hand out worksheet 3.1. Ask learners to read the three news reports and match each text with the correct photo. Then ask learners to answer this gist question:
Are these basically good or bad news stories?

Allow 1-2 minutes for this first reading. Check answers.

Now ask students to read the stories again and find answers to more detailed questions, for example:
How have the situations affected people?
What time periods are mentioned in the stories?
etc.
Allow 1-2 minutes for this second reading. Check answers.

L Learners read news reports, find answers and compare with partners.

3

Reading comprehension: global and detailed comprehension

WS 3.1 Tasks 2 and 3

T Lead up to the grammar focus of the lesson. Ask questions about the reports, e.g.
1. Where might you read stories like these?
2. Are the events recent or long past?
3. How do you know?
4. Which verbs tell you this? (Elicit a few examples.)

Ask learners to underline all the verbs in the present perfect simple and present perfect continuous in the stories. Then elicit a few examples.

L Learners give answers:

1. in newspapers
2. recent
3. verb tenses
4. e.g. have been suffering, have closed, has died

Learners underline all examples of both tenses in the text.

Key
1) Much awaited cool weather is likely to arrive in our area over the weekend. This is good news for the thousands of families who have been suffering day-time temperatures of around 45 for the last two weeks. During that time, many head teachers have closed their schools and there has been a significant rise in hospital admissions. Farmers in the area have been hoping for cooler weather and rain to help save this season's crops. As far as we know, no-one has died.

2) According to latest reports, people in some of the most mountainous areas of the country have been unable to leave their homes due to the heavy snow which has been falling continuously for five days. In the worst affected area the snowfall has reached 200 centimetres in depth, and although road maintenance crews have been working round the clock, they have not managed to reach motorists trapped in their cars.

4

Grammar focus

WS 3.1 Task 4

3) Reports are coming in that a volcano which has been dormant for the past 50 years has erupted in a popular tourist area in west of the country. During the initial explosion, which lasted just half an hour, rocks fell on nearby villages causing serious damage. Ever since, people have been getting into their cars and driving away from their homes as fast as they can. Many have left all but their most precious belongings behind and fled.

Draw a table on the board with a column for each form and ask learners to write the verbs in the correct column.

Ask concept questions, e.g.
1. Which column emphasizes the action?
2. Which column emphasizes the duration of the action?

Check that learners understand how these two verb tenses are formed. If they are not sure, illustrate it on the board.

Learners place verbs in the correct category.
Key

pres. perf. simple	pres. perf. cont.
have closed has been a rise has died have been unable has reached have not managed has been dormant has erupted have left … and fled	have been suffering have been hoping has been falling have been working have been getting … and driving

5

Post-reading

WS 3.1 Tasks 5 and 6a

Homework: Task 6b

T On the WS ask learners to fill in the gaps in the newspaper story with the correct form of one of the verbs in the box. Check answers.

Ask learners to work in pairs. They are news reporters sending a recent story to a news programme. Suggest they choose a story they are familiar with. Allow 5-10 minutes for this. Remind them to use present perfect verbs where appropriate.

Listen to pairs reporting their stories to each other, making a note of verb errors to pick up on later.

Ask learners to write up their news stories in 80-100 words as homework (Task 6b).

L Learners fill in the gaps.

Key
1) has been falling; 2) have burst; 3) has been flowing; 4) have left; 5) have closed; 6) have drowned; 7) have been; 8) have been warning

In pairs learners prepare a news report and then report their story to another pair.

Recent news

Task 1

Look at the photos and talk about them in pairs.

a) Have you ever experienced these events?

b) What is happening now? What has happened?

Task 2

Read the following news reports. Match each story to a photo. Are these basically good or bad news stories?

1

Much awaited cool weather is likely to arrive in our area over the weekend. This is good news for the thousands of families who have been suffering day-time temperatures of around 45° for the last two weeks. During that time, many head teachers have closed their schools and there has been a rise in hospital admissions. Farmers in the area have been hoping for cooler weather and rain to help save this season's crops. Forest fires have already burned an estimated 2,000 square miles and destroyed over 100 buildings. As far as we know, no one has died.

2

According to latest reports people in some of the most mountainous areas of the country have been unable to leave their homes due to the heavy snow which has been falling continuously for five days. In the worst affected area the snowfall has reached 200 centimetres in depth, and although road maintenance crews have been working round the clock, they have not managed to reach motorists trapped in their cars

3

Reports are coming in that a volcano which has been dormant for the past 50 years has erupted in a popular tourist area in the west of the country. During the initial explosion, which lasted just half an hour, rocks fell on nearby villages causing serious damage. Ever since, people have been getting into their cars and driving away from their homes as fast as they can. Many have left all but their most precious belongings behind and fled.

Task 3

Read the stories again. How have the situations affected people? What time periods are mentioned in the stories?

ISBN 978-3-12-501628-6

Task 4

a) In the news stories underline all the verbs in the present perfect simple and present perfect continuous.

b) Put the verbs you have underlined in the right column.

present perfect simple	present perfect continuous

c) How are these verb tenses formed:

present perfect simple = ...

present perfect continuous = ...

Task 5

In the following news story fill in the gaps with the verbs from the box. Choose the correct form: present perfect simple or present perfect continuous.

be • burst • close • drown • fall • flow • leave • warn

In the north of the state, heavy rain (1)............................... for almost a week. In the last few days, two rivers (2)............................... their banks with the result that water (3)............................... through the streets of low-lying towns and villages. In Madison, many families (4) .... their homes and are camping in the town's sports centre. Police (5)............................... all the roads in the area apart from one and this is being kept open to allow people to escape. Although some farm animals in the affected area (6)............................... , there (7)............................... no deaths or serious injuries to people. The story should come as no surprise as weather experts (8)............................... for many years that flooding is likely.

Task 6

a) Work in pairs. You are news reporters and have to prepare a report on a recent story for a news programme. Choose a story you are both familiar with. Note down the most important facts.

Report your news story to another pair of students – remember to use the present perfect simple and continuous where appropriate!

*b) **Homework**: Write your news story in 80-100 words.*

ISBN 978-3-12-501628-6

Add your notes here!

Unit 4 – Looking forward

How to recognize it

Based on the notes below compose a voicemail to someone (Josh) who has offered to pick you up at the station. (You and Josh have never seen each other before.)

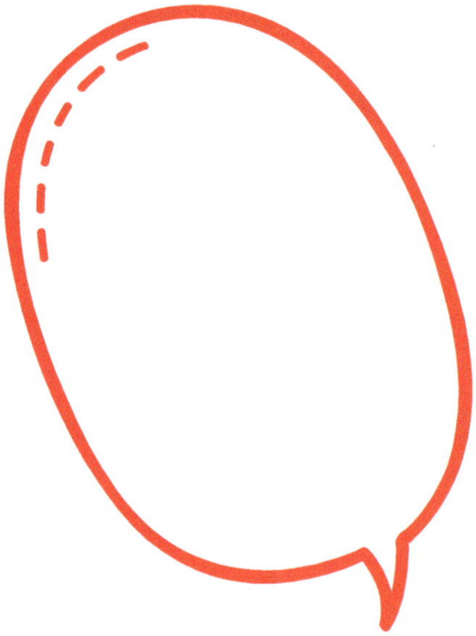

*The present simple and continuous can be found on page 16.

No doubt you will have noticed that there are various verb forms which we use to refer to the future: the **present continuous**, the **present simple***, **the future simple (will)** and **going to. Will** also has continuous and perfect forms.

Your message probably reads along these lines:

Hi Josh, it's … I'm catching the 10 am train from Liverpoool street, which gets into Ipswich at 11.05. I'll look out for a tall guy in a green jacket who will be waiting by the coffee cart near the exit. I'll see you on Monday!

How to use it

	future simple *= will + infinitive*	**future continuous** *= will + be + -ing*
affirmative (+)	*I / You / She / We …* ***will arrive*** *tonight.*	*I / You / She / We …* ***will be arriving*** *tonight.*
negative (-)	*I / You / She / We …* ***will not / won't arrive*** *tonight.*	*I / You / She / We …* ***will not / won't be arriving*** *tonight.*
question (?)	***Will I*** */ You / She / We …* ***arrive*** *tonight?*	***Will I*** */ You / She / We …* ***be arriving*** *tonight?*

	future perfect = *will + have + past participle*	future perfect continuous = *will + have been + -ing*
affirmative (+)	*I / You / She / We … **will have lived** here for ten years.*	*I / You / She / We … **will have been living** here for ten years.*
negative (-)	*I / You / She / We … **will not / won't have lived** here for ten years.*	*I / You / She / We … **will not / won't have been living** here for ten years.*
question (?)	***Will** I / You / She / We … **have lived** here for ten years?*	***Will** I / You / She / We … **have been living** here for ten years?*

	going to future = *going to + infinitive*
affirmative (+)	***I am going to learn** to dance.* *You / We / They **are going to learn** to dance.* *He / She is **going to learn** to dance.*
negative (-)	***I am not going to learn** to dance.* *You / We / They **are not going to learn** to dance.* *He / She **is not going to learn** to dance.*
question (?)	***Am I going to learn** to dance?* ***Are** you / we / they **going to learn** to dance?* ***Is** he / she **going to learn** to dance?*

When to use it

will (simple, continuous, perfect)	Possible teaching contexts / themes, examp-les
for decisions made at the moment of speaking	**Sudden responses** *A There's someone at the door.* *B **I'll go**.* *A Oh no – there are no eggs left.* *B **I'll get** some.* *A I'd love to go out tonight, but I'm broke.* *B That's okay – **I'll pay.*** *A I'm really cold.* *B **I'll put** the heating on.*
for future predictions	**Predicting your personal future** *Q What **will you be doing** this time next year / in ten years' time?* *A **I'll** probably **have** a family of my own. Hopefully **I'll have** a well-paid job. I expect **I'll be working** very hard.* **Making predictions about your town's / country's future** *The population **will have doubled** by 2050.* *I expect **they'll build** more houses.*

See lesson plan 4.

	Aspects of life 50 years from now: science and technology, education, health, food, life expectancy, space exploration ***We'll have found*** *a cure for diabetes.* *People will* ***have landed*** *on Mars and* ***be living*** *there.*
for promises and offers	**Making promises** ***I'll phone*** *as soon as I get there. / (I promise)* ***I'll give*** *you the money back when I get paid.*
	Organizing a party / holiday – sharing out the jobs ***I'll order*** *the food. /* ***I'll book*** *the room. / Paul and I* ***will organize*** *the music.*
	Moving into a new house / apartment – sharing out the jobs ***I'll get rid*** *of the rubbish. /* **I'll help** *with the decorating.*
	Volunteering in an emergency ***I'll call*** *for an ambulance. /* ***I'll phone*** *the police. / We'****ll look*** *after the children.*
for future facts and theoretical certainties	**Dates and places of events** *The next Olympic Games* ***will take*** *place in Tokyo in 2021.*
	Personal dates *On May 25th* ***I'll be*** *26.* *In two weeks' time* ***we'll have known*** *each other for a whole year.*
(won't) for refusals and things that aren't functioning	**For refusals** *He* ***won't do*** *anything I say.* *I* ***won't buy*** *anything that's wrapped in plastic.*
	Non-functioning *My car won't start – probably because it's so cold.* *Come on, why* ***won't*** *you just* ***print****?!*

going to	Possible teaching contexts / themes, with examples
for intentions, plans or resolutions	**Personal plans and intentions** *I'****m going to apply*** *for a job in advertising.* ***We're going to live*** *abroad next year.*
	Resolutions because of bad habits *I'm overweight – so* ***I'm going to eat*** *less and do more exercise.* *I'm not sleeping well.* ***I'm going to stop*** *playing games on my phone before I go to bed.*

for predictions when there is evidence	**Asking for predictions about what's going to happen next (in a film, book etc.)** *Q So, what's **going to** happen?* *A (I think) He's **going to** jump off.* **Amateur weather forecasting** *Look! The sky's red. **It's going to be** fine tomorrow.* *The cows are all lying down – it's **going to rain.*** *It's **going to snow** – look at those black clouds.*

Present continuous	Possible teaching contexts / themes, with examples
for arrangements already made	**Checking diaries trying to arrange a time to meet** *A Sorry, I can't do Monday evening. **I'm working** late.* *B What about Tuesday morning?* *A No, **I'm taking** my son to the dentist.* *B Wednesday?* *A That should be okay – **I have no plans** at all on Wednesday.* **Making an excuse** *Sorry, I can't come out. **I'm helping** my brother with his homework.*

Present simple	Possible teaching contexts / themes, with examples
for scheduled events	**Travel times** *We need to hurry. The train **leaves** in 10 minutes.* *We **take off** at 10.30 tomorrow morning.* **Sports events** *France **play** Spain in Madrid tomorrow night. Kick-off **is** at 7.30.* **Timetables (of lessons)** *This evening's lesson **starts** at 6.00 and **finishes** at 8.30.*

Good to know

shall / shan't

In the past, **shall** was sometimes used instead of **will** when referring to the future. This is now considered old-fashioned except in some negative expressions like these (**only** after *I* and *we*):

*We **shan't be** long. / **I shan't tell** you again.*

However *shall* is normal usage in questions used for the following:

• Making a suggestion	***Shall we go** swimming this afternoon?*
• Making an offer	***Shall I drive** you to the airport?*
• Asking for an instruction	***Shall I lock** the door?*

Adverbs expressing certainty or uncertainty

To express degrees of certainty add these adverbs to modify the verb form: *probably, definitely, hopefully.* Notice how they are used in sentences:

*I'll **probably / definitely** be there by 10 o'clock.*
***Hopefully**, I'll be there by 10 o'clock.*

Add your own notes here!

How to teach it

Practical matters

- As was pointed out in respect of past verb tenses, don't try to present too many future forms at once. It makes more sense to introduce one form at a time and then compare two forms. So for example, you might start by teaching *going to* for plans and intentions and once that has been established you could introduce the present continuous for arrangements.

  Another possibility would be to teach *will* for predictions and then contrast this with *going to* for predictions with evidence.

- If English is your first language, you will probably become aware that you use the various forms of the future without thinking and this means that you sometimes "break the rules" outlined in the **When to use it** section above. These are not errors, but the rules are intended to make it easier for learners to make choices which will always be correct. (Some learners tend to want to use the future simple *(will)* in all situations when there are better options.)

What to watch out for

- If learners use the contracted forms *I'll / he'll* etc., it may be very difficult to hear the "-ll", so *I'll see you later* may be impossible to distinguish from *I see you later*.

- Learners often adopt one tense and use this almost exclusively when referring to the future. Often this is *will*. Learners may use *will* rather than the present simple in subordinate clauses like this:
  As soon as I ~~will~~ get there, I'll tell you what happened.

- Learners may avoid using the future continuous form because the form itself seems complicated or because they don't understand the difference in meaning between the simple and continuous forms. The difference in meaning between pairs of sentences like this may need to be explained.
  We'll be sleeping when you arrive. (which is a statement of fact)
  We'll sleep when you arrive. (which is a promise or an offer)

- Learners may try to use the continuous form to describe conditions rather than actions.
  ~~You'll be knowing~~ where I am at all times. rather than
  You'll know where I am at all times.
  You may need to remind them *know* is a **stative verb and that stative verbs are not used in the continuous** form.

- Learners may confuse statements such as
  I'm going to Paris tomorrow. (which refers to a future arrangement) with
  I'm going to go to Paris. (which refers to a plan or intention).
  This may occur because *going to go* sounds awkward or unnaturally repetitive.

- Some learners – and possibly even some teachers (!) may be reluctant to use the unstressed form, which is sometimes written as *gonna*. Point out that in everyday speech the deliberate pronunciation, *going to,* sounds very formal.

- Some learners may not remember that *going to* can be used for predictions as well as intentions.

  I think I'm going to be sick. (prediction with evidence, not an intention)
  I'm going to lose weight. (intention not a prediction)

Suggestions for classroom activities

1 Topic Foretelling the future / Horoscopes
Language *will / going to* for predictions (with or without evidence)
Activities Read horoscopes in newspapers or magazines. How do they compare with learners' own ideas about their future.
Learners could write horoscopes for a partner. If they are simple predictions, they should use *will, will be + -ing,* or *will have + past participle*. If predictions are based on evidence, they should use *going to* and mention what their evidence is.
*You **will meet** a mysterious stranger.*
*You **are going to live** to be very old, like your parents and grandparents.*

2 Topic Arranging a get-together with friends / colleagues, e.g. a party, or an important meeting
Language Present continuous – for arrangements
Activities Using their (phone) diaries, learners, working in small groups, could try to find a time they are all free to get together. This will generate conversations such as this:
A How about Monday evening?
*B That's okay for me. **I'm not doing** anything then.*
*C Sorry I can't. **I'm working** late on Monday.*
Note: If learners do not have a busy diary, provide them with a completed ready-made diary for next week with some of the times filled in. (Make sure learners have different times filled in.)

3 Topic Future newspaper headlines
Language *will* and *will have + past participle*
Activities Present the class with possible future news headlines and ask them to predict in which year they might see these. You give them some possible dates: 2030, 2040, 2050, 2060, 2500, 3000. Examples:
World gas supplies run out
Earth abandoned because of pollution
Bees extinct
Robots replace 50% of human jobs
First human colony on Mars established
Worldwide ban on smoking
Diabetes wiped out
Get learners to discuss ideas in pairs or groups and make sentences like this:
*I think gas supplies **will run out** in 2030. / Gas supplies **will have run out** by 2040.*

4 Topic Your hopes and fears for the future
Language *will, won't, will / won't be + -ing*
with
I hope …, I'm confident …, I'm pretty sure …, I expect …, I doubt if …
Activities Ask students to think about personal or professional aspects of their future life in 10, 20 or 30 years' time. *What will they be doing? What will they have done?*

5	**Topic**	The foreseeable future
	Language	All future forms
	Activities	Pair or group work – exchange ideas about your future. Include arrangements, plans and predictions. This could be time-limited: the next six months / year / five years etc. The discussion could be followed by a short writing activity. Learners email a friend telling them about the future they see for themselves.
6	**Topic**	Offer help
	Language	*will*
	Activities	1. Make a set of cards which state problems such as these: *"I'm really tired." / "It's so hot in here." / "I've got a terrible headache." / "I'd like to go out tonight, but I can't afford to." / "Aren't you cold? I'm freezing."* Learners work in pairs or small groups. They take turns to read the cards and offer help. A picks up a card and reads what it says: *It's so hot in here.* B offers help: *I'll open the window if you like.* C offers: *I'll turn the heating off, shall I?* 2. When they have worked through the cards, encourage learners to come up with their own problems for which they need help.
7	**Topic**	Film predictions
	Language	*will* or *going to*
	Activities	Play enough of a film / YouTube clip for learners to get the idea of what's happening and then pause the film and ask the class So, *what happens next?* Elicit predictions. If learners use *going* to rather than *will* ask what evidence they have for their prediction. Each time you pause the film elicit several predictions. Continue the film to show whether the predictions were correct. Silent films, action films or cartoons with the sound muted work well for this activity.
8	**Topic**	An imaginary trip
	Language	Any future verb forms / *shall* questions
	Activities	1. In small groups, learners plan an imaginary trip. This will involve making suggestions, plans and decisions and could involve conversations like this. *A So where **shall we go?*** *B How about Australia?* *C Good idea. **We'll go** to Australia. **Shall we fly** or go by boat?* *B Let's go by boat – **we'll see** more of the world that way.* *A Okay, so **we'll sail** to Australia.* *C **I'll find** out the best routes, **shall I**?* 2. When they have come up with a plan, let groups report to the rest of the class. Once decisions have been made they could use *going* to for plans and present continuous for arrangements already made. *A So, **we're going to go** by boat to Australia. **We're leaving** in September.* etc.

9	**Topic**	Resolutions
	Language	*going to / not going to* for intentions; *will* for predictions
	Activities	1. In pairs or small groups learners discuss any habits they have that they'd like to break. Introduce the idea of resolutions with a list of typical examples. *Turn phone off for five hours a day. / Make new friends. / Learn something I didn't learn as a child. / East less meat. / Walk to work or college. / Spend less. / Visit relatives. / Stop smoking. / Lose weight. / Join a gym.* etc. 2. On the basis of their discussion of bad habits, each learner writes down six resolutions, three starting *Next year, I'm going to …* and three starting *Next year, I'm not going to …* 3. Back in the group learners tell each other their resolutions and they ask each other how they intend to keep their resolutions. This might lead to conversations like this: *A* ***Ok, so I'm*** *going to turn my phone off for five hours every day.* *B* ***That'll be*** *really difficult – you're on it all the time.* *C* ***How are you going to do*** *that?* *A* ***I'm going to turn it off*** *and* ***leave*** *it at home when I go to work / college.*
10	**Topic**	Optimist / Pessimist
	Language	All future verb forms
	Activities	Ask the class to suggest some topics that might become issues in their country in the future. Examples: air travel / weather / wealth and poverty / employment / housing Learners work in pairs. A is an optimist, B a pessimist. When they discuss each topic, A should express optimistic views and B a pessimistic view. For example, on the subject of travel: *A* *I think air travel will be cheaper and less damaging to the environment because scientists will have discovered new, safer types of fuel.* *B* *I disagree. In my opinion, the government will restrict air travel by putting up prices. Many people will no longer be able to afford to fly.*

Lesson plan 4

Lesson profile

Description	Presentation → Practice → Production (See Introduction)
Topic	Predicting future changes in the city
Grammar point	*will* or *going to* for predictions
Aims	To revise and clarify differences in use between the *will* and *going to* forms.
Material	WS 4.1 *Urban changes*

PRESENTATION: 1

Photo-based speaking activity

WS 4.1 Task 1

T Show learners two photos of a town or city they know well: one photo from the present and one from the past – the greater the contrast, the better.

Ask what has changed and elicit answers.

L Learners discuss how the town / city has changed, e.g.

There used to be more green spaces / trees here. Now there are tall office blocks / more skyscrapers.

2

Listening comprehension

WS 4.1 Task 2

T Either play a recording of several people predicting how the town will improve / change in the future or tell them your own thoughts. There should be a mixture of *will* and *going to* in the predictions.

Ask learners whether they agree or disagree with each prediction they hear, but don't at this stage expect them to use the target language.

L Learners listen to the predictions and think about whether they agree or not.

Learners agree or disagree with the predictions:

Yes, I agree. / No, I disagree.

3

Grammar focus – modelling the target structures

T On the board write two examples of predictions with *will* and two with *going to*, e.g.

I think the roads will be widened.
I expect they'll build more parks.
They're going to ban cars from the city centre. I've seen the plans.
There's going to be a new bridge. I read it in the paper.

L

	Model and ask students to repeat these sentences. Insist on contractions ***'ll*** and ***gonna.***	Learners repeat the model sentences, using the contracted forms: *The roads'll be wider.* *There'll be more parks.* *They're gonna ban cars.* *There's gonna be a new bridge.*
4 Grammar focus – understanding the differences in use WS 4.1 Task 3	**T** Check that learners understand the idea of predictions – and point out that we can make predictions in two different ways, using ***will*** or ***going to.*** Ask learners to underline the future verb forms *will* and *going to* in the script (Task 3a). See if they can work out themselves when we use each form by asking them to look back at the four sentences on the board. Elicit their ideas. (Task 3b) Clarify how the two pairs of sentences are different.	**L** Learners suggest when we use *will* and when *going to* for predictions. (Hopefully they will understand from examples that *will* is used when we're saying what we think or expect to happen, and *going to* is used when we have evidence or prior knowledge.) The first pair: You ***think*** this will happen. The second pair: You ***have evidence*** it's going to happen.
PRACTICE: 5 Grammar practice WS 4.1 Task 4	**T** Elicit more predictions of both types from the class. If they use *going to*, ask what evidence there is for their idea. Give learners a short gap fill activity asking them to fill the gaps with the correct form of a given verb. Check answers.	**L** Learners make more predictions of both types, providing evidence in the case of *going to*. Learners complete the gap fill exercise and then compare their answers in pairs. **Key** *I expect massive changes* ***will*** *take place in the city in the next 20 years. People from all over the world move here to live, study and work. Experts say the population* ***is going to*** *grow even more. I think they* ***will*** *build more houses – but because so much of the land here is mountains, I expect they* ***will*** *reclaim land from the bay and the river. I also read in the newspaper that they* ***are going to*** *improve transport links and introduce greener vehicles. Air quality and people's health* ***will*** *continue to be a problem if they don't find greener solutions.*

T	L	
Outline a new scenario and ask learners to come up with their own predictions, e.g. *Predict how the town you are studying English in / your school / the country you live in / the way and place people work / … could be different in 25 years' time.*		**PRODUCTION: 6** Speaking activity: formulating own predictions WS 4.1 Task 5
First elicit a few ideas in the group and then get learners to continue working in pairs or groups. Remind them to use *will* and *going to* appropriately.	Working in pairs / groups learners make their predictions.	
Monitor but remember this is a free practice activity, so do not interrupt discussions. Simply make a note of any errors you hear (these could be the wrong choice of will or going to, a badly formed verb etc.).		
Round off the activity by eliciting a few ideas from the class.	Learners share some of their predictions with the class.	
Finally, focus on the most serious errors you heard in the group discussions and ask students to correct the errors themselves.	Learners suggest corrections for the errors.	

Urban changes

Task 1

Compare the two photographs below. The top photo shows Hong Kong harbour in 1971 and the bottom one shows a recent view of the harbour.

What has changed?

Task 2

Listen to the recording. Three people are discussing how Hong Kong might change in the future. Do you agree with their predictions?

Task 3

a) Read the script of the conversation on the next page. Underline the future verb forms.

b) Formulate rules for the future verb forms. Highlight examples in the text, using three different colours.

- *Use the **will future** for* ....
- *Use the **going to** future for* ....
- ***Going to** can also be used for* ....

ISBN 978-3-12-501628-6

A So how do we think our city will change in the next 25 years?

B Hong Kong will continue to be a popular place to work, so it's likely that the population will grow. All the signs are that the traffic's going to get worse – more people, more cars. I guess it'll probably get worse gradually and if that happens, more people will suffer the effects of air pollution.

C I imagine many families will want to move to somewhere on the outskirts of the city, where it's quieter and greener and the air is better.

B I agree that will happen if they don't do something about the air pollution. But I think they're gonna ban buses and private cars from the city centre.

A That'll certainly make the city a better place to live in.

C When are they going to do that?

B I don't know.

A So until that day, everything will get steadily worse – that's my prediction.

Task 4

Fill in the correct future verb form in this short text.

I expect massive changes .... (take place) in the city in the next 20 years. People from all over the world move here to live, study and work. Experts say the population .... (grow) even more. I think they .... (build) more houses – but because so much of the land here is mountains, I expect they .... (reclaim) land from the bay and the river. I also read in the newspaper that they .... (improve) transport links and introduce greener vehicles. Air quality and people's health .... (continue) to be a problem if they don't find greener solutions.

Task 5

Work with a partner or in a group. Choose one of the following and predict what could be different in 25 years' time in:

a) the town you are studying English in
b) the country you live in
c) the way and place people work
d) ...

ISBN 978-3-12-501628-6

Unit 5 – Shades of Meaning

How to recognize it

Which of these everyday expressions do you use or have you heard other people using?

The highlighted verbs are **modal auxiliary verbs**, or **modal verbs** for short.
What do all these verbs have in common? Could you replace any of them?

How to use it

	subject + can / could *+ infinitive without* **to**	**subject + could have + past participle**	
	present	**past**	**perfect**
affirmative (+)	*She* ***can run*** *fast.* *She* ***could run*** *even faster.*	*She* ***could walk*** *when she was less than a year old.*	*She* ***could have walked*** *instead of going by car.*
negative (-)	*He* ***can't / cannot run*** *fast.* *He* ***couldn't / could not run*** *any faster.*	*He* ***couldn't walk*** *until he was two.*	*He* ***couldn't have walked*** *with a broken leg.*

question (?)	***Can they run*** *fast?* ***Could*** *they* ***run*** *faster?*	***Could you walk*** *to school when you were a child?*	***Could they have walked*** *or was it too windy?*

	subject + must + *infinitive without* **to**	**subject + must have** + **past participle**
	present	**perfect**
affirmative (+)	*I* ***must finish*** *this job as soon as I can.*	*They* ***must have finished*** *early.*
negative (-)	*You* ***mustn't / must not take*** *things without asking.*	*They* ***mustn't have arrived*** *yet.*
question (?)	***Must*** *you* ***leave*** *so soon?*	form not used

The question form *"Must you…?"* sounds quite formal or old-fashioned, so *have to* is often used instead, e.g. *Do you have to leave so soon?*

	subject + should + *infinitive without* **to**	**subject + should have** + **past participle**
	present	**perfect**
affirmative (+)	*She* ***should get*** *more sleep.*	*They* ***should have thought*** *about the consequences.*
negative (-)	*You* ***shouldn't go*** *to bed so late.*	*I* ***shouldn't have said*** *anything.*
question (?)	***Should*** *you ask someone for help?*	***Should*** *they* ***have asked*** *for permission first?*

	subject + might /may + *infinitive without* **to**	**subject + might / may have** + **past participle**
	present	**perfect**
affirmative (+)	*We* ***might / may*** *go by train.*	*They* ***might / may have missed*** *their flight.*
negative (-)	*You* ***might / may not get*** *there on time.*	*They* ***might / may not have finished*** *lunch yet*
question (?)	***Might / May I make*** *a suggestion?*	***Might*** *she* ***have caught*** *the wrong train?**

*A more common (that is, less formal) question form would be: **Do you think she might / may have caught** the wrong train?

When to use it

There are many possible uses and meanings of modal verbs. Here are just a few of the more important uses.

Modal verb uses	**Possible teaching contexts / themes, with examples**
can / could / be able to → ability	Talking about current abilities now and when younger *I* ***can drive*** *a car.* *I* ***could ride*** *a bicycle when I was six.* *I* ***could swim*** *at the age of three but* ***I've never been able to swim*** *underwater.*

NOTE
will and **would** are sometimes considered to be modal verbs and they do have much in common form-wise with the verbs covered here. **Will** is covered in the unit on the future (Unit 4, p. 58) and **would** is dealt with in the section on conditional forms (Unit 6, page 90).

Talking about abilities or skills to be proud of
*I **can play** the accordion / piano.*
*I **can speak** three languages.*

Things you can't do but would like to be able to do
*I'd love **to be able to yodel / dance** the tango.*

See lesson plan 5.

can / can't / could / couldn't
→ permission or prohibition

What you can do at certain ages
*In my country **you can't get married** until you're 17.*
*In the past **you could drive** without a taking a test.*

Childhood "rules"
***I can't / couldn't play** computer games for more than 2 hours a day.*
***I can / could stay** out until 10 o'clock.*

What you can / can't do in these places: on planes, on trains, on roads
*In parks you **can play** games on the grass, but you **can't ride** motorbikes*

can / could / could have
→ possibility

(use *can* if you think something is likely and *could* for something less likely)

Referring to outcomes of particular actions
*Eating too much rich food… **can make** you feel ill.*

Possible explanations for sets of circumstances, e.g.
- **Your car is making strange noises**
  *It **could need** a new exhaust pipe. / It **could be** out of oil.*
- **One of your fellow students is not in class today**
  *He / She **could be** ill. / She / He **could have missed** the bus.*

may / might
→ less likely possibilities

Planning a holiday (optimistic and pessimistic views)
A What about going to Thailand? The weather will be great.
*B I'd rather not. I'm not keen on flying – our plane **might crash**.*
A OK, then how about Spain? We could drive there.
*B I'd love to go to Spain, but our car **may break down**.*

must / mustn't
→ obligation

(use *should* to sound less authoritarian)

Safety rules for children – things parents tell their children
*You **must look** left and right before you cross the road.*
*You **mustn't talk** to strangers.*
*You **must** share things with your friends.*
*You **mustn't hit / bite / kick** other children.*

When travelling to another country
*You **must respect** the laws of the country.*
*You **mustn't expect** everyone to speak your language.*

have to
→ necessity or obligation

Current duties and responsibilities
__I have to__ get to work by 9 o'clock every morning.
What time __do you have to get__ to work?

Childhood duties / jobs
__I had to clean__ my dad's car every Sunday. What __did you have to do__?

What certain groups of people don't have to do
Children and old people __don't have to go to work__.
Adults __don't have to go__ to school.

should / ought to
→ advice or suggestions

Asking for and giving advice
Q I'm fed up with my job. What __should I do__?
A __You should look__ for another job.

A I can't afford to pay the rent on my apartment.
B __You should find__ someone to share with.

B I've found a very expensive-looking phone in the street.
A __You ought to take__ it to a police station.

Q What's the best advice you were ever given?
A Someone said "__You shouldn't worry__ too much about what people think of you."

Good to know

Possibility vs ability

When referring to possibilities, *can* and *could* refer to the future:
I __can / could meet__ you for lunch tomorrow.
However, when referring to abilities, *be able to* is used instead:

future	past	infinitive
I hope __I'll be able to speak__ three or more languages one day.	*Eventually, __I was able to break down__ the door and escape.*	*I'd love to __be able to come__ to your party, but I'm afraid I'm busy that day.*

Obligation and necessity

In certain situations the verb *have to* + infinitive is used instead of *must:*

1. When referring to future obligations, e.g.
   __You will have to find__ a new job next year, won't you?
2. When referring to past obligations, e.g.
   She __had to pay__ a $100 fine for speeding.
3. In the negative to mean lack of obligation or necessity (*need to* is also possible here), e.g.
   I __don't have to wear__ a suit for work. / I __won't have to apply__ again. / He __didn't have to give__ the money back.
   I __don't need to wear__ a suit for work. / I __won't need to apply__ again. / He __didn't need to give__ the money back.

Suggestion and moral obligation

Ought to + infinitive and *should* have similar meanings, but there is a slight difference. *Should* usually relates to **advice or suggestions** while *ought* to suggests a **rule or a moral obligation:**
*You **should get** more sleep.* (Advice)
*You **ought to be** more polite on occasions like this.* (Moral obligation)

Bear in mind the following:
- (The negative form of *ought to* + infinitive is *ought not to* + infinitive:
  *We **ought not to leave** the window open if we go out.*
- There is no past form of *should* or *ought to*.
- *Ought to* is rarely used in questions, as it is extremely formal. *Should* is used instead.
  ~~***Ought** we **to be***~~ *more worried?* → ***Should** we **be** more worried?*

Asking for permission

The forms *might* and *may* can both be used to ask for permission. However, *might I / we / they…?* is extremely formal and rarely used. *May I / we / they …* is also polite and formal but still used more often (in most everyday contexts it is usual to use *can I / we / they …*). It is not possible to say *May / Might you…?*

Continuous forms

are only possible for some modal verbs and in certain uses (mainly possibility, probability, in suggestions and recommendations), e.g.
*They **could be coming** by train. / He **could have been driving** too fast.*
*We **may be flying** there – we haven't decided yet. / They **might have been visiting** their friends.*
*He **must be finishing** work soon. / She **mustn't have been looking** where she was going.*
*You **shouldn't be staying** out so late. / They **should have been thinking** about what to say next.*
*We **ought to be looking for** a bigger place to live now that we're expecting twins.*

How to teach it

Practical matters

- Limit how much new language you introduce at any one time, and certainly don't try to cover all the uses of a particular modal verb in one go as this is certain to cause confusion. Remember teaching grammar like this is as much about showing learners when to **use it appropriately** as how to form it accurately. There is no single correct order of introducing modal verbs, but a beginner-level syllabus might look like this:

Can I have?	*asking for things*	Unit 3
can / can't	*talking about possibility*	Unit 6
can / can't	*talking about ability*	Unit 10
should / shouldn't	*giving advice*	Unit 13

- Lessons should highlight the **function of the verbs** you are going to introduce rather than the grammatical form. For example, it makes more sense to say you are doing a lesson on *permission and prohibition* rather than on *can, can't, must, mustn't.* Doing this you will avoid confusing learners by explaining that *can* and *can't* are also used to talk about *ability and possibility.*
- However, don't be surprised if you have to **explain some of the functional terminology** such as *obligation* or *prohibition*. If words like these are problematic for your learners, find thematic or situational terms which might help to clarify the concepts. For example, if you are teaching the language of obligation and prohibition, you could say your lesson is about strange laws, or workplace regulations.
- Try to teach modal verbs in **realistic communicative contexts** which provide learners with opportunities to practise using the target language in ways they may find useful in real life situations.
- Make sure learners understand that **modal verbs** have no meaning of their own but are used to **convey the attitude or feeling of the user**. Compare these three sentences:
  *You **could work** harder.* (a gentle suggestion, perhaps by a friend)
  *You **should work** harder.* (advice, perhaps from a critical parent)
  *You **must work** harder.* (firm advice, perhaps from a teacher)
- Make sure you point out early on that modal verbs are different from other verbs learners have learned. For example, you may have taught some basic rules of verb formation so well that learners make errors like these:
  *My friend Josh **cans** swim very fast.* or
  *Last week, we **musted** revise for our exam.*

What to watch out for

- Learners may try to use *to* before the infinitive after modal verbs. For example
  *She looks very tired. She should **to** get more sleep.*
- Learners may try to make forms of these verbs which do not exist. Some examples:
  She musts … (instead of *must*)
  He cans … (instead of *he can*)
  Did you must … (instead of *Did you have to…?*)
- Unless they are quite advanced, learners will be unaware of all the possible shades of meaning that can be conveyed by modal verbs which are commonly used by English speakers as a way of conveying information in an indirect way. Some learners may regard this as pointless politeness or even hypocrisy. For example:

Polite use with modal verbs	Possible real meaning
*We **might not** be able to make it to your party at the weekend.*	*We can't come to your party at the weekend.*
*You **must** come and see us when you're next in town.*	*We'd quite like to see you again.*
***Shouldn't** we close the window?*	*Can you close the window?*
***You may** need to think more carefully about what you say.*	*Think before you speak.*
***May I take** your name, please?*	*What's your name?*

4. Learners may assume that *mustn't* is always the opposite of *must*, when in fact the opposite is sometimes *don't have to*. Example

*I **must** renew my passport next month.*	(It is important to do this.)
***I don't have to / needn't** renew my passport next month.*	(It is not necessary to do this.)
*I **mustn't** renew my passport next week.*	(This is prohibited.)

What else do you need to bear in mind when teaching modal verbs? Make a note here!

Suggestions for classroom activities

1 Topic Abilities – things you have learned to do
Language *can / can't / be able to*
Activities 1. Learners make a list of things they have learned to do. Example: play the trombone / speak four languages / make French onion soup …

2. Referring to their lists, learners have conversations like this:
A ***Can you play** any instruments? I **can play** the trombone.*
B *Yes, I **can play** the violin, but I **can't play** the trombone.*
A *How many languages **can you speak**? I **can speak four**: French, Spanish, Italian and English.*
B *I **can speak** English, Japanese and French, but **I can't speak** Spanish.*

3. Learners discuss in pairs or small groups things they would like to be able to do:
A *I'd like to **be able to cook** well.*
B *I **can cook** ordinary things, but I'd really like **to be able to cook** Indian food.*

Note: To make this activity less controlled or drill-like, tell students to talk to each other about things they are proud of being able to do.

See lesson plan 5.

2 Topic Rules and regulations
Language *can / can't / must / mustn't / could / couldn't / had to* – for permission and prohibition
You may also wish to introduce *be allowed to*. *We're (not) allowed to …*
Activities 1. Learners exchange information about rules and regulations

- In public places such as: libraries, hospitals, restaurants, bars, sports clubs
  *We **can only smoke** in special areas.*
- For certain groups of people: students, police officers, parents
  *Police officers **can carry** guns but they **mustn't use** them unless they are at risk.*
- The ages at which people can get married, join the army, smoke, vote
  *You **can't vote** until you're 18 but you **can join** the army at 16.*
- In workplaces or college
  *We **must get** there by 8.30 every morning and we **can't be** late more than once a month.*

2. Talking about the past rules and regulations

- Learners discuss the rules and regulations that were imposed by their family or their teachers when they were younger. (Silly school rules often work well.)
  *My brother and I **had to go** to bed at 8 o'clock until we were 10 years old.*
  *We **could only watch** one hour of TV every evening and we **couldn't go out** until we'd finished our homework.*
  *We **had to walk** on the left along corridors and up and down stairs.*
- What people could and couldn't do in the past (100-200 years ago)
  This could cover these topics: education / clothes / social behaviour / love and marriage

3 Topic Possible results and explanations
Language *can / could / could have* – for possibilities (Remind learners to use *can* if they think something is more likely and *could* if less likely.)
Activities 1. Learners discuss different ways of finishing sentences like these. (This should be more of a discussion activity than a simple one-answer drill.)

- *Watching too much TV can / could …*
- *Eating too much can / could …*
- *Not getting regular exercise can / could …*
- *Driving too fast can / could …*

2. Learners discuss possible explanations for the situations described in sentences such as the following examples. Encourage them to make up their own situations.

- *"My car won't start."*
- *"There's a terrible queue of traffic on the motorway."*
- *"My sister is not answering her phone."*

3. Ask learners to speculate about what's happening in a photograph or cartoon using *could / could be + -ing / could have + past participle*. For example

4 Topic Sensory memories
Language *could + see, hear, smell*
Activities 1. Ask learners to think back to an occasion or a situation in the past which sticks in their memory because of something they could hear, see or smell. Some possible situations:
a visit to a farm or zoo / arriving at a party / travelling on a crowded train / a first day at a new school or in a new job

2. *Learners work in pairs with one partner describing what she/he could see, hear or smell and the other trying to guess the occasion or situation. They could make conversations like this:*
A I ***could hear*** *the noise of engines.*
B Were you in a traffic jam?
A No. I ***could see*** *people with suitcases.*
B Were you at a train station?
A No. I ***could smell*** *fuel.*
B Were you at an airport?
A Yes, I was.

5 Topic Asking for and giving advice
Language *should / shouldn't / ought to / ought not to*
Activities 1. Present learners with a set of problems. These could be made up or taken from newspapers and magazines, where problems are often about relationships or money.

2. Individually, learners make notes about what they would say to these people. There is no need to suggest the use of modal verbs at this stage.

3. Learners then work in pairs, one outlining a problem, the other giving the advice based on the notes they made, this time using the target language.

4. Monitor these discussions and encourage learners to go beyond this initial, rather controlled practice stage. The following might be an example discussion:

A *My flatmate and I get on very well, but she never does any tidying or cleaning. I do everything. I can't stand it any more, but I don't know what to do.*
B *You* ***should / ought to tell*** *her you're going to move out if things don't improve.*
A *I tried that and she tidied and cleaned for a few days and then things went back to normal.*
B *You* ***shouldn't / ought not to let*** *her get away with it.*
A *I know but she's my best friend.*
B *But best friends don't behave like that, do they?* etc.

5. As a follow-up, students could ask each other for advice about real problems they have. Suggest they discuss relatively straightforward issues rather than anything too serious or personal.

6 Topic Language Activities

Retrospective advice
could have / should have / shouldn't have
1. Learners read newspaper stories which could have ended differently.
Examples

High speed idiots
Two thieves escaped from police after a high-speed car chase through the streets of a small town in the north of the country. They were going so fast that they crashed their car into the wall of a car park. In an attempt to escape from the police officers, they climbed over the wall straight into the police station.

Crash for cash
A van driver got his revenge on a bank's cash machine which had kept his debit card. He stole a tractor, attached it to the cash machine and then pulled it out of the wall of the building. Unfortunately, he couldn't get the money from the machine, but he did major damage to the bank. Revenge is sweet, but anger cost the van driver three years in prison.

What a catch!
A French fisherman got into trouble when he unexpectedly caught a giant fish. The monster fish dragged the man a kilometre out to sea before the fishing line broke.

2. Learners then consider how things could have ended differently by answering these questions with sample answers:
a) What mistakes did the people in the stories make?
The van driver stole the cash machine and damaged the bank.
b) What could he/she have done differently?
He ***could have gone*** *into the bank and* ***asked*** *for his card back.*
c) What should or shouldn't they have done?
He ***should have complained*** *to the bank. / He* ***shouldn't have lost*** *his temper.*

3. They could then discuss their answers to these questions in pairs or small groups and arrive at a joint decision.
NOTE: The discussions could equally well be about stories learners had heard. The activity could also be personalized by asking learners to tell each other about a problem they handled badly. Partners suggest what they *could have / should have done differently*.

7 Topic
Language
Activities

Stressful situations
may, might (may suggests a more likely possibility than *might)*
1. Outline stressful situations people sometimes find themselves in. Suggest situations like this:
- Charlie has lost his job. He's 62 years old.
- Anna has just split up with her boyfriend.
- Emma's car has broken down on the motorway and she doesn't have her phone with her.

2. Ask learners to discuss some of the problems people in these situations might experience.
*It **might be** difficult for Ben to find another job. He **may be** too old.*
*Anna **may decide** to move to another area. She **might not want** to risk seeing her boyfriend again.*
*Emma **might be** worried about getting out of her car, but she **may have to walk** to the nearest phone.*

Note: You may need to remind learners of the difference in use between *must* and *have to*:
- *must* is used when the speaker feels the obligation
- *have to* is used when the obligation is from another source.

8 Topic
Language
Activities

Evening and weekend obligations
must / have to
1. Learners think about the next few days and make two lists:
Things I must do
go to the hairdressers / buy new shoes / put up a shelf in the kitchen …
Things I have to do
apply for a new passport / pay a tax bill / work late on Friday …

2. They compare lists in pairs or small groups and discuss their various obligations. Each use of *have to* could be queried or questioned by other learners:
Why do you have to do that? Who says you have to do that? What would happen if you didn't do that?

9 Topic
Language
Activities

Speculating
must / must have; can't / can't have; might / might have
1. Present learners with a series of lateral thinking puzzles and ask them to discuss them using the target language. Examples:
a) A woman lives on the tenth floor of a building. Every day she takes the lift to go down to the ground floor to go to work or to go shopping. When she returns she takes the lift to the seventh floor and walks up the stairs to reach her apartment on the tenth floor. She hates walking so why does she do this?
*A She **might be doing** it to keep fit.*
*B She **can't be doing** it to keep fit. She only walks up the last three floors.*
*A She **must be** a masochist!*

b) A man walked into a bar and asked the barman for a glass of water. The barman took out a gun and pointed it at the man. The man said 'Thank you' and walked out smiling.

A "A glass of water" might have been a secret code.
B The man might have taken the gun with him when he left.
A No, he can't have taken the gun – that wouldn't make any sense. The man might have been an inspector who wanted to check that the barman could protect the bar in case of robbery.

c) There were six eggs in a basket. Six people each took one of the eggs. One egg was left in the basket? How and why?

2. If learners run out of ideas you could give them clues. Allowing these discussions to go on too long can be frustrating and annoying so, when you feel learners are tiring of talking about one of the problems, give them a clue to the answer.

Answers

a) The woman in the lift is very short.
b) The man who went into the bar had hiccups. The barman recognized this from his speech and pointed the gun at him to give him a shock. This cured the hiccups, so the man no longer needed the water.
c) The last person took the basket with the last egg still in it.

3. Ask learners if they know any other lateral thinking puzzles. (You can find lots of examples on various internet sites.)

10 Topic Language Activities

Parent / teenage child role play
may / can for polite requests and asking for and giving permission
1. Allocate roles: A is a parent and B is a teenage son or daughter. Give out role cards

A
Your son or daughter wants to go on holiday with a friend but needs your help. They haven't been very helpful or pleasant to you recently, so you are not inclined to help them unless they improve their ways. Only give your permission if they do something to help you.

B
You'd like to go on a short holiday with a friend, but you need a parent's permission. You'd also like to borrow their car and some money. You know they are not very pleased with you at the moment, so you have to ask them very politely.

2. Learners prepare their roles for a few minutes and then perform the role play. Remind them to use *may* for polite requests (and *please*). (If they use *can,* their parent may not help!) The parent should use *can / can't* when giving or refusing permission. (In this situation *may* would sound over formal.)

3. Monitor the conversations, listening for learners' use of polite language.

4. Round off the activity by asking a few pairs to perform their role play for the rest of the class.

Lesson plan 5

Lesson profile

Description	Test → Teach → Test (See Introduction)
Topic	What you can do at different ages
Grammar point	*can / can't* for permission / prohibition; *be allowed to*
Aims	To clarify the use of *can / can't / (not) be allowed to (and mustn't)* and compare age restrictions in different countries
Material	WS 5.1 *At what age?*

TEST: 1

Photo-based speaking activity

WS 5.1 Tasks 1 and 2

T Introduce the topic by asking learners to think and talk about the ages at which young people can do certain things in their country, e.g.

- work part-time job (A)
- vote in elections (B)
- play the lottery (C)
- get married (D)
- join the army (E)

Note: If your learners are of different nationalities, this will probably take considerably longer than if they are of the same nationality.

As far as learners are concerned this should be suggested as an interesting discussion about a possibly contentious topic. At this stage, don't tell them what language you want them to use. This will mean that their conversations go beyond the *can / can't* stage.

Monitor discussions, listening for learners' use of the target language. Make a note of any of this language that is being used incorrectly or is not being used at all. For example they may use *mustn't* when *can't* would be better. Check that they are not using *to* before the infinitive.

L Learners talk about these questions in pairs or groups.

If they are interested in the topic, they will also discuss the rights and wrongs of limiting certain activities to certain age groups. They may talk about the reasons why for example in some countries young people can join the army at 16 but cannot vote until they are 18.

Allow the discussions to continue for as long as you need to get a clear picture of how familiar or unfamiliar learners are with the target language.

TEACH: 2

Grammar focus - modelling the target structures and clarifying use

T The length and nature of this part of the lesson will depend on how well the learners used the target language in the first stage of the lesson. It may be that some learners are familiar with *can / can't* for permission and prohibition, but others may need extra study and practice.

If learners have not used *allowed to / not allowed to*, introduce this as an alternative.

They may overuse mustn't instead of can't.

Write some model sentences on the board to clarify appropriate use. Include affirmative and negative sentences, e.g.

In the UK, you can get a part-time job when you're 14, but you can't work for more than two hours a day.
You can't vote in elections until you're 18.
You're allowed to get married when you're 16 with your parents' consent.
You're not allowed to drive until you're 17.

Ask questions about these example sentences, e.g.
What can you do when you're 18?
How long are you allowed to work for when you're 14?
etc.

L Learners ask questions if the grammar or use of the target language is not clear.

Learners answer questions about the model sentences.

3

Grammar practice - gap-fill

WS 5.1 Task 3

T Set a short practice task. Gap-fill exercises are not communicative but they are quick and efficient.

L Students complete the sentences with *can / can't / allowed / not allowed.*

Key
a) *In the UK you are **allowed** to go into a bar and order soft drinks when you're 14.*
b) *You **can't** see an adult film until you're 18.*
c) *You **can** become a blood donor at 17.*
d) *You are **not allowed** to fly a glider until you're 16.*

TEST: 4

Speaking activity – comparing age restrictions in different countries

WS 5.1 Task 4

T For this final activity, set a similar task to the one you started the lesson with. Here are more topics learners could discuss:

- get a tattoo (A)
- join a social media site like Facebook (B)
- serve on a jury (C)
- get a credit card (D)
- take a driving test (E)
- drink alcohol (F)

This time remind them to use the target language.
Monitor the discussions, listening for learners' use of the target language, but do not interrupt.

L Discuss the topics suggested and any others which seem interesting and perhaps contentious.

5

Class discussion

T Round off the lesson with a general class discussion of one of the issues that provoked most debate.

L Again the discussion may widen to include ideas about how these restrictions may change in the future.

Want to adapt the lesson plan? Feel free!

At what age?

Task 1

What is happening in these photos? Describe each photo using the words below.

A

B

C

D

E

join army • vote elections • part-time job • play lottery • get married

Task 2

Discuss these questions in pairs.

1. *At what age are young people able to do these things in your country?*
2. *Do they need permission from their parents or other people?*
3. *Do you think these age limits are sensible?*

Task 3

Complete these sentences with one of the following:

can • can't • allowed • not allowed

a) *In the UK you are .... to go into a bar and order soft drinks when you're 14.*

b) *You .... see an adult film until you're 18.*

c) *You .... become a blood donor at 17.*

d) *You are .... to fly a glider until you're 16.*

ISBN 978-3-12-501628-6

Task 4

Talk about these photos with a partner.

1. *What is happening in each photo?*
2. *At what age can young people do these things in your country?*

A

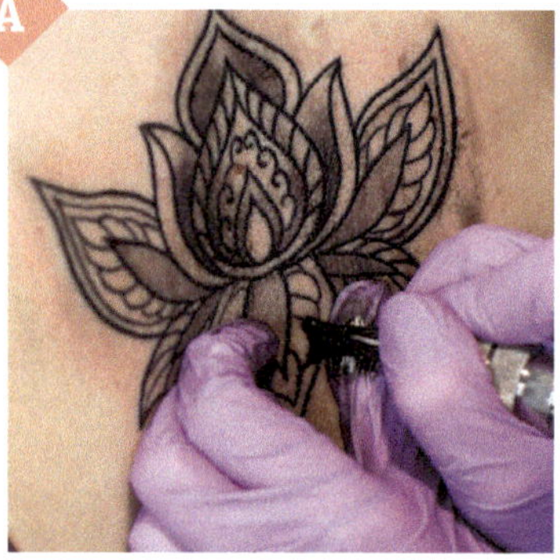

B

C

D

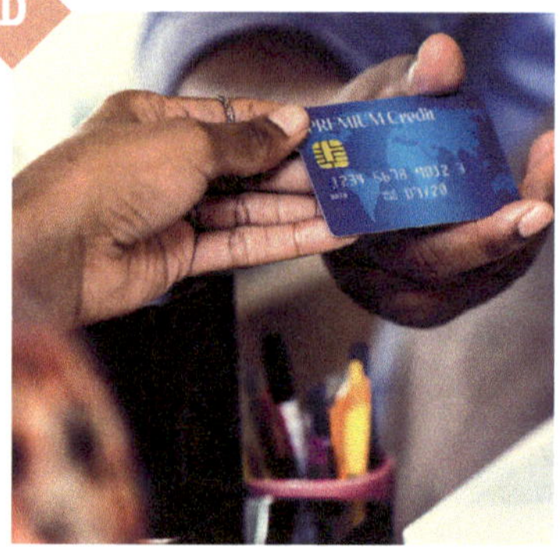

E

F

ISBN 978-3-12-501628-6

Add your notes here!

Unit 6 – What if?

How to recognize it

Finish these sentences in ways which are true for you.

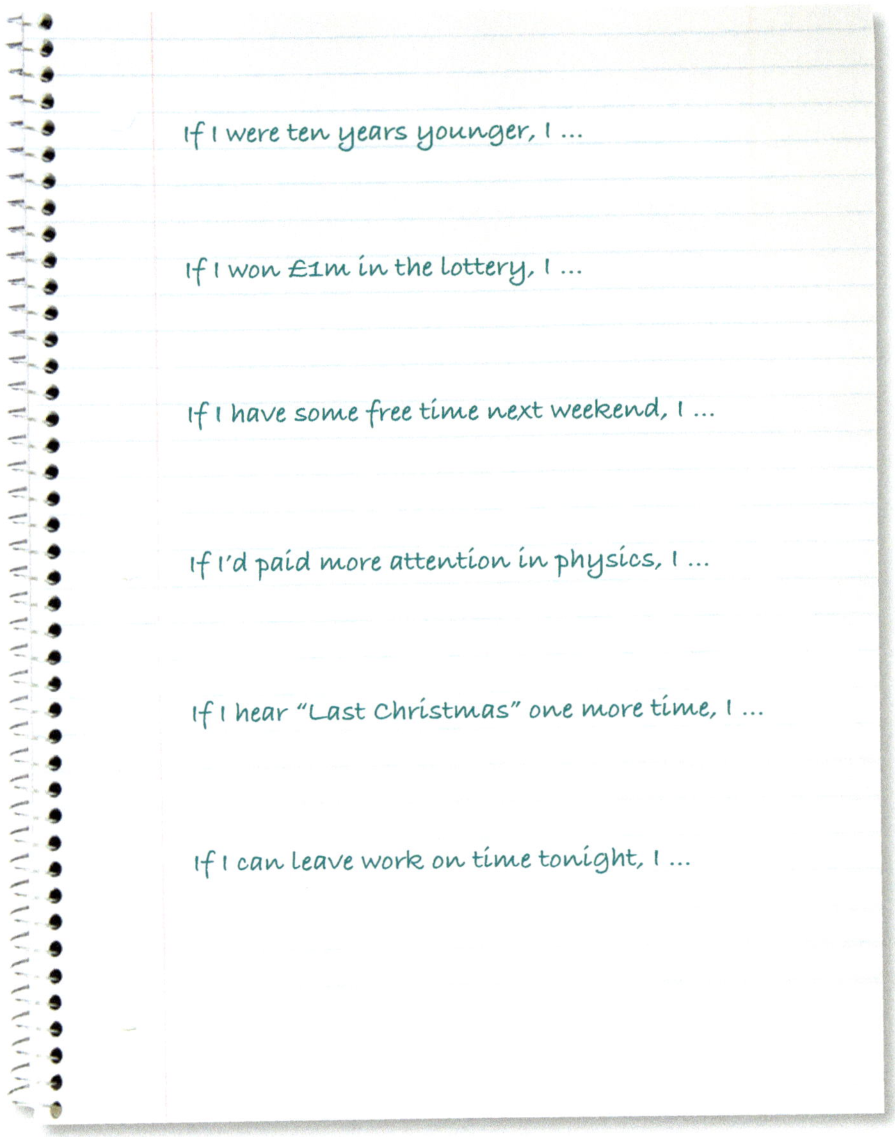

What do you notice about the verbs you have used in your sentence endings?
Most sentences which include the word **if** are called **conditional sentences**. There are four main conditional sentence patterns, *zero, first, second, third* and the additional *mixed* – a combination of the other four.

How to use it

if clause	conditional clause
zero conditional	
If + present simple	present simple / continuous
If I have *a headache,*	***I take*** *paracetamol.*
If the pavements look *wet,*	***it's*** *probably raining.*
first conditional	
If + present simple	***will future / may / might / could***
If we get *there on time,*	***we'll have*** *a meal in the pub beforehand.*
If the weather's *good tomorrow,*	***I may / might / could go*** *for a hike.*
second conditional	
If + past simple	***would / could + infinitive***
If we got *there on time,*	***we could have*** *a meal in the pub before-hand.*
If the weather was *good tomorrow,*	***I'd go*** *for a hike.*
third conditional	
If + past perfect	***would / could + have +*** past participle
If we had got *there on time,*	***we could have had*** *a meal in the pub beforehand.*
If it had been *sunny yesterday,*	***I would have gone*** *by bike.*
If I hadn't reminded *you,*	***you'd have forgotten.***
mixed conditional	
There are other conditional forms. These are called "mixed conditionals" because, unlike the others, they do not follow set patterns Here are a few examples.	
If you're driving *into town tomorrow,*	***I'll come*** *with you.*
If anyone has found *your keys,*	***I'll let*** *you know.*
If you don't apologize *immediately,*	***I'm never going to speak*** *to you again.*
If it was raining,	***I'd wear*** *a coat and take my umbrella.*
If you could lock *the door when you leave,*	***I'd be*** *most grateful.*
If he hadn't been looking *at his phone,*	***he wouldn't have walked*** *into that lamp post.*

Good to know

Generally speaking we can change the order in conditional sentences – the ***if*** clause can precede or follow the main clause. If it precedes the main clause, it is followed by a comma.
If the weather's good tomorrow, I'll go for a hike.
I'll go for a hike if the weather's good tomorrow.

Using other conjunctions

There are other words and phrases with similar meanings to *if*:
unless (*unless* + an affirmative verb can sometimes replace *if* + a negative verb)
***Unless you take** it easy, you'll have a breakdown.* (= **If you don't take** it easy, you'll have a breakdown.)
as long as
***As long as you have** the correct password, you will be able to log on anywhere.*
provided that
*You can borrow my car **provided that you check** with me first.*

When to use it

Conditional uses	Possible teaching contexts / themes, with examples
zero conditional Zero conditional sentences describe general conditions or rules; one action always follows another. *If* can be replaced by *when* or *whenever* with no change of meaning.	**Health questions** *What **do you do*** ***… if you have** a headache? / **if your nose bleeds?** / if you **can't sleep**? / **if you have** hiccups? / **if you have** a cold?* **Crime and punishment** *What happens in your country* ***… if you steal** something from a shop? / **if you drive** too fast?* **The laws of nature and science** ***If you stroke** a cat, **it purrs**.* ***If you throw** something in the air, **it falls back down** again.* **Giving directions in your country / town** ***If you travel** north on the A9, **you come** to Inverness.* ***If you turn** right at the traffic lights, the castle **is** on your left.* **Describing someone's character** ***If you argue** with him, **he gets** very angry.* ***He doesn't cope** very well **if someone criticises** him.*

first conditional
First conditional sentences refer to future time and are used to refer to things which we think are quite likely to happen in the future.

Think about possible everyday future situations
*What **will you do***
*… **if you have** some free time this evening / at the weekend?*
*… **if you get** a pay rise?*
*… **if you lose** your job?*
*… **if the weather's** bad tomorrow?*

What to do in imaginary situations
- You get home and realise you don't have your key

***If I don't have** my key, **I'll go** to my parents' house and **stay** the night there.*
- Your phone needs charging

***If my phone needs** charging, **I'll borrow** a charger.*
- Your friend is out

***If my friend is out, I'll wait** till he gets home.*

second conditional
Second conditional sentences also refer to future time. They are used in two different ways:
- for possible but unlikely future conditions
- for impossible conditions

Hypothetical situations
*What **would you do***
*… **if you were** in bed and your realized the house was on fire?*
*… **if** the brakes on your car **didn't work**?*
*… **if someone broke** into your house and **demanded** money?*
*… **if you lost** your mobile phone?*
*… **if you met** Chris Pine?*
*… **if you won** first prize in a competition?*

See lesson plan 6.

Impossible conditions: finish these sentences about yourself
***If I had** more money, **I'd / I might** …*
***If I didn't have to** go to work / college every day, **I might** …*
***If I was / were** a man / woman, **I'd** …*
***If I was / were** five years younger, **I might / I'd probably**…*
***If I was / were taller, I'd** …*
***If I could change** my appearance, **I'd**…*

How honest are you?
What would you do
*… **if** a shop assistant **undercharged / overcharged** you for something you bought?*
*… **if you found** a wallet with money and credit cards in it?*
*… **if you crashed** into a parked car and the owner was not there?*
*… **if** a good friend who was not well off **gave** you an expensive present which you didn't like?*
*… **if you** saw someone steal something from a shop?*
*… **if a friend left** a diary or mobile phone in your room?*

third conditional
Third conditional sentences refer to past time, to hypothetical past actions.

Different lives (e. g. think about how your life would have been different if something had / hadn't happened)
If I hadn't worked *so hard,* ***I wouldn't have got*** *into university.*
If I hadn't got *into university,* ***I'd have ended up*** *in a low-paid job.*
If I'd ended up *in a low-paid job,* ***I wouldn't have met*** *Josh.*
If I hadn't met Josh, we wouldn't have got married and had *seven children.*

Explaining actions
If I hadn't broken *a window,* ***I wouldn't have got*** *into the house.*
If I hadn't got *into the house,* ***I wouldn't have been able*** *to turn off the water.*
If I hadn't turned off *the water,* ***the house would have been*** *flooded.* etc.

mixed conditionals

Changing the past (Think about what you could or couldn't do in the present or the future if something had or hadn't happened in the past.)
If I hadn't caught *the flu last week,* ***I'd*** *…*
If I'd worked *harder,* ***I wouldn't*** *…*
If I hadn't learned *to read and write, …*
If I'd been born *into a very poor / rich family, …*
If my mother hadn't met *my father, …*

Add your own ideas for possible teaching contexts here!

How to teach it

Practical matters

- Don't introduce conditional sentences **until learners are familiar with the present simple, past simple and the *will* future**. Once they know these, they will be able to form zero, first and second conditionals.

- As with other points of grammar, only introduce **one conditional form at a time**. Starting with zero conditional sentence patterns will establish the idea of two-clause sentences comprising main and subordinate clauses. It is important to establish that the subordinate *if* clause make no sense without a corresponding main clause.

- Teach the second conditional in separate sessions. Start by focusing on the possible but unlikely future use: *If we left now, we'd see him.* This contrasts well with the first conditional form (*If we leave now, we'll see him.*) Once learners are familiar with this use, introduce the unreal or impossible use: *If I were 10 years younger, I'd … / If I were you, I'd …* The verb pattern is the same but the meaning is quite different.

- Many conditional sentences are long and structurally complicated. If learners are to become fluent, they will need plenty of oral practice so that the tense sequences become second nature. If learners find it difficult to repeat conditional sentences by starting at the beginning, try **back-chaining**. Imagine you are trying to get learners to speak this sentence fluently:

  If I hadn't been tired, I wouldn't have fallen asleep on the train.

  Follow this procedure:
  T *Repeat … asleep on the train*
  Ls *asleep on the train*
  T *… fallen asleep on the train*
  Ls *fallen asleep on the train*
  T *… have fallen asleep on the train*
  Ls *have fallen asleep on the train*
  T *… I wouldn't have fallen asleep on the train*
  Ls *I wouldn't have fallen asleep on the train*
  etc.

  Back-chaining makes it easier for learners to imitate the correct stress and intonation pattern of long complex sentences.

What to watch out for

- Learners may use *will* in the *if* clause of a first conditional sentence. Example:
  *If I ~~will~~ **pass** the exam, **I'll go** to Cambridge University.*

- Learners may confuse the first and second conditional forms, not realizing the difference in meaning. For example, someone who says
  *If **I see** him, I'll …*
  thinks it is quite likely they will see him, whereas if they say
  *If **I saw** him, I'd …*
  they think seeing him is not very likely. This distinction needs emphasizing.

- Learners may be reluctant to use *were* instead of *was* in second conditional sentences because it sounds wrong. In fact native speakers use both forms in these sentences, so either form is acceptable, e.g.
  ***If he was / were coming**, he'd be here by now.*
  ***If I were / was** you, I'd get an early night.*
- Learners may be reluctant to use a past verb form to refer to the future. For example *If I **went** there tomorrow, I'd probably see some of my old schoolfriends.* It needs to be pointed out from time to time that there is no one-to-one correlation between the name of the verb form and the time to which it refers.
- In third conditional sentences learners may make the mistake of using *would have* in the *if* clause, e.g.
  ***If we ~~would have~~ got** there on time, **we could have** had a meal at the pub.*
- Learners may try to avoid using the third conditional altogether because they are unsure of the correct sequence of tenses. They may prefer to use a different structure altogether. For example, instead of saying ***If we had got** there on time, **we could have** had a meal at the pub.* they may prefer to say: *We didn't get there on time, so we didn't have a meal at the pub.*

What if my students ...?

Suggestion for classroom activities

1 Topic Family remedies / Folk cures
Language Zero conditional
Activities 1. Show photos of common, non-serious illnesses. For example *hay fever, nose bleed, back pain, headache*. Get learners to talk about which of these ailments they, or people they know have suffered from.

2. Pairs of learners compare what they do if they suffer from any of these.

3. Elicit learners' ideas. Discussing headaches they may say *If I have a headache, I make myself a cup of tea.* or ... *I take paracetamol.*

4. Introduce the zero conditional sentence pattern and get learners to practise using it to talk about what they think about the remedies suggested.
If I have a headache, I make myself a cup of tea and take two paracetamol tablets.

2 Topic Everyday scientific facts
Language Zero conditional
Activities 1. Introduce the topic of science and tell learners they are going to think about scientific facts, things that are always true. Start by eliciting answers to this question: *What happens if you freeze water?*
Ask learners to repeat the answer: *If you freeze water, it turns to ice.*

2. Ask learners to discuss similar questions in pairs or small groups.
Examples:
What happens
... if you don't water plants?
... if you heat water to 100 degrees?
... if you cut yourself?
... if you mix oxygen and hydrogen?
... if you close your eyes?
... if you touch fire?
Elicit learners' answers, checking they are using the present simple in their answers. Encourage unusual answers as well as the obvious ones.

3. Challenge learners to think of similar questions to ask each other.

3 Topic Problems and Warnings
Language First conditional sentences
Activities 1. Learners discuss what they would say to friends who had confided that they had these problems:
"I love junk food – I eat it at least once a day."
"I'm lazy and can't be bothered to exercise regularly."
"I'm a terrible driver. I find it impossible to keep to speed limits."
"I haven't see a dentist for three years. I'm too frightened."
"I've got an exam coming up and I've done hardly any revision."
"I'm addicted to computer games. I often play for 12 hours a day."

2. In pairs, learners take turns reading out and answering each other's problems. Once they have spoken a first conditional sentence, encourage them to continue to discuss the topic more freely. They should aim to make conversations like this.
A I love junk food – I eat it at least once a day.
B ***If you eat too much junk food, you'll put on weight or you'll be***

ill.
A I know, I think I'm addicted. I don't know what to do.
B Could you cut down – to just twice a week, perhaps?

4 Topic Superstitious beliefs
Language First conditional
Activities 1. Show the students this photo or write on the board:
Don't break a mirror.

2. Ask learners why someone might say this. Elicit the idea that breaking a mirror will bring bad luck. If learners don't know this, tell them and explain that this is a superstition. Use a sentence like this:
If you break a mirror, you'll have seven years of bad luck.

3. Ask learners to tell you about any superstitions they know about that bring good or bad luck. They should express them as first conditional sentences. If they can't think of any, ask them to complete these sentences. There is likely to be some difference of opinion!
If you open an umbrella inside a house, …
If the palm of your hand itches, …
If you see a black cat walking towards you, …
If one of your ears is red and burning, …
If you catch a leaf as it is falling from a tree, …
You will have bad luck if …
You will have good luck if …
You will have a visitor if …
Tomorrow the weather will be fine if …
Don't eat lettuce if …

4. Round off the activity with a short discussion about superstitions in general. Who believes in them? Why? Why not?

5 Topic Imaginary situations
Language Second conditional
Activities 1. Ask students to complete these sentences which get them to think about imaginary situations. They could think of one or more endings.
If I were a woman / man, …
If I had more money, …
If I were the president / prime minister of my country, …
If I were ten years younger, …
If I had more time, …
If I were taller, …
If I became very famous, …

2. Learners compare their answers in pairs or small groups. They should give reasons for their answers.

3. Ask learners to report what others said to produce answers in the third person. For example:
If Emma had more money, she'd open a shop selling flowers and plants.

4. Monitor and correct conversations, then round off the activity with a class discussion about some of the more interesting answers.

6 Topic How honest are you?

Language Activities

Second conditional (What would you do if …?)
1. Ask learners to think individually what they would do in the following situations:

A *Imagine you were shopping in a supermarket and found a wallet or a purse full of money and credit cards.* ***What would you do?***
B *Imagine you were trying to park in a small space in a multi-storey car park. You scraped another car.* ***What would you do?***
C *Imagine you were buying something in a large shop and when you came to pay, the assistant undercharged you by £20.* ***What would you do?***
D *Imagine a very good friend of yours gave you an expensive present which you really didn't like.* ***What would you say / do?***

2. Learners compare answers to the four questions.

3. Ask them to discuss the same questions again in new pairs but now taking this extra information into account:

A *There was also a slip of paper in the purse or wallet giving the owner's name and contact details on it.*
B *There was also damage to your car and a CCTV camera close to where you were parking.*
C *The assistant actually undercharged you by £200.*
D *Your friend has very little money and never buys anything for himself/ herself.*

4. Monitor discussions listening out for the correct use of the second conditional.

7 Topic

Chain of events (Well known national or international events or personal stories) – well known 'butterfly effect' stories could also be used for this purpose (see box below).

Language Activities

Third conditional
1. Tell learners a story with a series of clear stages or linked events. Personal stories work quite well for this. For example:
Peter was from a poor background but he did very well at school. He did so well in the exams that he got into Cambridge University. On his second day there, he met Gina and they fell in love. Three years later, Peter and Gina got married. Soon after this they had twin daughters, Amy and Cara.

2. Ask learners to think what would have happened if Peter had not done well at school. Elicit this third conditional sentence:
If Peter had not done well at school, he wouldn't have got into Cambridge University.
Then ask learners to make the rest of the sentences in the chain:
If Peter hadn't got into Cambridge University he wouldn't have met Gina.

3. Ask learners to think or write about a sequence of related events in their own lives.

Other examples of 'butterfly effect' stories

At primary school, when I was 7, everyone in my class went in for a national junior poetry competition. We all had to write an extra verse to the nursery rhyme 'Old Mother Hubbard'. Our teacher sent our entries off and we all forgot about it. Six months later, I was told that I had won second prize and I was invited to go to London to receive my prize. This gave me a taste for writing and for the next 10 years or so I wrote poems – just for fun. Later I wrote a play which was performed by an amateur group, and then some children's stories which were broadcast on national radio. Ever since then I have made my living writing school textbooks and magazine articles. If I hadn't won that poetry competition at the age of 7, I might never have written anything else!

I heard this First World War story on the radio the other day. Apparently, a French soldier saw a young German soldier trying to escape. But because he noticed that the German was injured, he couldn't shoot him and instead let him go free. It turned out that the German soldier's name was Adolf Hitler.

8 Topic
Language
Activities

What would you have done if …?
Third conditional
1. Ask learners to think of and note down their answers to this question *Imagine you had been in charge of the government of your country for the past five years. Think of three things you would have done and three things you wouldn't have done.*
For example:
I would have built more houses that poor people could have afforded.
I wouldn't have cut taxes paid by rich people.

2. Learners now discuss their ideas in pairs or small groups. Each learner tells the others one of the things they would or wouldn't have done. The others can then ask more questions. Example
A I wouldn't have cut taxes paid by rich people.
B Why wouldn't you have cut their taxes?
A Because they have enough money already.
B What would you have done with the money you'd have saved?
A I'd have spent it on health and education.

3. Allow the whole class to discuss what would have happened if any of the measures they talked about had been carried out.

9 Topic
Language
Activities

Present result(s) of past actions
Mixed conditionals
1. Ask learners to make a list of turning points in their lives, points when they made important decisions. For example
At the age of 14, I chose to study German instead of Science.
When I was 18, I decided to start work instead of going to university.
When I was 22, I decided to work abroad instead of staying in my own country.

2. Pairs of learners interview each other about the present results of their past decisions. Suggest they include the adverbs *definitely* or *probably* in their conversations. Example conversations:

A Tell me about one of your decisions.
B Okay – at the age of 14, I chose to study German instead of Science.
A So how would your life be different if you'd chosen Science?
B I ***definitely*** *wouldn't be a German teacher.*
A What would you be doing?
B I'd ***probably*** *be earning a lot more money!*

3. Monitor their conversations, checking their correct use of tenses.

10 Topic
Language
Activities

Questionnaire
All conditionals
1. Ask learners to give personal answers to miscellaneous questions like these.

a *What will you do if there's a transport strike tomorrow?*
b *What would you do if you lost your passport / identity card?*
c *What do you do if there's a power cut?*
d *What would you have done if you hadn't come here today?*
e *Who do you talk to if you have problems?*
f *Who would you be if could choose to be another person?*
g *What will you do if you run out of money this week?*
h *If your apartment was on fire, what two things would you take with you?*
i *If you were a time traveller, which year in the past or the future would you travel to?*
j *What would you do if you saw a UFO landing?*
k *How would your life be different now if you had won 1 million dollars in the lottery?*

2. Learners compare their answers in pairs or small groups and discuss any similarities or differences.

Lesson plan 6

Lesson profile

Description	Presentation → Practice → Production (See Introduction)
Topic	Hypothetical situations: winning a prize/in the lottery
Grammar point	First and second conditionals
Aims	Understanding the contrast between the first and second conditionals.
Material	WS 6.1 *And the winner is …*

PRESENTATION: 1

Photo-based speaking activity

WS 6.1 Task 1

T Show learners some pictures of various people with trophies and awards etc. Ask them what the pictures have in common.

L Learners discuss in pairs what the pictures have in common.

T Ask learners to tell each other about any prizes or awards they have won. These could be educational, for sport or as a result of chance (e.g. a lottery). Elicit a few examples from the class – highlighting the idea of winning by chance.

L Learners tell each other and then the whole class about things they have won.

2

Speaking activity

T Hand out raffle tickets for a local charity: two for each member of the class. (Tell them there are only 40 tickets in total.)
Tell them there are three cash prizes:
1st - £50
2nd - £25
3rd - £10

Ask them these questions
1. *Imagine you win 1st, 2nd, or 3rd prize. What will you do with the money?*
2. *Do you have a good chance of winning?*

Elicit answers to the two questions. Establish the idea that it is **quite likely** they will win one of the prizes.

L Learners take the tickets and discuss the questions in pairs.

T Now give them model conditional sentences based on their answers to Question 1.
If Maria wins 1st prize, she'll buy new clothes.
If Abdul wins 2nd prize, he'll go out for a meal.
If Jan wins 3rd prize, he'll go for a drink.

Ask concept questions about model sentences:
Has Maria won 1st prize?
Has she bought new clothes?
Does she want to buy new clothes?
Is it possible for her to win 1st prize?
How likely is it that she'll win a prize?

Check learners know the tenses that are used in 1st conditional sentences and understand when this form is used.

L Learners repeat model sentences.

Learners answer concept questions:
No
No
Yes
Yes
Quite likely

3

Grammar focus – modelling the target language (1st conditional)

T Ask learners to have 1st conditional conversations in pairs, starting with e.g.
What will you do if you win 1st prize?
...

Monitor conversations and correct any errors.

Ask a few pairs to report back, using 3rd person sentences.

L In pairs, make conversation using 1st conditional questions and answers, e.g.
A What will you do if you win 1st prize?
B I'll buy some new trainers. What about you?
A If I win, I'll save the money for my next holiday.

Some of the pairs report back to class, e.g.
A If Ben wins 1st prize, he'll buy some new trainers.
B If Hannah wins, she'll save the money for her next holiday.

PRACTICE: 4

Grammar practice – speaking activity using the 1st conditional

T Introduce the topic of the national lottery (most countries have something similar). Ask students to have a short discussion in pairs:
Who does the lottery? Have you ever won?
How much have you won? Is it likely that you will win the first prize?
What are the chances of winning the top prizes?

Explain that you have bought everyone in the class lottery tickets and tell them about this week's prizes:
1st - $10m
2nd - $5m
3rd - $1m

L In pairs students discuss the subject of national lotteries and exchange experiences of winning etc.

PRESENTATION: 5

Speaking activity – introducing the 2nd conditional

WS 6.1 Tasks 2 and 3

Ask them these questions
1. Imagine you won 1st, 2nd, or 3rd prize. What would you do with the money?
2. Do you have a good chance of winning?

Elicit answers to the two questions. Establish the idea that it is **very unlikely** they will win one of the prizes.

Students discuss the two questions in pairs.

6

Grammar focus – modelling the target language (2nd conditional)

T Now give students model conditional sentences based on their answers to Question 1.
If Maria won 1st prize, she'd buy a small island.
If Abdul won 2nd prize, he'd buy a house for his parents and a Rolls Royce for himself.
If Jan won 3rd prize, he'd start his own business.

L Learners repeat model sentences

Ask concept questions about the model sentences:
Has Maria won 1st prize?
Has she bought a small island?
Does she want to buy a small island?
Is it possible for her to win 1st prize?
How likely is it that she'll win a prize?

Learners answer concept questions:
No
No
Yes
Yes
Extremely unlikely

Check learners know the tenses that are used in 2nd conditional sentences and understand when we use this form.

PRACTICE: 7

Grammar practice – speaking activity using 2nd conditional

WS 6.1 Task 4

T In small groups, learners have 2nd conditional conversations, starting e.g.
What would you do if you won 1st prize?

Monitor conversations and correct any errors.

L In small groups, students make conversations using 2nd conditional questions and answers, e.g.
A What would you do if you won 1st prize?
B I'd buy houses for all my relatives. What about you?
A If I won, I'd give most of the money to a charity.

Ask a few groups to report back, using 3rd person sentences.

Report back to class.
A If Ben won 1st prize, he'd buy houses for all his relatives.
B If Hannah won, she'd give most of the money to charity.

T Get learners to think of a new type of competition where the prizes are opportunities to do something or go somewhere of their choice.

Elicit their ideas. For example:
You can / could…
- *… go anywhere for a week*
- *… have lessons in a language of your choice*
- *… have a holiday in space*

Remind learners to use 1st conditional sentences to indicate that they think something is quite likely and 2nd conditional sentences when they think something is very unlikely.

To avoid this becoming just another controlled practice activity, encourage more wide-ranging discussions in which learners ask each other about reasons for their choices.

Monitor discussions, listening for correct use of both conditional forms, but without interrupting the flow of the discussions.

L The class comes up with a list of unusual competition prizes.

Pairs of learners work through the list discussing what they would or wouldn't do if they won each competition.

PRODUCTION: 8

Speaking activity

T Round off the lesson with a whole class discussion, perhaps covering some of these topics:
- why people go in for competitions
- the danger of winning large sums of money
- addiction to gambling

Allow students some time to discuss the issues in pairs or groups and prepare some notes for the debate.

L Students discuss the issues in pairs or groups and make notes on one or more of the topics. Following this, the class discuss the issues together.

9

Class discussion

WS 6.1 Task 5

T WS 6.1 Task 6 offers extra practice for students to do as homework.

L Students complete the sentences using the 1st or 2nd conditional as appropriate.

10

Extra practice / Homework

WS 6.1 Task 6

And the winner is ...

Task 1

Look at these photos and discuss the questions with a partner.

a) What do they have in common?

b) Have you ever been in a similar situation?

Task 2

Look at these photos and discuss the questions below with a partner.

a) Why do people play the lottery on a regular basis?

b) Do you do this? Have you ever won? How much did you win?

c) Is it likely that you will win the first prize?

d) What are the chances of winning the top prizes?

ISBN 978-3-12-501628-6

Task 3

Discuss these questions with a partner.

a) Imagine you won 1st, 2nd, or 3rd prize in the lottery. What would you do with the money?

b) Do you have a good chance of winning?

Task 4

In groups discuss what you would do if you won 1st prize. Remember to use the second conditional (if + past simple -> would / could + infinitive). Make some notes and then report back to the class.

....

....

Task 5

Discuss one or more of these related topics with a partner or in a group. Make some notes and prepare to discuss the topics with the rest of the class.

a) Why do so many people go in for competitions they are unlikely to win?

b) What are the dangers associated with winning large sums of money? Do you know of any situations in which winning has caused unhappiness?

c) How serious a problem is an addiction to gambling? What problems can it cause to people and their families?

Task 6 – Extra practice

Finish these sentence with your own ideas.

a) If my computer stops working, ...

b) If I was lost in a big city, ...

c) If I had more time, ...

d) If I work really hard, ...

e) If I don't understand a word, ...

f) If I was abroad and someone stole my wallet / purse, ...

ISBN 978-3-12-501628-6

Unit 7 – Who does what?

How to recognize it

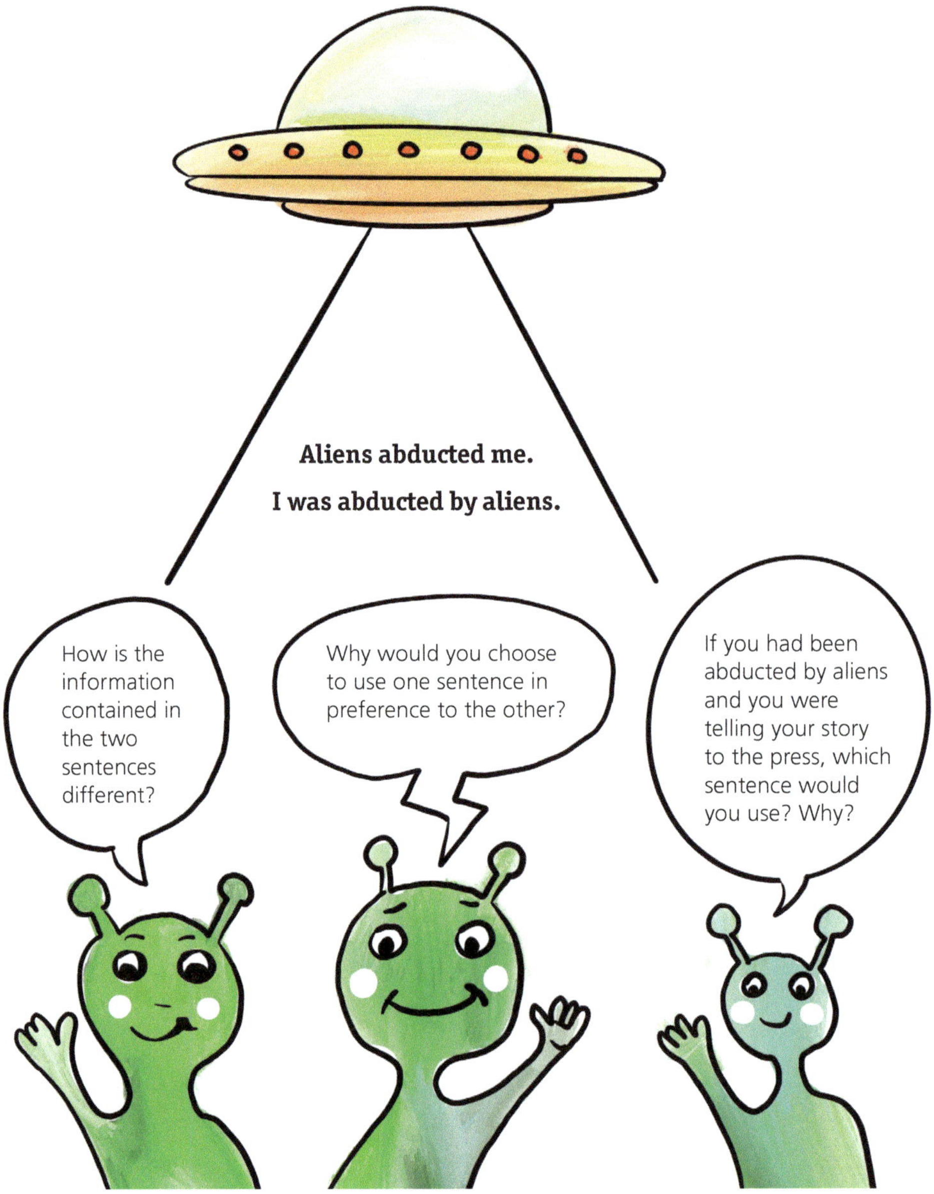

Aliens abducted me.
In the first sentence, the verb is **active**
→ the subject – *aliens* – is the doer of the action – *abducted*. The object of the action is *me*.
I was abducted by aliens.
In the second sentence, the verb is **passive**
→ the subject – *I* – is the person affected by the action. (*By*) aliens is the agent.

How to use it

The passive has all the same forms as the active although not all are commonly used.

Tense / Form	Active	Passive = appropriate tense of *to be* + *past participle* of main verb
present simple	*They **grow** rice in India.*	*Rice **is grown** in India.**
present continuous	*The wind **is blowing** the leaves off the trees.*	*The leaves **are being blown** off the trees.**
past simple	*They **told** him to get there by 6.00 pm.*	*He **was told** to get there by 6.00 pm.**
past continuous	*The postman **was delivering** letters and parcels.*	*Letters and parcels **were being delivered** by the postman.*
present perfect simple	*The airline **has lost** our luggage.*	*Our luggage **has been lost** by the airline.*
present perfect continuous	***They've been repainting** their house.*	*Their house **has been being** repainted.***
past perfect	*She **hadn't cleaned** her car for three months.*	*Her car **hadn't been cleaned** for three months.*
past perfect continuous	***They'd been looking** after Amy's cat.*	*Amy's cat **had been being** looked after.***
future simple - *will*	***They'll send** me the results soon.*	***I'll be sent** the results soon.**
future continuous	***They'll be visiting** us next week.*	***We'll be being visited** next week.***
modal verbs	*We **must tell** everyone.* *They **might fine** us for parking here.* *They **should have told** us about the strike.*	***Everyone must be told**.** ***We might be fined** for parking here.** ***We should have been told** about the strike.**

* In these types of passive sentences an agent is not usually mentioned.

** These continuous forms sound awkward so are often avoided. The active form is normally used instead.

Good to know

Transitive or Intransitive?

A **transitive** verb is one which is used with an object, e.g. *speak* (a language), *throw* (a ball, a tantrum), *buy* (a house, a newspaper) etc. An **intransitive** verb on the other hand cannot have an object, e.g. *laugh*, *live*, *arrive* etc.
Only **transitive** verbs have a passive form. For example:
Active: *They **speak** English here.* (*English* is the object of the verb *speak*.)
Passive: *English **is spoken** here.*

Intransitive verbs only have an active form. For example:
*Everyone **laughed**.*
*We've **lived** here for ten years.*

Some verbs can be transitive or intransitive depending on the meaning or how they are used in a sentence, e.g. *run*, *change*, *eat* etc.

	Active	Passive
Transitive	*My father **ran** this hotel.* *He **changed** the name of the hotel.*	*This hotel **was run** by my father.* *The name of the hotel **was changed.***
Intransitive	*I **run** twice a week.* *The town **has changed** very quickly.*	– –

Causative verbs

The constructions ***have / get** something **done*** can be used to emphasize an action rather than who did the action. These are referred to as *causative verbs* and they are similar to using a passive verb. They express the idea of someone causing something to happen or take place. *Get* is used in less formal situations than *have*.

Compare the information in these three sentences:

***I'm repairing** my bike.*	(active → I'm doing the repairing myself)
*My bike **is being repaired**.*	(passive → sb else is doing the repairing)
***I'm having / getting** my bike **repaired**.*	(causative → I'm causing sb to repair my bike, e.g. by paying them)

Recognizing whether a past participle is being used as an adjective or in a passive form

It is sometimes difficult to distinguish between sentences which describe actions and those which describe situations. This is because the past participle form of verbs can be used to form the passive or as adjectives, for example:

*My house is **flooded**. / The window was **broken***
→ *flooded* and *broken* are adjectives which describe the condition of the house and the window.
*My house **is flooded** twice a year.*
→ *flooded* is the present simple passive describing an action.
*The window **was broken** yesterday morning.*
→ *was broken* is the past simple passive describing an action.

When to use it

These contexts and themes are not limited to particular times or verb forms..

Passive forms	
Context / Theme	**Examples**
Facts about famous buildings and land-marks When? / Why? / Who? (Based on photos of landmarks such as the Eiffel Tower, Stonehenge, the Statue of Liberty, the Pyramids, the Sydney Opera House, the Taj Mahal etc.)	*When **was it built**?* *Who **was it designed / built by**?*
In newspaper stories and headlines	*A man **was killed** by a falling tree as he was driving home.* *Man **killed** by falling tree*
To describe the stages of a technical process e.g. making wine, describing a recipe, creating a TV programme, making a vase etc.	*First the grapes **are picked / harvested**. This **can be** done by hand or mechanically. The grapes **are then taken** to the winery, where **they are sorted** into bunches. Rotten or under-ripe grapes **are removed**. After the grapes **have been sorted**, they **can be de-stemmed** and **crushed**.*
Towns and cities Suggesting improvements (for residents / tourists)	The passive form of modal verbs: *The town centre **should / could be pedestrianized**.* *The main street **should be widened**.* *Traffic **should be banned** from the town centre.* *Road signs **must be made** clearer.* *New car parks **should be built** on the outskirts of town.*

See lesson plan 7.

Describing changes already made	Past or present perfect passives: *The old bridge **was replaced** in 1980.* *The town centre **has** recently **been redesigned**.* *New estates **have been built** on the outskirts.*
Quizzes e.g. Question & answer	Arts quiz (active questions and passive answers) *Who wrote Hamlet?* *Hamlet **was written by** William Shakespeare* *Who painted the Mona Lisa?* *The Mona Lisa **was painted by** Leonardo Da Vinci*
e.g. True / False quiz	*Ice cream **was** first **made** in Italy.* *True ☐ False ☒ → in China* *The first underground railway **was opened** in New York.* *True ☐ False ☒ → in London* *Mirrors **were invented** by the ancient Egyptians.* *True ☒ False ☐*
Written description of places (a school, a hotel, the HQ of an office etc.) This could be in the form of a gap-fill exercise.	*The school, which ________(build) in 1900, ________ (locate) on the outskirts of the city. We invite interested parents to visit at any time. First you ________ (will show) round the buildings and then ________ (will give) the opportunity to observe a lesson.*

Causative verbs	
Context / Theme	**Examples**
Thinking about what you do for yourself and what you have done for you. E.g. cutting / dying your hair, washing the car, repairing sth, changing a tyre, cleaning / decorating your apartment / house, washing/ cleaning clothes, preparing food for party etc.	***I have** my hair **cut**, but I dye it myself.* ***We had** a new bathroom **fitted**, but I did the painting myself.* *James fixed his punctured tyre himself, but **got** the brakes **repaired** by a bike mechanic.*

How to teach it

Practical matters

- It is sometimes thought that passive verbs are more common in writing or formal speech than in informal everyday conversation. Here are some common examples which disprove this idea:
  *My brother **was born** in 2005.*
  *I **was brought up** in Germany.*
  *French **is spoken** in Algeria.*
  *My ring **is made** of gold.*

- The mechanics of changing verbs from the active to the passive form are quite simple, so this should not be a problem for learners as long as they know the past participle of the verbs they want to use. Learners are frequently asked to do this as a practice exercise, but a more important issue is to clarify when it is appropriate to use the passive rather than the active. For this reason, it is important to choose a context or a theme in which the use of the passive sounds normal.

- It is important to focus on why we would use the passive rather than the active. The main reason for using the passive is **to focus on the person or thing to whom the action was done**, rather than the person or thing who did the action. There may, however, be specific reasons for using a passive without mentioning the agent or actor. For example:

a. We don't know who did the action	*My car **has been stolen**.*
b. It is obvious who did the action	*Six people **were arrested** after the match.*
c. We don't want to say who did the action	*The president **has been accused** of lying.*
d. It is not important who did the action	*The match **has been postponed**.*

What to watch out for

- Some learners are not confident about forming the passive correctly or may not be sure about when to use it. They may think it is only used in writing or formal speech and use an active sentence where a passive would be more natural. For example:
  My parents brought me up in Germany. rather than *I was brought up in Germany.*

- The passive may be more common in English than in a learner's L1 or it may be used in different ways. It might be useful to make it clear that the passive is useful when we do not know or can't say who did an action.

- Some learners may avoid using the passive because they think it is more natural to use the active. In certain circumstances, however, using the passive form is more natural:
  As he was crossing the road, he was hit by a car. (passive)
  As he was crossing the road, a car hit him. (active)

Suggestions for classroom activities

1 Topic Crime and punishment
Language *should be / should have been* + past participle
Activities 1. In pairs learners discuss how they would order crimes in regards to their seriousness, e.g.
burglary / drink driving / mugging / pick-pocketing / shoplifting / vandalism

2. Elicit ideas from the class and note down the order most learners decide.

3. Ask pairs to recommend suitable punishments for each crime, using passive sentences with *should be*. For example
People who drink and drive ***should be banned*** *from driving for a year.*

4. Tell students about very light or very heavy sentences imposed by judges in cases you know about. Example cases:
a) Someone who stole two loaves of bread from a supermarket to feed his children was sent to prison for a month.
b) A drunk driver who knocked over and killed a child was fined £1000.

Ask learners to discuss what their punishments should have been. For example:
a) *The person who stole bread to feed their children* ***should have been fined*** *the price of the bread or* ***should have been asked*** *to work for two days in the supermarket without pay.*
b) *The driver killed the child* ***should have been sent*** *to prison for 10 years.*

2 Topic The Arts (Films, plays and books)
Language present & past simple passive
Activities 1. Ask learners to list their two favourite books, films and plays

2. They then try to find other learners who have chosen one of the same books, films or plays as them.

3. Elicit choices from the class.

4. Learners write short reviews of their favourites, using present and past simple passive verbs. They should include the following details:
- The year it was written, made or first performed
- The writer, the director
- The setting
- A sentence or two about what happens

Encourage learners to research the information they need on the internet. They should aim to produce short reviews like this:
Indiana Jones and the Raiders of the Lost Ark ***was made*** *in 1984 and* ***was directed*** *by Stephen Spielberg.*
The film ***is set*** *in India. After he arrives in India, Indiana Jones* ***is asked*** *by villagers to find a mystical stone.*

Note: Learners could be asked about the worst book, film or play they've ever seen.

3 Topic Waste disposal
Language present simple passive / *could, should, shouldn't be* + past participle
Activities 1. Learners discuss how waste is disposed of in their town, region or country.
Get them to focus on questions such as these, but do not insist that they use passive verbs at this stage.

- How much is recycled? How much is burnt or goes to landfill?
- Is it collected regularly? Can people take it somewhere themselves?
- Do people have to sort the rubbish into different types, for example paper, metal, glass, plastic etc.?

2. Elicit their ideas in a short follow-up session, this time asking them to produce passive sentences. Example:
75% of our rubbish ***is recycled****. I don't know much* ***is burnt*** *or* ***taken*** *to landfill sites.*

3. Now ask learners to discuss how waste should be disposed of. Give one or two model sentences, such as:
I think 95% of rubbish ***should be recycled*** *and none* ***should be sent*** *to landfill.*
5% ***could be burnt*** *if energy* ***was produced****.*

4. Finish with a class discussion about the topic. If you intend this to be a mainly fluency activity, don't insist the learners use passive verbs – just hope they do!

4 Topic Environmental damage
Language present and past continuous passive / future passive
Activities 1. Ask learners to read or listen to you reading this (1990) extract from a report on the environment. Ask them to guess when it was written.
In recent years, we have become aware that our planet is in danger.
All over the world, forests are being destroyed at an alarming rate and deserts are advancing. Lakes, rivers and even seas are being polluted so that the fish and other creatures that lived in them are being poisoned. Perhaps, most seriously of all, the air that we breathe is being polluted dramatically – for the worse.

2. Now ask learners to rewrite the part of the text in blue, looking back from the current date to 1990, like this:
All over the world, forests were being destroyed at an alarming rate and deserts were advancing. Lakes, rivers and even seas were being polluted so that the fish and other creatures that live in them were being poisoned. Perhaps, most seriously of all, the air that we breathed was being polluted dramatically – for the worse.

3. Have a short whole class discussion summarizing the current situation. Some things may be different, others the same.

4. Now ask learners to look forward and predict what will be done in the future to save the environment. Learners may use the future continuous passive, but point out that the simple form sounds more "normal".
New forests ***will be planted****. The seas, oceans and rivers* ***will be cleaned****. Petrol and diesel cars* ***will all be replaced*** *by electric vehicles.*
etc. Encourage optimism!

See lesson plan 7.

5 Topic Famous buildings / landmarks
Language Past simple passive
Activities 1. Show learners photos of famous buildings or landmarks, such as the following:
Eiffel Tower, Stonehenge, Statue of Liberty, Taj Mahal, Sydney Opera House, Colosseum, Burj Khalifa, Empire State Building, Leaning Tower of Pisa, the Great Mosque of Djenné, the Sagrada Familia

2. Ask learners to talk to a partner. They should tell each what they know about the buildings. Don't ask them to use the passive verbs yet.

3. Now get learners to find out as much as they can about the buildings. For example:
- when they were built
- who they were designed by
- what they are / were used for

This could be an internet research project. This time, ask learners to use passive verbs.

6 Topic Newspaper headlines
Language Various tenses of passive
Activities 1. Show the class some news headlines which use shortened passive verbs.
Examples:
*East coast **hit** by heavy snow storm. (hit = has been hit)*
*£3m **stolen** from High Street bank. (stolen = has been stolen)*
Point out that newspaper headlines often take this form instead of being written as longer active sentences, such as
A heavy snow storm has hit the East coast.
Thieves have stolen £3m from a bank in the High Street.

2. Ask students to make up similar passive headlines from these active sentences.
A falling tree has killed a woman as she was driving home.
Lifeboats have rescued two men from a boat in the Mediterranean Sea.
Strong winds have blown the roofs off many houses in the city.
An overturned lorry blocked the motorway for several hours yesterday.

3. Check answers
*Woman **killed** by falling tree (as she was driving home).*
*Two men **rescued** (by lifeboats) from a boat in the Mediterranean (Sea).*
*Roofs **blown** off many houses in the city (by strong winds).*
*Motorway **blocked** by (an) overturned lorry (for several hours yesterday).*

4. Finally ask learners to make up their own active sentences and exchange them with partners to be turned into passive headlines.

7 Topic Improving your town
Language *could be / should be* + past participle
Activities 1. Ask learners to think about their town and discuss in pairs or groups what they could do to improve it.

2. Elicit their ideas. If learners are all from the same place, this could lead to an interesting discussion. Allow the discussion to progress naturally for a few minutes without mentioning the target language.

3. Ask *What could be done to improve the town for the people who live here or for tourists?*
Write a model answer on the board:
Traffic ***could be banned*** *from the town centre.*
Allow the class to discuss the question and come up with more passive sentences.

4. Elicit as many ideas as the class can produce and then ask for decisions to be made. Which three changes **should be made**? Allow the class to discuss this and come to an agreement.

8 Topic Thoughts and beliefs
Language *It is known, thought, believed* + past participle
Activities 1. Provide examples of passive sentences like this:
It is known that *bees are in danger in the northern hemisphere.*
(= we / people know that)
It is thought that *five cars were involved in the accident.*
(= we / people think that)
It is believed that *hundreds of families have been made homeless by the storms.*
(= we / people believe that)

2. Ask learners to produce similar sentences about what is known, thought and believed. Once they have got used to producing sentences like these, suggest that they discuss some of the most contentious thoughts and beliefs.

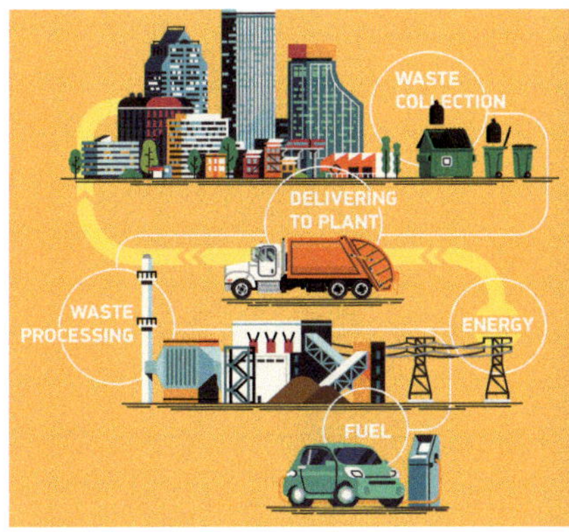

9 Topic Processes
Language Present simple passive
Activities 1. Show learners a flow diagram illustrating several stages of a process.

2. Check understanding of vocabulary and then ask learners to explain the process using passive sentences. Examples:
Waste can be used to generate energy. First, people throw away their rubbish / waste into bins. Then the waste is collected by dustcarts / garbage trucks and delivered to a waste processing plant, e.g. an incinerator. Next it is burnt. The heat from the fire is used to generate electricity or to heat buildings.

3. Ask learners to research another process which involves several stages and describe this using passive verbs. They might choose a cooking recipe, an agricultural process or a scientific or technical process. This could start as a speaking activity and be followed up by a writing task.

10 Topic The perfect holiday
Language *will* future passive
Activities 1. Tell the class they are managers of hotels in the same holiday resort. These hotels are in competition with each other. Ask learners to work in pairs to find out which hotel can offer the most services to their tourist customers. They should make promises like these:
You will be met *at the airport by one of our representatives.*
You will be driven *to the hotel in a chauffeur-driven limousine.*
You will be welcomed *at the hotel reception and given a glass of champagne.*

2. All pairs discuss their ideas and form similar promises using the *will* future passive form.

3. Elicit learners' ideas, correcting errors in the formation of the *will* future passive.

4. Ask the class to vote on the most ridiculous set of promises.

Got a brilliant idea how to teach the passive? Make a note of it here!

Lesson plan 7

Lesson profile

Description	Authentic → Restricted → Clarifying (See Introduction)
Topic	Famous buildings and landmarks
Grammar point	The passive
Aims	To practise forming the passive and understanding when specifying an agent is necessary.
Material	*WS 7.1 Famous landmarks*

AUTHENTIC (1)

Photo-based speaking activity

WS 7.1 Task 1

T Show photos of famous places, for example: the Eiffel Tower, Stonehenge, the Statue of Liberty, the Pyramids, Sydney Opera House, the Taj Mahal, Notre Dame de Paris etc., and ask learners to note down or discuss what they know about each place:

- its age
- where it can be seen
- its purpose etc.

(Don't mention grammar at this stage.)

L In pairs or small groups, learners discuss what they know about each place and note down any facts they agree about.

Elicit learners' ideas and write in note form on the board, e.g.
Eiffel Tower: In Paris / 19th century / Gustave Eiffel designer / closed during the German occupation of Paris.

Learners report information they have gathered (and agree about).

Ask learners to make sentences using these facts. (Assuming learners have not yet learnt the passive, these will have active verbs.)

Learners make sentences like these:
The Eiffel Tower is in Paris. / They built it in the 19th century. / Gustave Eiffel designed it. / The tower closed during the German occupation of Paris.

Key to Task 1 (top to bottom, left to right): Uluru (central Australia), Christ the Redeemer statue (Rio), Taj Mahal (Agra), Stonehenge (Wiltshire), Tower Bridge (London), Bagan (Myanmar), Golden Gate Bridge (San Francisco), Sphinx (Giza), Sydney Opera House, Statue of Liberty (New York), Great Mosque of Djenné (Mali), Hagia Sophia (Istanbul), Saint Basil's Cathedral (Moscow), Great Wall of China, Colosseum (Rome), Machu Picchu (nr. Cuzco), Table Mountain (Cape Town), Moai stautues (Easter Island), Eiffel Tower (Paris), Acropolis (Athens)

CLARIFICATION (1)

Grammar focus – modelling the target structures

T Write sample simple past passive sentences on the board using learners' sentences that can be made passive:
*It **was built** in Paris in the 19th century*
*It **was designed** by Gustave Eiffel.*
*It **was closed** to the public during the German occupation of Paris.*
*It **is made** of steel.*

Ask concept questions about these sentences, e.g.
Do we know who designed it?
Do we know who built the Eiffel Tower?
Do we know who closed it during the Occupation?

Ask learners why we would say one of these sentences rather than the other:
Gustave Eiffel designed the Eiffel Tower.
The Eiffel Tower was designed by Gustave Eiffel.

Establish that the second sentence chooses to put the emphasis on the famous building rather than the now long-dead designer.

L Learners answer concept questions.

Learners may answer the question.

CLARIFICATION (2)

Grammar focus – clarifying how the passive is formed

T Using two sentences (one with a regular verb and one with an irregular verb), check that learners understand how the passive is formed.
If necessary, write the rules of formation on the board.

L Learners answer teacher's questions to show their understanding of the formation of the appropriate tense of the verb to be followed by the past participle of the main verb.

RESTRICTED (1)

Grammar practice – writing activity

WS 7.1 Task 2

T Ask learners to change some active sentences about other buildings into the passive:

a) *They built the Taj Mahal between 1632 and 1653.*
b) *They made it out of white marble.*
c) *They repaint the Eiffel Tower every seven years.*
d) *In 2019, a fire partially destroyed Notre Dame cathedral in Paris.*
e) *Can you see the Great Wall of China from space?*
f) *They have discovered 130 pyramids in Egypt.*
g) *They built pyramids as tombs for Pharaohs and their families.*
h) *The French gave The Statue of Liberty to America in 1886.*

L Students work out the answers:

a) *The Taj Mahal **was built** between 1632 and 1653.*
b) *It **was made** out of white marble.*
c) *The Eiffel Tower is **repainted** every seven years.*
d) *In 2019 Notre Dame cathedral **was** partially **destroyed** by a fire.*
e) *Can the Great Wall of China **be seen** from space?*
f) *130 pyramids **have been discovered** in Egypt.*
g) *The pyramids **were built** as tombs for Pharaohs and their families.*
h) *The Statue of Liberty **was given** to America by the French in 1886.*

T Explain that passive sentences can but do not always need to mention the agent – the person who did the action.

Elicit learners' ideas about why these passive sentences do not tell us who did the action:

a) The men were arrested in the town centre.
b) A serious fire was started near the palace yesterday morning.
c) The president has been accused of lying.
d) Tomorrow's Grand Prix has been cancelled.

L Learners suggest ideas

a) It is obvious who arrested them: only the police can make arrests.
b) The arsonist is unknown so we can't say who started the fire.
c) It is confidential – we don't want to say who accused the president.
d) Only motor racing authorities can cancel races. Everyone knows that.

CLARIFICATION (3)

Grammar focus – explaining the agent

WS 7.1 Task 3

T Ask learners to convert sentences from active to passive, deciding whether or not to mention the agent:

a) They closed the roads around the building.
b) They asked people to stay indoors.
c) The president donated £1m to the charity.
d) They used 18,000 different parts in the building of the tower.

L Learners convert sentences to passive:

a) The roads around the building ***were closed****. (no agent)*
b) People ***were asked*** *to stay indoors. (no agent)*
c) £1m ***was donated*** *to the charity by the president. (agent included because it is important to know who made the donation)*
d) 18,000 different parts ***were used*** *to build the tower. (no agent)*

RESTRICTED (2)

Grammar practice – writing activity

WS 7.1 Task 4

T Ask learners to research and write about buildings and other landmarks in their neighbourhood / hometown / country. These can be ancient or modern.

Monitor student activity, answering any queries from learners

L Learners prepare a (short) presentation on buildings and other landmarks in their home neighbourhood or country. As many of their sentences as possible should be in the passive.

Students present the results of their research to the class.

AUTHENTIC (2)

Writing activity leading into oral presentation

WS 7.1 Task 5

Famous landmarks

Task 1

Work with a partner. How many of these world landmarks do you recognize? What do you know about them?

a) What are their names?

b) Which countries are they in?

c) How old are they?

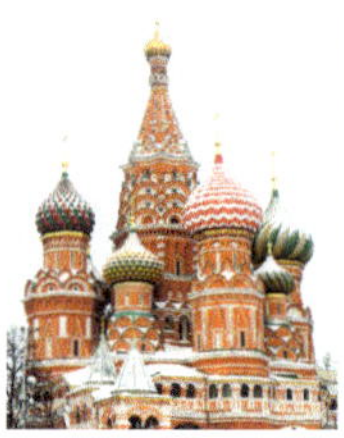

ISBN 978-3-12-501628-6

Task 2

Rewrite these sentences using passive verbs.

a) They built the Taj Mahal between 1632 and 1653. *The Taj Mahal* ***was built*** *between 1632 and 1653.*

b) They made it out of white marble. ....

c) They repaint the Eiffel Tower every seven years. ....

d) In 2019, a fire partially destroyed Notre Dame cathedral in Paris. ....

e) Can you see the Great Wall of China from space? ....

f) They have discovered 130 pyramids in Egypt. ....

g) They built pyramids as tombs for Pharaohs and their families. ....

h) The French gave The Statue of Liberty to America in 1886. ....

Task 3

Passive sentences don't always mention the ***agent****.*

The agent is the person who did the action!

Why do you think the agents are not mentioned in these sentences?

a) The men were arrested in the town centre.

b) A serious fire was started near the palace yesterday morning.

c) The president has been accused of lying.

d) Tomorrow's Grand Prix has been cancelled.

Task 4

Change these sentences from active to passive. Decide where an agent is necessary and why.

a) They closed the roads around the building ....

b) They asked people to stay indoors. ....

c) The president donated £1m to the charity. ....

d) They used 18,000 different parts to build the tower. ....

Task 5

Choose a building or landmark in your hometown or home country. Do some research and prepare a short presentation on it. Use as many passive sentences as possible in your presentation.

ISBN 978-3-12-501628-6

Unit 8 – People, places, things and abstract ideas

How to recognize it

Which of the words in this paragraph are **nouns**?

Now think about these questions:

- Is the first noun you have chosen *palm* or *palm oil*?
- How could you describe *horseradish sauce*?
- How are the nouns in list A different from those in list B?

A	B
biscuits / shelf / toast / supermarket	ice cream / horseradish sauce / shoe polish / chocolate spread

- How could you describe "the rich" and "the poor" in this Oscar Wilde quotation? "There is only one class in the community that thinks more about money than the rich, and that is the poor. The poor can think of nothing else."

How to use it

A **noun** is a word that names a person, place, thing or an idea (i.e. more abstract things such as feelings, qualities etc.). There are different categories of nouns.

compound noun

A noun which is made up of two or more words. Combinations may be:

- noun + noun — *car park / shareholder*
- adjective + noun — *supermarket / greenhouse*
- verb + noun — *driving licence / fishing rod*
- verb + adverb — *take-off / break out*
- adverb + noun — *outbreak / downfall*

Compound nouns can be written as oneword, two words or hyphenated.

countable noun

A noun which has singular and plural forms: *cat → cats / man → men / child → children*

- singular or plural verbs — *My car **is** green. / My cats **are** black.*
- a / an or a number — *She has **a** 6-year-old child.* *He has **three** children.*
- not many / a few — ***Not many** people are here tonight.* ***A few** people were late.*

uncountable noun

See lesson plan 8.

A noun which has no plural form: *cheese / money / water / air / bread*

However, some generally uncountable nouns can be countable in certain contexts, e.g.

- to express a quantity — *Would you like **a chocolate**?* *We'll have **two beers** and **a cider**, please.*
- to express a type or kind of sth — *I love **all** French **cheeses**.*

Uncountable nouns are used with:

- singular verbs — *Time **is** precious.* *Money **is** scarce.*
- definite or zero articles — ***The water** is freezing.* *I love drinking **water**.*
- not much / a little — *I don't have **much time**.* *Could I borrow **a little money**?*

adjectival noun

An adjective used as a noun to refer to a group:
the rich, the poor, the needy, the blind, the British, the French, the Irish

Adjectival nouns are used with the definite article and plural verbs:
*Every day the gulf between **the rich** and **the poor** widens.*
*Traditionally **the British celebrate** Christmas on December 25th.*

collective noun

A singular noun which refers to a group of individuals:
team, crew, staff, government, herd, shoal

Collective nouns can be used with:

- singular verbs if they are regarded as a unit or single mass
  My ***team is*** *doing very well this year.*
  The ***government is*** *going to lose the election.*

- plural verbs if they are regarded as a number of individuals
  The school ***staff are working*** *extra hard at the moment.*
  The ***audience are thoroughly enjoying*** *the show.*

- many of these nouns have plural forms
  There are twenty ***teams*** *in the English Premier League.*

proper noun

Nouns used as names for specific people, places, organizations, brand names, shops etc.:
Elvis, Athens, the United Nations, Pepsi Cola, Harrods

They are spelt with a capital letter.
Nouns which are not proper nouns, i.e. that refer to people, places, things etc. that are generic are called "common nouns".

When is a noun not a noun? When it is being used a verb, e.g. *elbow* (someone out of the way), *friend* (someone on social media), *chair* (a meeting). Know anymore useful facts about nouns? Add them here!

Good to know

Using the definite article

The definite article *the* is used:

• to refer to something which has been mentioned before	*I bought my first car 3 years ago.* ***The car*** *was red.*
• when there is only one of something	***The*** *moon is really bright this evening.*
• in superlative expressions	*That's* ***the best pizza*** *I've ever eaten.*
• with the names of oceans, seas, rivers and mountain ranges	***the*** *Atlantic,* ***the*** *Mediterranean,* ***the*** *Nile,* ***the*** *Alps*
• with the names of some countries and groups of islands	***The*** *United States,* ***The*** *Netherlands* ***The*** *West Indies,* ***The*** *Seychelles*
• with the names of newspapers (but not magazines)	***The*** *Times,* ***The*** *Independent (but Cosmopolitan)*

Using the indefinite article

The indefinite article *a / an* is used with singular nouns:

• to refer to a person or thing, but not a specific person or thing	*There's* ***a*** *large bird in our garden. I think it's* ***a*** *seagull.*
• to refer to something for the first time	*There's* ***a*** *man at the door. It's the man I told you about yesterday.*
• to classify what something / someone is or does	*She's* ***a*** *French woman. He's* ***a*** *teacher. You're* ***an*** *optimist.*

Zero article Ø

No article is used:

• with plural countable nouns when we are speaking generally	*Ø Lions and Ø tigers can be dangerous. Ø Rainforests are being cut down at an alarming rate.*
• with uncountable nouns when we are speaking generally	*Ø Money is the root of all evil. Ø Time is precious*
• with certain types of places	*He's been to Ø prison. They're at Ø home. She's in Ø hospital.*
• with the names of towns and some countries	*Ø Liverpool / Ø Madrid / Ø Thailand*
• with **by** + means of transport	*They went by Ø train. We're coming by Ø car.*

When to use it

Using a noun in English means making a decision as to whether it requires an article. If it does, it is important to choose the right article: *a / an / the / Ø*. Whether or not an article is necessary (and if so, which one) depends on factors such as meaning, context, whether it is a singular or plural noun, countable or uncountable or whether it is a fixed expression.

Context / Theme	Examples
Jobs / Talking about careers	Your ideal job *I'd like to be a doctor because Ø **doctors** help Ø **people**.* Going for a job interview *Make sure you wear Ø **suitable clothes**.* *Ask Ø **questions** about **the job**.* *Find out about **the company**.*
Food and drink	My favourite foods / Addictions / Pet hates *I love Ø **potatoes** but I can't stand Ø **mashed potato**.* In a recipe (listing the ingredients) *In my recipe for paella, I use Ø **rice**, Ø **chicken**, Ø **mussels**, Ø **prawns**, Ø **oil**, Ø **tomatoes**, and Ø **garlic**.* (method) *Fry **the chicken** in **the** oil, then add **the tomatoes** and **the garlic**. Finally add **the rice** and **the water** and cook for 30 **minutes**.* Dietary advice: Healthy and unhealthy foods *You should eat **fruit** and **vegetables** every day.* *Don't eat too much red **meat**.* *Ø **Fruit** is good for you.* Deciding on food and drinks for a party or a picnic *Most people like Ø **bread** and Ø **cheese**.* *We need Ø **milk**, Ø **tea**, Ø **coffee**, Ø **crisps** and Ø **eggs**.* Foods that remind you of your childhood *We always had Ø **fish** on Fridays – usually with Ø **chips**.* ***The bread** we buy now isn't as tasty as **the bread** my mother made.*
Materials (countable and uncountable nouns)	Talk about what things are made of in your home / college / town *Everything in **the room** is made of Ø **metal** or Ø **wood** except **the windows** which are made of Ø **glass** and **the curtains** which are made of **cotton**.*

See lesson plan 8.

Sports

Explaining a sport
(what you need and how to play)
You need to join ***a tennis club*** *or find* ***a public court****.*
You play with ***a racket*** *and* ***tennis balls****.*
You have to hit ***the ball*** *with* ***the racket*** *over* ***the net****.*

Superlative events, experiences etc.

Describe …
The most dangerous thing *that has happened to you.*
The funniest thing *you've ever seen.*
The worst book / film / TV programme *you remember.*

Towns and cities

In discussions of subjects such as
Pollution / Traffic / Public transport / Waste disposal / Housing / Employment etc.
Ø ***Pollution*** *is increasingly becoming* ***a problem*** *in Ø major cities around* ***the world****. Ø* ***Traffic*** *is increasing in volume and emissions are rising. However, most major cities have excellent Ø* ***public transport networks*** *…*

Which contexts and topics might appeal to your students? Add some ideas here!

How to teach it

Practical matters

- Nouns are taught and learnt from the very beginning of a course of language study, but unlike verb forms, they are not taught as part of a system where form and function are significant issues.

- You will rarely devote a whole lesson to teaching nouns, except perhaps to teach the **grammatical differences between countable and uncountable nouns**. However, there are certain basics to be established very early on. These include the following:
  - how to make singular nouns plural
  - pointing out that uncountable nouns do not a have plural form
  - establishing that in English nouns do not have genders or cases. The first language of some learners may have three genders and six cases. This means that, in English, adjectives do not have to "agree" with the nouns they qualify. Having said that, it is worth pointing out that inanimate objects are referred to with the pronoun "it".
  - how apostrophes are used to make the possessive form of nouns

- Rather than regarding nouns as individual words, encourage learners to see them as part of noun phrases, collocations or idioms. These groups of words are sometimes referred to collectively as "chunks". Here are some examples of chunks which include the word *business*
  - Noun phrases: ***business*** *executive* / ***business*** *studies* / ***business*** *affairs* / *a start-up* ***business*** / *the city centre* ***business*** / *run*
  - Collocations: *big* ***business*** / *drum up* ***business*** / *family* ***business*** / *run a* ***business***
  - Idioms: *funny* ***business*** / *get down to* ***business*** / *to mean* ***business*** / *to mind one's own* ***business***

  This is not to suggest that learners learn all these chunks when they come across the word business, merely that they should **learn the word in context rather than in isolation**.

- Recommend that learners use a good English-English dictionary which will provide them with "chunks" which include the word they are looking up (online dictionaries will also "speak" the word and help learner's pronunciation).

What to watch out for

- Learners may find it difficult to understand the difference between countable and uncountable nouns, especially if their first language does not use articles.

- Nouns which are uncountable in English may be countable in other languages. This may lead to mistakes such as these.
  What advices can you give me?
  We bought a lot of new furnitures for our flat.

  You will need to point out that advice and furniture are uncountable in English. This could lead on to teaching learners how to make such nouns plural. For example:
  pieces of advice / pieces of furniture / loaves of bread / slices of toast / bottles of wine

- Some nouns have countable and uncountable forms with different meanings. The differences between the two will need to be pointed out and explained. For example:
  I love ***chickens*** *so I don't eat* ***chicken****.*
  "Would you like ***a chocolate****?" – "No thanks. I don't like* ***chocolate****."*
  "I'm going to have ***the lamb****, what about you?" – "No, I'm having* ***the chicken****. And* ***a beer****."*

- Learners may have problems remembering irregular plural forms and use a regular but incorrect form, e.g. *childs* instead of *children* or *mans* instead of *men*.

  It sometimes helps to show them singular → plural patterns but not always. For example, this pattern works:
  knife → *knives* / *life* → *lives* / *wife* → *wives*
  But not these:

mouse → *mice* / *louse* → *lice*	BUT *house* → *houses* / *grouse* → *grouse*
foot → *feet*	BUT *boot* → *boots*
goose → *geese*	BUT *mongoose* → *mongooses*

- Learners may find forming compound nouns counter-intuitive and make groups of words using prepositions instead. For example:

the headlights of the car	instead of ***car headlights***
services on the motorway	instead of ***motorway services***
the capacity of the fuel tank	instead of ***the fuel tank capacity***

See lesson plan 8.

Suggestions for classroom activities

1 Topic Recipes
Language countable and uncountable nouns
Activities 1. In pairs learners tell each other about their favourite meals.

2. Learners ask each other what the main ingredients of their meals are: probably a mixture of countable and uncountable nouns. The teacher could provide an example list like this:
a tin of fava beans, two onions, two cloves of garlic, vegetable stock, spices (1 teaspoon each): oregano, cumin, turmeric

3. Make sure learners understand the vocabulary and can distinguish between countable and uncountable nouns.

4. Introduce the method of preparation, like this
Fry the onions and the garlic, then add the spices, the vegetable stock and the fava beans. Stir well and simmer for 30 minutes
Check learners understand the words *fry, add, stir* and *simmer.*

5. Ask learners to tell each other their how to make their recipes.

6. Follow-up writing task: write recipe including quantities.

2 Topic Healthy and unhealthy food
Language countable and uncountable nouns and quantities / *more, less, fewer*
Activities 1. Show photos of various popular foods.
Ask learners to name as many as they can. They could make sentences like this:
There are some apples and there's some cheese.

2. Learners work in pairs talking about which foods they like and which they don't.

3. Ask which food is healthy and which is unhealthy. Elicit learners' answers.

4. Present learners with a list of food an unknown person eats every day. For example: 200g crisps / 100g sweets / 100g chocolate / 1 apple / five slices of bread / 50g green beans etc.
Ask them what advice they would give this person. Elicit answers like these using *more, less, fewer.*
He should eat more fruit and vegetables.
He should eat less chocolate and fewer sweets.

5. Learners tells each other what they eat every day and then give each other dietary advice. (It may be more fun if they exaggerate the amount of unhealthy food they eat.)

3 Topic Describing people in a crowd
Language noun phrases which include prepositions
Activities 1. Show learners a photograph or illustration of a crowd and ask them to choose one person in the crowd (books such as *Where's Wally* work very well for this as well).

2. Working in pairs, learners ask each other questions to find out who their partner is looking at. Their questions should include noun phrases. E.g.
*Are you looking at **the man in the blue suit carrying a briefcase**?*
*Are you looking at **the woman pushing the red pram**?*
*Is it **the man with dark hair and a checked shirt crossing the road**?*

3. Monitor learners' conversations, helping them to construct correct noun phrases.

4 Topic Materials quiz
Language uncountable nouns for materials (wood, metal, plastic, glass etc.) and countable nouns for places
Activities 1. Tell the class you are thinking of an object. They have to guess the object by finding what it's made of, where it can be found and what it's used for. They should ask Yes/No questions like this:

Q	*Is it made of metal?*	*A*	*No*
Q	*Is it made of wood?*	*A*	*Yes*
Q	*Can I find it in a house?*	*A*	*Yes*
Q	*In the bedroom?*	*A*	*No*
Q	*In the dining room?*	*A*	*Yes*
Q	*Could I eat at it?*	*A*	*No*
Q	*Could I sit on it?*	*A*	*Yes*
Q	*Is it a chair?*	*A*	*Yes*

2. Learners now follow the same procedure in pairs.

3. A follow-up activity might be to ask learners to compile lists of things in a house made of particular materials. Perhaps like this:
*These things are made of **wood**: beds / tables / cupboards / chairs*
*These things are made of **metal**: cutlery (uncountable) / waste bins / taps*

5 Topic Mobile phone collocations
Language Verb + noun collocations
Activities 1. Learners compare how they use their mobile phones. Allow 3-4 minutes discussion and then elicit some of their ideas.

2. Write these nouns on the board
app / button / call / contact list / film / game / message / phone / screen / text
Check that learners understand their meaning then ask them to suggest verbs that could be used with these nouns. Elicit a few sentences like these
download + app *You can **download apps** onto your phone.*

3. Now write these verbs on the board and ask learners to make sentences using appropriate verb + noun collocations from the two lists.
download / look at / make / play / press / read / send / set up / tap / turn off / turn on

6 Topic Dictionary check
Language Words which can be countable and uncountable
Activities 1. Write these two sentences on the board and ask learners if they can explain the difference in meaning between the underlined phrases.
Would you like a <u>chocolate</u>? / Would you like <u>some chocolate</u>?

2. Make sure learners understand the differences in grammar and meaning between *a chocolate* and *chocolate*, ask them to use their dictionary to check the difference in meaning between the following

a glass / glass	*a wood / wood*
a paper / paper	*a lamb / lamb*
a room / room	*a memory / memory*
a coffee / coffee	

3. They should then make sentences using both words of each pair, e.g. *The glass I dropped on the floor broke and now the floor is covered in broken glass.*

7 Topic Towns and cities
Language Compound nouns on this topic
Activities 1. Show a photo of a city centre, e.g.
Ask learners to say what they can see. Elicit as many nouns as possible *street corner / traffic lights / lamp post / pedestrian crossing / shop fronts …*

2. Ask learners to make as many compound nouns as they can from the following lists. They should follow a word from list A with a word from list B to make compound nouns. The nouns they make may be one word or two.

A art / bus / cash / cross / foot / pedestrian / petrol / railway / sky / street / town / traffic
B centre / corner / gallery / hall / jam / light / lights / line / path / point / precinct / roads / scraper / station / stop

3. Elicit compounds from the class and ask them what happens at each place or point. For example

art gallery	*You can see paintings and sculpture here.*
bus stop	*You can wait for or get off buses here.*

8 Topic Magazine article
Language Different types of nouns
Activities 1. Remind learners of the different kinds of nouns they have studied and elicit examples from them:

plural countable noun – *dogs*	uncountable noun – *water*
compound noun – *bus stop*	adjectival noun – *the young*
collective noun – *team*	proper noun – *London*

2. Hand out a short newspaper or magazine text and ask learners to find at least one of each of the above types of noun. For example

It's become a cliché, hasn't it? When someone shows excitement or surprise about something pretty mundane, we say: "You should get out more!" I took this advice years ago and thought you might like to hear about some of my visits to musical events. I ought to declare an interest before we start, though; when I mention the band I'm in – The Hosepipe Band – it is not for purposes of blowing my own trumpet – it is simply to present a full picture of my gettings-out. I should also declare that I am not a fan of the rich and famous and I don't frequent stadiums which house hundreds of thousands of people. My band play in village halls and farm barns.

Key	
singular countable nouns	*cliché / interest / band / trumpet / picture / fan*
plural countable nouns	*visits / events / purposes / gettings-out / stadiums / people / halls / barns*
uncountable nouns	*excitement / surprise / advice*
compound nouns	*village halls / farm barns*
adjectival nouns	*the rich / the famous*
collective noun	*band*
proper noun	*Hosepipe Band*
noun phrases	*some of my visits to folk-related events / the band I'm in / a full picture of my gettings-out / stadiums which house hundreds of thousands of people*

3. Elicit learners' ideas. There are some words and phrases which can be classified in different ways. For example: *some of my visits to musical events* can be regarded as a noun phrase, but *visits* and *events* are also plural countable nouns.

9 Topic Language Activities

Kim's game
countable and uncountable nouns with definite and indefinite articles
1. Gather together 10 random items, a mixture of countable and uncountable nouns, on a large tray. Tell the class they are allowed to look at it for ten seconds. They should remember as many items as possible.

2. Elicit items learners have remembered. There will be a variety of answers, e.g.
there are some keys / there's a pair of scissors
there is some water / there is a glass of water

3. Now tell learners you're going to remove one of the items and they have to say what is missing the next time you show them the tray. Elicit their answers, this time with the definite article. For example
the clock is missing

10 Topic Language Activities

Names
proper nouns vs common nouns
1. Write a selection of nouns on the board (or a handout) and ask learners which should start with a capital letter. For example:
amazon / arctic / asia / car / continent / country / eiffel tower / ford / iceland / june / month / ocean / river / tourist attraction
Elicit answers and remind learners of the difference between proper nouns and common nouns.

2. For each of the proper nouns they have identified, ask learners to find the common noun category to which the proper noun belongs. For example
Amazon = continent

Now ask learners to work in pairs to makes lists of proper nouns which are examples of the common nouns in your original list. Examples:

car	*Ford, Toyota, Volkswagen, Volvo*
continent	*Asia, Europe, North America, South America*

country	*Iceland, Indonesia, Wales, Jordan*
month	*June, April, August, October*
ocean	*Atlantic, Pacific, Indian, Arctic*
river	*Amazon, Nile, Rhine, Thames*
tourist attraction	*Eiffel Tower, Big Ben, Statue of Liberty, Sydney Opera House*

3. Learners now research one of the countries on the internet and write a few sentences about it, including major towns and cities, rivers and any tourist attractions. Remind learners that proper nouns start with a capital letter.

Any more ideas?

Lesson plan 8

Lesson profile

Description	Engage → Study → Activate (See Introduction)
Topic	Food, dishes, recipes
Grammar point	countable and uncountable nouns, quantity words
Aims	To revise the use of quantity words for items of food and drink.
Material	WS 8.1 *It's party time!*

ENGAGE

Speaking activity

WS 8.1 Task 1

T Tell learners they are going to organize a party together. Ask them to discuss these general questions in pairs or groups:

What's the occasion? Will your party have a theme?
Where will you hold the party?
How many people will you invite?
What kind of music will you play?

L Learners discuss their answers to these questions and try to come to an agreement.

Now ask learners to think about the kinds of food and drink they want to have at the party and to prepare for a visit to the supermarket by making a shopping list.

Learners discuss food and make a simple shopping list.

Elicit food and drink items needed and make a simple list. Example:
bread / crisps / salad / cheese / fruit / biscuits / chocolate / orange juice

STUDY

Grammar practice

WS 8.1 Task 2

T Work through the items on the shopping lists asking learners to write a more detailed shopping list with quantities of each item. This may involve specifying:

- weight: *1kg cheese* or
- number: *8 loaves of bread*

Sometimes they may wish to keep quantities vague, e.g.
some apples / some wine

You may need to remind them of words like *loaf, packet, bar, box* etc.

L Learners rewrite their lists with appropriate quantities and using quantity expressions such as *loaves of, bottles of* etc. where necessary.

	T	L
ACTIVATE Speaking activity: agreeing on a dish Writing activity: writing a recipe	Ask learners to discuss in their groups which dish they are going to bring to the party. They should discuss: *What are you going to bring?* *Which ingredients do you need?* *What do you need to buy?*	In pairs or groups, learners plan which dish to prepare for the party and write their shopping list specifying quantities as before in Task 2.
WS 8.1 Tasks 3 and 4	As a follow-up writing activity (or as homework) ask students to write down the recipe for the dish they are bringing to the party.	Individually learners write down the recipe, listing the ingredients and their quantities and describing the method as a series of steps.
	At this point it may be necessary to refresh or introduce vocabulary such as *cut / chop, add, mix, fry, bake, simmer, stir* etc. Ask students to swap their work with a partner and correct each other's work.	Students work in pairs and read each other's recipes. They make suggestions how mistakes could be corrected
	If time allows, ask some of the students to read out their recipes to the class.	Students tell the rest of the class about their party plans and read out some of their recipes. The class holds a vote on which dish sounds the tastiest.

It's party time!

Task 1

You're going to organize a party in your class. Discuss these questions in pairs or groups.

a) What's the occasion?

b) Will your party have a theme?

c) Where will you hold the party?

d) Who will you invite? How many people will you invite?

e) What kind of music will you play?

Now discuss this question. Make notes.

f) What kinds of food and drink will you serve at the party? Make a note here.

PARTY MENU

1. ....
2. ....
3. ....
4. ....
5. ....
6. ....
7. ....
8. ....
9. ....
10. ....

Don't forget to cook

Task 2

Write a shopping list to take to the supermarket. Include the quantity or weight you need for the number of people you are planning to invite.

TO BUY *before* PARTY

1. cheese 2 kg
2. bread 8 large loaves, 20 rolls
3. Fruit some apples
4. ....
5. ....
6. Drinks
7. 5 cartons of fruit juice
8. 7 bottles of ...
9. ....
10. ....

ISBN 978-3-12-501628-6

Task 3

Each group should prepare a dish to take to the party. In your group decide:

- what you are going to bring (a cake, a salad, a tortilla etc.)
- what ingredients you need for the recipe
- what you need to buy. Write a shopping list that includes numbers or quantities.

TO BUY *before* PARTY

1. ....
2. ....
3. ....
4. ....
5. ....
6. ....
7. ....
8. ....
9. ....
10. ....

Task 4

Write down the recipe and describe how to make it. These words can help you:

cut • add • mix • fry • bake • stir • simmer

My recipe

ISBN 978-3-12-501628-6

Add your notes here!

Unit 9 – Describing people, things and actions

How to recognize it

1. Describe this scene using sentences which include some descriptive words.

2. Reorder each of these groups of words into a sentence which makes sense.

a	*cottage*	*grandmother*	*in*	***little***	*lives*	*my*
pretty	***thatched***	*at*	*frames*	*look*	***old***	*our*
rotten	*window*	*an*	***ancient***	*city*	*Florence*	
is	***Italian***					

The words in blue are **adjectives** – words we use to describe a person, place, object or abstract idea or concept. They give extra information about a noun and provide answers to the questions *which?*, *what kind of?* and *how many?* What do you notice about their position in the re-ordered sentences? Can you put the adjectives in a different order?

Words which qualify adjectives or describe actions are called **adverbs**. They provide answers to questions such as *how?*, *when?*, *where?* and *how often?* For example your sentences for the scene above may read:
The car is parked very badly. (*very* and *badly* are both adverbs)
The garden of the house is absolutely delightful. (*absolutely* is an *adverb*, *delightful* is an adjective)

How to use it → Adjectives

Bear in mind the following:

Form

Strictly speaking we **identify adjectives by their function** in a sentence rather than by their form. There are, however, some suffixes that are typical of adjectives, e.g.:
-ful *(careful, harmful, fruitful),* ***-ish*** *(churlish, foolish, Scottish),* ***-able, -ible*** *(incredible, reputable, responsible, adorable),* ***-less*** *(hairless, careless, endless),* ***-ic*** *(romantic, problematic, artistic),* ***-ical***, *(political, theoretical, economical),* ***-ative, -ive*** *(communicative, manipulative, alternative, active),* ***-(i)ous*** *(pious, religious, famous),* ***-y*** *(busy, misty, silly, crappy)*

Position

Most adjectives can be used in two positions: **before the noun** they describe and **after a verb** such as *be, become* as well as sense verbs such as *look, seem* etc.:
This is an ***endless*** *book.* *This book is* ***endless****.*

There are, however, some adjectives that can only be used **before the noun** they describe:
My ***eldest son*** *is 44 this year.*
It was a ***mere scratch****.* (Not ~~the scratch is mere~~)

And other adjectives may only be used after a verb:
The children ***were afraid****.* (Not ~~the afraid children~~)
Eva ***was asleep*** *when Raoul arrived.*

Order

When more than one adjective is used in front of a noun, there is a normally **accepted order**. Adjectives that express an opinion normally come before more neutral ones. The most usual sequence of adjectives is:

determiner	*that*
1. opinion	*fantastic*
2. size	*huge*
3. physical quality	*rusty*
4. shape	*long*
5. age	*ancient*
6. colour	*black*
7. origin	*Japanese*
8. material	*metal*
9. purpose	*ceremonial*
noun	*sword*

(Obviously a sentence that included all types would be extremely rare!)
It's a ***beautiful warm sunny*** *morning.* not ~~*a sunny warm beautiful morning*~~
He's wearing a ***long black woollen*** *coat.* not ~~*a black woollen long coat*~~

Possessive adjectives

Words like *my, your, his, her, our* and *their* are possessive adjectives. They show **who** something **belongs to**.
Is that ***your*** *red car? No* ***my*** *car is black*

Note: *mine, yours, his, hers, ours, theirs* are possessive pronouns and cannot be followed by a noun.
Jo and I have similar cars. Mine is green and hers is black.

Making comparisons

Adjectives have **comparative** and **superlative forms** which are used when things are compared:

- one-syllable adjectives add *-er / -est* at the end (or simply *-r* if the adjective ends in *-e*)
  *large – **larger – largest***

- one-syllable adjectives with one vowel + one consonant double the final consonant and add *-er / -est*
  *big – **bigger – biggest***

- two-syllable adjectives ending in –y change *y* to *i* and add *-er / -est*
  *heavy – **heavier – heaviest***
  *easy – **easier – easiest***

- some two-syllable adjectives add *-er / -est* and others *more / most*
  *quiet – **quieter – quietest***
  *useful – **more useful – most useful***

- adjectives of three or more syllables take *more / most*
  *important – **more important – most important***

- some adjectives are irregular
  *good – **better – best***
  *bad – **worse – worst***

Grading adjectives

Most adjectives are gradable, that is they express qualities that can be measured, e.g.
warm, cold, frightened, hungry
These can be used with the words such as *very, slightly, rather, pretty, quite, extremely* etc., adverbs which intensify their meaning or make it weaker, e.g.
*It's **rather warm** today.*
*She's **very frightened**.*
*It's **extremely expensive**.*

Some adjectives, however, are ungradable. These include:
- adjectives that describe the absolute quality of someone or something, e.g.
  vegan, male, finished, dead, necessary
- adjectives that express extreme qualities, e.g.
  boiling, frozen, terrified, ravenous

These cannot be used with *very, rather, pretty* or *quite*. It is not possible for someone to be *rather vegetarian* or for a project to be *very finished*! It is only possible to make adjectives such as these stronger, so they can be used with words such as *absolutely, completely, totally, really* etc.
*It's **absolutely boiling** today.*
*She was **completely terrified**.*
*They're **absolutely ravenous**.*

Compound adjectives

Compound adjectives – adjectives made up of more than one word – are very commonly used. Here some examples:
*a **five-star** hotel / a **half-eaten** apple / a **well-known** singer / a **sugar-coated** tablet / a **rarely-seen** bird / a **half remembered** dream / **handmade** furniture / a **six-hour** flight / the **post-war** period*

How to use it → Adverbs

There are many types of adverbs. In fact, it is sometimes said that if you can't decide what class a word is, it is probably an adverb! The most important things to bear in mind are:

Function

Adverbs can **qualify verbs, adjectives** or other **adverbs**

*She played the piece **beautifully**.*	*beautifully* tells us how she played.
*It was a **really** beautiful piece.*	*really tells* us how beautiful the piece was.
*He ran **incredibly** quickly.*	*incredibly* tells us how quickly he ran.

Types of adverb

Manner adverbs answer the question "How …":
*She spoke **slowly** and **precisely.***
*He walked **carefully** down the narrow path.*

Many manner adverbs are formed by adding the suffix *-ly* to an adjective, e.g.
*slow – **slowly***
*deep – **deeply***
*interesting – **interestingly***

Some words that end in *–ly*, however, are adjectives as well as adverbs, e.g.

*Most people used to buy a **daily** paper.*	vs	*We get a paper delivered **daily.***
*This is your **early** morning call.*	vs	*I have to get up **early** tomorrow.*

Frequency adverbs answer the question "How often …?":
*I **often** go shopping on Friday evenings. I **always** buy bread and I **usually** buy milk. **Sometimes**, I buy fruit and vegetables and **occasionally** I buy butter. I **rarely** buy alcohol and I **never** buy cigarettes.*

Place adverbs answer the question "Where …?":
*The dog was **here** a moment ago. I think it's gone **upstairs.***

Time adverbs answer the question "When …?":
*He **recently** bought an old car, but he **soon** regretted it.*

Degree adverbs answer the question "To what extent …?" or "How much?":
*I'm **very** interested in your ideas and I'd **quite** like to discuss them with you.*
*It's **highly** unlikely they'll be here in time.*

Comment adverbs tell us something about the user's thoughts or opinions:
***Hopefully**, we can discuss our differences.*
*We solved the problem **amazingly** quickly.*

Position in sentences

Adverbs can be at the front, in the middle or at the end of a clause. Unfortunately, there is no simple rule which tells us the correct position of adverbs in sentences, and it often depends on the type of adverb and/or which information the speaker wishes to emphasize.

Some adverbs can be put in different positions:
*I **sometimes** go swimming after work.*
***Sometimes** I go swimming after work.*
*I go swimming after work **sometimes**.*

But others can only go in one position:
*I **always** go swimming after work.* but not
~~***Always** I go swimming after work.*~~
~~*I go swimming after work **always**.*~~

Comparisons

Like adjectives, adverbs have **comparative** and **superlative** forms.
The comparative and superlative form of adverbs ending in *-ly* includes *more* and *most*
slowly → more slowly → most slowly

The comparative and superlative form of short adverbs is the same as the related adjectives
hard → harder → hardest

Good to know

Some adverbs have two forms:

- the same form as adjectives. Commonly used examples include *hard, rough, tight, quick, late:*

*He's a **hard** worker.*	*He works **hard**.*
*They're **rough** sleepers.*	*They sleep **rough**.*
*It was a **tight** squeeze.*	*Hold it **tight**!*
*I'm taking the **late** train.*	*The train arrived **late**.*
*He gave a **wrong** answer.*	*Where did we go **wrong**?*

- a form ending in -ly, e.g. *tightly*, *quickly*, *wrongly*, *hardly*, *roughly*:
  *The room was **tightly** packed with her supporters.*
  *He was **wrongly** accused of fraud.*

  Sometimes the *-ly* form has a different meaning:
  *He **hardly** sleeps most nights.*
  *There were **roughly** 20 people at the meeting.*
  *The trains have been running on time **lately**.*

When to use it

Context / Theme	Examples
Describing people	A detailed description of a missing person *Police are looking for a 26-year-old man. He is **quite tall** and has **short dark** hair.* Comparing yourself with classmates *I'm **taller than** Juan, but he's **slimmer than** me. **The tallest** member of the class is Jorge.* Describing encounters with memorable people *I met the **most interesting** person at a demo the other day. She's only 14 but already **very knowledgeable** about climate change and **totally committed** to the cause.*
Describing places	Describing a house, apartment or room *It's a **three-storey** house and our apartment is on the **second** floor. It has a **very large** living room, three **medium-sized** bedrooms, a kitchen and an **absolutely tiny** bathroom.* A description of a hotel or building *The **totally unique** location of The Grand, in a **secret** corner of the city, makes this **intimate** 5-star hotel **very special**.* A description of a town or tourist resort for a brochure *Lavenham is an **ancient** market town, full of character and history, set in the **lush**, **fertile** valley of the River Brett. West of the town the land rises **sharply** to **arable** fields and copses filled with pheasants and partridges. To the east, the slope is **shallower**, and it is **here** that most of the town's housing has been built.*
Describing things	A description of something you're trying to sell on eBay, to make it sound as good as you can *This is a **beautiful**, **original** 1970's **Danish** armchair in **absolutely superb** condition. We have just had the frame, seat and fabric **fully** refurbished. It has been **professionally** re-upholstered in a **lovely, hard-wearing green** fabric.*

Adjectives especially are usually learnt as **units of vocabulary** with a particular semantic function, rather than as a specific grammar form.

See lesson plan 9.

Describing events

Watching and describing something to someone who can't see it

*This magician is asking if he can borrow Tom's T-shirt. It's **quite** a **small red** T-shirt. He's taking the T-shirt, then shaking it **very hard**. As it moves it changes into a **large blue** flag much **bigger** than Tom's T-shirt. Tom is **clearly** amazed, and **obviously** he's wondering where his T-shirt is. The magician is pointing to the building behind him where Tom's **red** T-shirt is fluttering **gently** between two **brightly coloured** flags, **similar** in size to the **yellow** flag.*

Commentating on a sports event

*It's quite a **scrappy** game at the moment with a series of **surprisingly late** challenges. Only one **yellow** card, but I suspect that will increase. The **latest** foul has just seen Messi deliver a **free** kick into the PSV box, but Zoet was **there** to collect. Still **goalless** with 31 minutes on the clock.*

Which other contexts will appeal to your students? Describing this year's fashion styles? Where's Wally activities? Add your ideas here!

How to teach it

Practical matters

Adjectives and adverbs are more likely to be **taught as items of vocabulary** rather than as parts of a grammatical system. However there will be lessons where the grammar of adjectives needs to be dealt with. These are some of the "grammatical features" of adjectives (for more details see the section **How to use it** on page 143):

- The **position** of adjectives in sentences:
  - in front of the noun they describe: *I have a **red** car.*
  - after certain verbs: *My car looks **red**, but it's actually **brown**.*
- The formation of **comparative** and **superlative** forms:
  - forming comparative and superlative adjectives
  - using *than* in a comparative form when explicitly comparing two things or people
    *I'm **taller than** my sister.*
    *My sister is **shorter than** me.*
  - using the superlative form *the …-est* when explicitly comparing more than two things or people
    *That's **the funniest** book I've ever read.*
    *That was **the most expensive** meal I've ever eaten.*
- The difference between **gradable** and **ungradable** adjectives and the adverbs that can be used with each.
  *I'm **very tired**.*
  *I'm **absolutely exhausted.***
- The **order** of adjectives if several are used in front of a noun. Although we rarely use more than three adjectives at a time, there is a generally accepted order.
- The position of adverbs in sentences will need to be taught on a case by case basis.

What to watch out for

1. The **normal position of adjectives** may be problematic for learners if, in their first language, adjectives are placed after the nouns they describe. So, for example, a Spanish learner might say *grass green (césped verde)* instead of *green grass*.

2. The exact **order of adjectives** before nouns is difficult for learners to learn and remember, so instead of asking them to memorise the entire list, suggest they learn a few set phrases which illustrate the correct order. For example,
a little old man
a beautiful pink rose
a small red Japanese car etc.

3. Adjectives in English only have one form. Speakers of languages where the adjective always "agrees" with the noun may, however, try to create plural adjective forms if the noun in question is plural, e.g.
Look at the ~~pinks~~ flowers.

4. Similarly, English nouns do not have genders, so adjectives do not have male and female forms, as is the case with many other languages. For example, the word for *white* in French is *blanc* or *blanche*, so *un camion **blanc*** (a white lorry) but *une voiture **blanche*** (a white car).

5. Some learners confuse adjectives ending in *-ed* and *-ing*, such as *interested / interesting*;

bored / boring; tired / tiring.
In most contexts, people are *interested, bored* or *tired,* while things and situations are *interesting, boring* or *tiring*. However, this is only a rough guideline – after all, people certainly can be boring and tiring!

6. Understanding the difference between **gradable** and **ungradable** adjectives and knowing which degree adverbs can be used to qualify these adjectives. For example:

Gradable adjectives	Ungradable adjectives
hot / cold / hungry / tired / frightened / small / big Appropriate degree adverbs: *very, really, extremely, a bit, quite*	*boiling / freezing / ravenous / exhausted / terrified / tiny / enormous* Appropriate degree adverbs: *absolutely, totally, really*

Make a note of any interesting / unusual / odd / amusing / alarming / hair-raising issues your students might have where adjectives (and adverbs) are concerned!

Suggestions for classroom activities

1 Topic Personal interests
Language frequency adverbs (and their positions in sentences)
Activities 1. Ask learners to tell each other about how they spend their evenings and weekends. Elicit endings to sentences like these:
I hardly ever … / Occasionally, I … / I sometimes … / Usually, I … / I always …

2. Now ask them to tell each other things that they would never do if they can possibly help it.
I would ***never*** *go swimming in the sea unless it was very warm weather.*

3. This might also involve using time phrases like these:
once a week, every day, every so often.

2 Topic Comparisons between two people, things or products
Language comparative adjectives
Activities 1. Ask learners to think about the differences and similarities between themself and one of their friends.

2. They now work in pairs and tell each other about their friend. They could make comparisons like this
I'm taller than Jorge, but Jorge's more intelligent than me.
Suggest that they qualify their comparisons with phrases such as *a bit, a little, a lot, much, slightly …*
I'm ***a bit taller*** *than Jorge, but Jorge can run much faster than me.*

3. Learners could then compare an object they now possess with the one they had before, e.g. a mobile phone, a car, a pair of trainers etc.
My old phone was ***much heavier*** *than my new one.*
My new phone is ***much lighter than*** *my old one.*

4. Learners could compare their favourite soft drinks. For example *Coca Cola* vs *Pepsi*. Ask them to give reasons for their choice.

3 Topic Personal experiences
Language superlative adjectives *the most / ever*
Activities 1. Learners answer questions such as
Who is the strangest / funniest / most interesting person you've ever met?
What is the most expensive item you've ever bought?
What is the most uncomfortable place you've ever slept in?
What is the funniest film you've ever seen?
What is the most interesting place you've ever visited?

2. When they've thought / answered for themselves, learners could compare their answers in pairs. Having done this, they could make up new questions of a similar kind to discuss with their partners.

See lesson plan 9.

4 Topic Detailed descriptions
Language adjective order / compound adjectives
Activities 1. Write a short sentence on the board. For example
My car came from a dealer.
My friend lives in an apartment.

Ask learners to add adjectives to this sentence. Suggest simple adjectives to start with, e.g.
*My **red** car came from a **reputable** dealer.*
*My **best** friend lives in a **small** apartment.*

They could then add an opinion adjective to this sentence, e.g.
*My **beautiful red** car came from a **reputable** dealer.*
*My **brilliant best** friend lives in a **small** apartment.*

Next they could add a compound adjective to their sentences, e.g.
*My **beautiful red** car came from a **reputable, long established** dealer.*
*My **brilliant best** friend lives in a **small, third-floor** apartment.*

2. Finally, they could add an additional sentence with two adjectives. For example:
*My **beautiful red** car came from a **reputable, long established** dealer.*
*It's **Japanese** and **second-hand**.*
*My **brilliant best** friend lives in a **small, third-floor** apartment.*
*It's very **light** and **airy**.*

3. Working in pairs, learners make up new short sentences and take turns to add adjectives. Remind them to think about the order of adjectives and suggest that they add no more than three adjectives to each noun.

5 Topic Describing personalities
Language personality adjectives and their opposites
Activities 1. Elicit 10-20 personality adjectives from the class and write them in a column on the board. Then elicit adjectives with the opposite meaning – like this:

hardworking	*lazy*
clever / bright	*stupid*
interesting	*boring*
extrovert	*introvert*
sociable	*unsociable*
reliable	*unreliable*

2. Ask learners to choose three adjectives that other people might use about them. They could write these in a sentence like this:
*Some people think I'm **interesting, hardworking** and **clever**.*

Now ask them to write a follow-up sentence using adjectives with the opposite meanings:
*... But actually I'm **boring**, **lazy** and **stupid**.*

3. Learners now mingle with others and ask questions like this:
*Do you think I'm **interesting** or **boring**?*

4. With some groups this may simply be a fun exercise not to be taken too seriously, whereas with others it might lead on to some interesting and more serious conversations.

6 Topic Making stories more interesting
Language Adding adjectives and adverbs / correct order of adjectives
Activities 1. Write the beginning of a story on the board. It should contain no adjectives or adverbs. For example:

It was a Thursday morning in January. My alarm clock woke me. I got up and looked out of my bedroom window. It was snowing.

2. Elicit learners' ideas about the next two of three sentences of the story. Write their ideas on the board but leave out any adjectives or adverbs they include.

3. Now ask learners to work in pairs to make the story more interesting by adding adjectives and adverbs.

4. After a few minutes elicit their ideas. Ask learners to choose / vote on the best suggestions and add these to the sentences on the board. For example:
*It was a **cold** Thursday morning in **late** January. My **cheap old plastic** alarm clock woke me **noisily**. I got up **reluctantly** and looked out of my **tiny** bedroom window. It was snowing **heavily**.*

5. If time allows, ask learners to continue the story orally in class, but if time is tight, suggest they finish the story in their own way for homework. They should finish the outline of the story before adding the adjectives and adverbs. Remind them that they may need to decide on the correct order of adjectives.

7 Topic Language Activities

What am I describing?
Adjectives and adverbs – including comparative forms
1. Tell learners they have to try to guess the person, animal or object you are thinking of. Start by giving them one simple clue:
I'm thinking about an animal.

2. Learners now ask questions about the animal but you can only answer *Yes* or *No*. You should probably limit the number of questions that can be asked.
Learners should include adjectives and adverbs in their questions. Here's an example:
*Q1 Is it **bigger than** a cat?*
A1 Yes
*Q2 Is it **grey**?*
A2 Yes
*Q3 Can it run **fast**?*
A3 No
Q4 Is it an elephant?
A4 No
*Q5 Is it **smaller than** an elephant?*
A5 Yes
Q6 Is it a squirrel?
A6 No?
Q7 Is it a wolf?
A7 Yes

3. Now ask learners to work in groups of 4 or more. Each learner takes it in turn to think of a person, an animal or an object. Other learners ask questions which should all include an adjective or an adverb. Monitor group work and help if necessary.

8 Topic Making reviews sound better
Language Gradable and ungradable adjectives
Activities 1. Show learners this review of a book and ask if they would be inspired to read it. (*Hopefully they will say Probably not!*)

Matthews is a reasonable writer and this is another well-written book from his collection. Some people just have a great gift for writing and his stories are hard to put down. I have watched all the films and they are also quite good.

2. Ask learners which words or phrases they would change to make the review sound more exciting, persuasive or interesting. Hopefully they will come up with: *reasonable, well-written, great, hard, quite good.*

Highlight these words and phrases in the review and ask learners to come up with alternatives using ungradable adjectives where possible. (You may need to remind them what ungradable adjectives are.)

Matthews is a reasonable (→ excellent / superb / first-rate / outstanding / exceptional) writer and this is another well-written (→ finely written / brilliantly-written) book from his collection. Some people just have a great (→ incredible / amazing / tremendous / wonderful) gift for writing and his stories are hard (→ impossible) to put down. I have watched all the films and they are also quite good (→ remarkable / fantastic).

3. Ask learners to write their own lukewarm reviews of a book, film or TV programme. They then swap with a partner and make their partner's review more exciting by changing adjectives.

9 Topic Qualities needed for people in certain jobs
Language Adjectives and their opposites
Activities 1. Write a selection of jobs on the board, e.g.

DOCTOR	SHOP ASSISTANT
TAXI DRIVER	TEACHER

Alternatively show photos.

2. Ask learners to think of two positive adjectives to describe someone doing one of these jobs. Example:
A good doctor is ***sympathetic*** *and* ***efficient***.
A good shop assistant is ***polite*** *and* ***knowledgeable***.

3. Now ask learners to work in pairs and make up positive descriptions of the other jobs listed.
Note: They should not use the same adjective twice.

4. Now ask pairs to describe the same jobs using negative adjectives, e.g.
A poor doctor is ***unsympathetic*** *and* ***inefficient.***
A poor shop assistant is ***impolite / rude*** *and* ***ignorant***.
Note: The negative adjectives need not be the positive adjectives with a prefix. So accept Positive: *polite* Negative: *impolite* or *rude*

10 Topic Language Activities

Find someone who …

Adjectives and adverbs of manner

1. Write these adjectives on the board and elicit from the class the related adverbs.

good (well) / bad (badly) / fast (fast) / daily (daily) / slow (slowly) / loud (loudly) / careful (carefully) / easy (easily)

(Note: *fast* and *daily* are adverbs as well as adjectives)

2. Tell learners they are going to do a mingle activity. They are going to find someone who does things in particular ways. Hand out this checklist and check that learners know how their conversations should run. When giving their answers learners can add an adverb of degree. For example:

Q What can you do well, May?

A I can sing quite well.

Set a time limit. Ask learners to note down the name(s) of their classmates and the activities they describe.

Find someone who does something …	Name / Activity
1 … well	May sings well.
2 … noisily	
3 … slowly	
4 … carefully	
5 … fast or quickly	
6 … badly	
7 … easily	
8 … daily	

3. Round off the activity with a reporting back stage. Each learner reports to the rest of the class something they found interesting or surprising about another learner.

Lesson plan 9

Lesson profile

Description	Engage → Study → Activate (See Introduction)
Topic	Memorable people and events
Grammar point	Superlative adjectives / Present perfect verbs with *ever*
Aims	To present and practise the use of the present perfect form to refer to memorable experiences.
Material	WS 9.1 *Pleased to meet you*

ENGAGE

Photo-based speaking activity

WS 9.1 Task 1

T

Show learners photos of famous people you think they will recognize. Ask them in pairs to discuss who the people are and what they do.

Point to each photo and ask questions such as
Who's this?
Do you recognize this person?
What does he/she do?

Then ask
What do these people have in common?
to elicit the answer:
They're all famous.

L

→ Task 1

Learners discuss what they know about the people in the photos.

Learners answer questions.

Key:
1 Emma Watson (British actor)
2. BTS (K-pop band)
3. Barack Obama (former US president)
4. Queen Elizabeth II (British monarch since 1952)
5. Billie Eilish (American singer)
6. Archbishop Desmond Tutu (South African Anglican priest)
7. Serena Williams (American tennis player)
8. David Beckham (English ex-footballer)

T

Ask if learners have ever met anyone famous. If they don't have much to say, move on to the next stage.

L

Learners exchange ideas in pairs.

T

Tell learners about interesting people you have met. For example:
I've never met anyone famous, but I've met some interesting people. I've travelled on the same plane as a Finnish rock band and I've been in a lift with a politician.

L

Learners listen.

T

Ask learners to tell each other about interesting people they have met.

L

Learners talk in pairs for a few minutes.

T Give the class an example of the target language pattern, e.g.
The most interesting person I have ever met is a 14-year-old girl on a climate change march / Anthony Gormley / my granddad / ...
(Provide more information about the person you choose to describe and invite learners to ask you questions.)

Write the target structure on the board:
The most interesting person I have ever met is ...
Ask learners to repeat, then ask concept questions, e.g.
Have I met a more interesting person than this?
Could I meet a more interesting person in the future?
Am I talking about one past event or my whole life?
Which word tells us this?
Which verb form is used?
Why is this the best verb form?

L

Learners listen.

Learners ask T questions, such as:
Where was she from?
Why was she interesting?

Learners repeat target structure and answer concept questions.
No

Yes

My whole life
'Ever'
Present perfect
It links something in the past with the present.

STUDY 1

Grammar focus - modelling the target structure

WS 9.1 Task 2

T Elicit similar sentences from learners. Correct any errors of grammar including word order and verb form.

Introduce similar questions for learners to talk about in pairs, using both the present perfect and present simple, e.g.
Who's ...
the most boring person you have ever met?
the funniest person you know ...

Monitor conversations, correcting where necessary. This may involve the correct form of the superlative adjectives, present perfect verbs and word order. Make sure they include the word *ever.*

L Learners produce their own sentences, e.g.
The most interesting person I have ever met is my basketball coach / my mum's boss / a violinist from Palestine ...

Learners talk about the sentences in Task 3 in pairs.

STUDY 2

Grammar practice

WS 9.1 Task 3

ACTIVATE

Speaking about own experiences

WS 9.1 Task 4

T Ask students to choose another topic to discuss using the same language structure. They could talk more about people that have been unusual in some way or a completely different topic. Examples on the worksheet include:

- journeys (most interesting / most boring / longest)
- experiences (frightening / funny)

but students may choose an entirely different topic if they wish.

Monitor pair or group work but do not interrupt this fluency activity. Listen for particularly interesting stories and elicit these from the group as a final activity.

L In pairs or small groups learners agree on the next subject for discussion and then spend time individually preparing what to tell their partner or the rest of the group.

After a few minutes, learners share their stories with the others.

T As a follow-up writing activity ask the students to write a few sentences about one of the topics they have been talking about in pairs.

L Based on the notes they made and the discussions they had in their group, students write the story of one of their experiences, journeys etc.

Pleased to meet you

Task 1

Look at the photos and discuss these questions with a partner:

a) Who are these people?

b) What do you know about them?

c) What do they have in common?

ISBN 978-3-12-501628-6

Task 2

The most interesting person I have ever met is a 14-year-old girl on a climate change march.

Answer these questions:

- *Have I met a more interesting person than this?*
- *Could I meet a more interesting person in the future?*
- *Am I talking about one past event or my whole life?*
- *Which word tells us this?*
- *Which verb form is used?*
- *Why is this the best verb form?*

Task 3

Note your answers to these questions and then exchange ideas with a partner.

Who is …

a) the most boring person you have ever met?
b) the most intelligent person you have ever met?
c) the strangest person you have ever known?
d) the kindest person you have ever met?
e) the funniest person you have ever met?
f) the best sportsperson you have ever known?
g) the oldest person you have ever met?
h) the most creative person you have ever met?

Task 4

Discuss one of these topics in pairs.

Journeys or trips: the most interesting / the most boring / the longest
Experiences: the most frightening / the funniest / the most embarrassing / the craziest
Meals: the tastiest / the most disgusting / the most expensive / the best

Choose one and write a few sentences about it here.

ISBN 978-3-12-501628-6

Add your notes here!

Unit 10 – Making connections

How to recognize it

Look at the short sentences below. If they were part of a story, it wouldn't be a particularly riveting one! How can you connect the sentences to form a single sentence and create a more natural sounding, fluent text? Use your own words and phrases or some from the suggestions below. You can rearrange the order of information however you wish.

I was sitting on the train.	I was reading Moby Dick.	Occasionally I was looking out of the window.
I looked at the green fields.	The green fields were flashing past.	I saw something truly astounding.

A text can be grammatically correct and full of 'good' words, but it is mainly how those words and phrases are connected that make a text (any text, a story, an article, a summary etc.) interesting and sound natural. It is likely your sentence reads something like this:

As I was sitting on the train, reading Moby Dick and occasionally looking out of the window watching the green fields (which were) flash(ing) past, I suddenly saw something truly astounding.

By adding conjunctions, joining sentences together and using *-ing* forms to form one complex sentence, the text stops being a list of short, abrupt statements and becomes more natural.

How to use it

There are many different ways of making connections between words, phrases, clauses and sentences. These are some of them.

Conjunctions

There are two main types of conjunction.

Coordinating conjunctions
Coordinating conjunctions link words or clauses of equal importance:

and	*The wind was blowing* ***and*** *it was pouring down.*
but	*He was shouting* ***but*** *I couldn't hear a word he said.*
so	*Pete was very tired* ***so*** *he went to bed early.*

Subordinating conjunctions
Subordinating conjunctions link two clauses, one of which is dependent on the other. The clause introduced by the conjunction is the dependent clause. The other is the main clause. Subordinating conjunctions can express meanings such as time, place, manner, reason, contrast, result etc. and include the following:

even though	***Even though*** *I've known her for years, she didn't recognize me.*
because	*He went home* ***because*** *he was ill.*
if / when	***If / When*** *I have a headache, I take paracetamol.*
when / while	*There was a knock at the door* ***when / while*** *we were having lunch.*
as	***As*** *I was getting in the bath, the doorbell rang.*
so	*The children were restless* ***so*** *I took them to the park.*

Adverbs (conjuncts)

Adverbs or adverbial phrases are used to link two clauses, sentences or paragraphs. They include the following:

however	*That's one possible answer to the question.* ***However****, there are others.*
as a result	*They found him cheating;* ***as a result,*** *he failed the exam.*
meanwhile	*Sarah was looking after the shop for her parents.* ***Meanwhile****, Jo was watching TV.*
eventually	*We'd walked for seven hours but* ***eventually,*** *we came to the border.*

Relative clauses

Relative clauses give additional information about a noun or noun phrase. These clauses start with a relative pronoun, such as *who, which* or *that*. There are two types of relative clause: defining and non-defining.

Defining relative clauses define the person or thing being referred to. It provides essential information and cannot be left out.

The car ***which is parked outside our block*** belongs to my sister.
The actor ***who first played James Bond*** was Sean Connery.

Non-defining relative clauses provide extra information about a person or thing and can be left out without affecting the meaning of the sentence. They are separated from the rest of the sentence by commas.

My brother***, who is four years younger than me,*** now lives in Australia.
The postman brought me a letter***, which I opened immediately***.

Good to know

Bear in mind the following:

- A dependent (or subordinate) clause can come before or after the main clause:

  Even though I've known her for years, she didn't recognize me.
  She didn't recognize me ***even though I've known her for years***.
  If the subordinate clause comes before the main clause, it is followed by a comma.

- If adverbs (conjuncts) start a sentence, they are followed by a comma.

  Jo was watching TV. ***Meanwhile***, Sarah was looking after the shop for her parents.

- The subordinating conjunctions *since* and *as* can be used to mean *because*.

  Since / As *you're obviously not interested, I won't go on trying to persuade you.*

- In defining relative clauses *who* refers to people, *which* refers to objects and *that* can refer to people or objects.
  The car ***which / that is parked outside our block*** *belongs to my sister.*
  The actor ***who / that*** *first played James Bond was Sean Connery.*

- Relative clauses can also refer to whole phrases or ideas.

  In many countries children do not have to wear a school uniform, ***which I think is a sensible idea***.
  (In this example the relative clause refers to the fact that in many countries children do not have to wear a school uniform.)

- The relative pronoun *whose* indicates possession.

  The people ***whose*** *Airbnb we're staying in are on holiday in Florida.*

- In formal language prepositions can be placed before relative pronouns.

  The story ***upon which*** *the novel is based took place in 19th century Austria.*

Note: Although these kinds of connecting devices are used in everyday speech, they are more commonly found in written English. Some of the suggestions below could be spoken or written activities.

When to use it

Making connections	Possible teaching contexts / themes with examples
to describe a sequence of actions	Reporting an event (conjunctions / relative clauses) *I was running late that morning* ***because*** *I'd over-slept,* ***which*** *meant I was walking faster than usual. Fortunately, my bus,* ***which*** *was always punctual, was five minutes late for a change* ***so*** *I got to work on time after all.*

	Telling a story (conjunctions / relative clauses) ***Because*** *Grandma was ill, the little girl was taking her some organically grown fruit and vegetables.* ***As*** *she was walking through the forest,* ***which*** *was full of endangered animals and plants, she met the wolf,* ***who*** *smiled and said …*
to talk about contrasts	Making life easier (finishing sentences using contrasting conjunctions) ***Instead of*** *spending so much time at work, we should …* *People are still short of money* ***even though*** *…* ***Whereas*** *Ben works 50 hours a week for very little money, his brother Pete …*
	Separating fact from fiction, talking about common myths etc. (contrasting conjunctions) *Some people believe sugar causes hyperactivity in children,* ***but*** *there is no proof of this.* ***Although*** carrots are healthy, eating them does not mean we can see in the dark.
to give reasons	Writing an email / a letter giving reasons *I didn't make the meeting on Friday afternoon* ***because*** *I was involved in a minor road accident. I'd taken photos on my phone and* ***as a result*** *the police wouldn't let me leave the area* ***until*** *they'd copied everything on to their computer.*
to make excuses	Making excuses *I'm late* ***because*** *I had to take the dog for a walk before I came to school.* *I dropped my phone down the toilet,* ***which is why*** *I couldn't phone you. Sorry.*
giving definitions	Defining people and things *A farmer is someone* ***who*** *…* *A good teacher is someone* ***who*** *…* *A router is a device* ***which*** *…*
adding extra information	Combining information about films or books to create complete relative clauses, e.g. 1) *Toy Story 4 / 2019 / stars Tim Hanks / computer animated comedy* *Toy Story 4,* ***which*** *was made in 2019* ***and*** *stars Tim Hanks, is a computer animated comedy.* 2) Brokeback Mountain / 2005 / American romantic drama / director Ang Lee / adapted from 1997 short story / by Annie Proulx 3) *Moby Dick / novel / 1851 / Hermann Melville* …

See lesson plan 10.

How to teach it

Practical matters

- Teaching conjunctions, both coordinating and subordinating is a key feature of sentence formation, so is likely to be an issue when learners start writing emails, letters etc.
- Some conjunctions and adverbs can be taught as an essential feature of functional lessons which focus on communicative purposes of language. For example:
    1. a lesson on reasons or purposes could include *because, as, so* and *in order to*
    2. a lesson on results could include *therefore, consequently, as a result*
    3. a lesson on contrasts could include *but, however* and *although*
- Conditional sentences may be the first examples of subordinate clauses learners come across in their learning. Teaching tends to focus on the verb form sequences in the conditional sentences, but these necessarily also involve the subordinating conjunction if at the beginning of the dependent clause. For example:

Conditional type	**Example** (Subordinate clause underlined)
First	***If** I see her, I'll ask her to call you.* *I'll ask you to call you **if** I see her.*
Second	***If** I told you the truth, you'd freak out.* *You'd freak out **if** I told you the truth.*
Third	*If she'd stopped, there wouldn't have been an accident.* *There wouldn't have been an accident **if** she'd stopped.*

Conditional sentences are as common in speech as in writing, so may work well as an introduction to subordinate clauses and subordinating conjunctions.

- Traditionally, relative clauses have been considered fairly advanced grammar, so appear quite late in many grammar syllabuses. However, defining relative clauses can be very useful in the early stages of learning. Imagine if a learner hears or reads the words *router* or *surgeon* and doesn't know what they mean.

  Learner *What's a **router**?*
  Teacher *It's the thing **that connects a computer to the internet**.*
  or
  Learner A *What's a **surgeon**?*
  Learner B *It's someone **who does operations in a hospital**.*
- Non-defining relative clauses, which add interesting but non-essential information, are mainly used in writing, so may be particularly useful when learners need to write complex sentences in articles, reports, letters or stories. They provide a way of combining different pieces of information in a single sentence and so make writing sound more economical and organised.
- The issue of omitting relative pronouns in defining relative clauses is probably best left until learners are thoroughly familiar with defining and non-defining relative clauses and the differences between the two.

  In brief, if the relative pronoun is the object (rather than the subject) of the relative clause it can be omitted, e.g.

  The film ~~that~~ I've enjoyed most this year is The Lunchbox.
  BUT
  *The film **that** has grabbed me most this year is The Lunchbox.*
  The people ~~who~~ we went with were work friends.
  BUT
  *The people **who** came with us were work friends*

- *where, when* and *why* are used in the same way as relative pronouns but are called relative adverbs:

  That's the village ***where*** *I was born and grew up.*
  1990 is the year ***when*** *I went to university.*
  He wouldn't tell me the reason ***why*** *he was annoyed.*

What to watch out for

- Learners may find it difficult to form complex sentences, especially when speaking English. They may prefer, instead, to use several short disconnected sentences or phrases and be happy simply to communicate their message successfully. Obviously, effective communication is the most basic requirement of language, but learners who wish to progress to more advanced levels and use language for work or study purposes will need to show they are able to use conjunctions and relative clauses correctly.
- Some learners may have little experience of organizing writing in their own language and so may not find it easy to do in English. In addition to providing them with the language they need to write coherent English, they will need first to be convinced that this is necessary and then be provided with plenty of practice. This may involve linking several short sentences using conjunctions and/or relative clauses, or establishing meaning links between sentences and paragraphs in longer pieces of writing.
- Conjunctions and adverbs may have similar meanings and uses but cannot always be used interchangeably. For example, *but* and *however* both express contrast, but are not used in the same way.
  I tried to drive home last night ***but*** *the road was blocked and I had to follow a diversion.*
  I tried to drive home last night. ***However****, the road was blocked and I had to follow a diversion.*
- When using relative clauses some learners may add an unnecessary subject or object to the clause, e.g.
  The people who came to dinner ***~~they~~*** *were our next-door neighbours.*
  They showed us round their garden, which we found ***~~it~~*** *very interesting.*
- *That* cannot be used in non-defining relative clauses. *Who* or *which* must be used instead.
  My son, ***who*** *won first prize in the international jazz competition, will receive a prize of €3000.*
  NOT
  My son, ***that*** *won first prize …*
- Some learners use *what* instead of *that*.

Suggestions for classroom activities

1 Topic Explaining human behaviour
Language Talking about reasons and purposes: because, so
Activities Ask the class why people do certain things. Suggest that they come up with humorous or original answers rather than the obvious ones. You could insist on full sentence answers. For example:

Q *Why do people climb mountains?*
A1 *(They climb mountains)* ***because*** *they have too much free time.*
A2 *(They climb mountains)* ***so*** *they can show how fit they are.*
Q *Why do people sneeze?*
A1 *(They sneeze)* ***because*** *no one is paying them any attention.*
A2 *(They sneeze)* ***so*** *they can exercise their lungs.*

To explain current actions show a few photos of people doing unusual things, e.g.
Learners could work in pairs explaining what is going on by asking and answering "Why" questions.

2 Topic National stereotypes
Language Contrast: *but, although, however*
Activities 1. Learners make a list of some of the positive and negative characteristics attributed to people of their nationality by people from other countries. For example

People say that English people …
… are always very polite.
… are all hardworking.
… love animals more than people.
… are quite unfriendly.
… don't mean what they say.
… make and eat terrible food.

2. Learners talk in pairs and discuss ideas which contrast with the stereotypes they have listed, using contrasting conjunctions and adverbs, e.g.
People say that they're very polite ***but*** *in private many of them are extremely rude.*
Although *some people love animals more than people, others don't have pets and can't stand animals.*
Many people are unfriendly when you first meet them. ***However****, when you've known them for a while, they can become good friends.*

3 Topic Imaginary situations (See also Chapter 6 What If? Activity 5)
Language *If* clauses (second conditional)
Activities 1. Show a photo of a car broken down at night in the middle of nowhere, e.g.
2. Ask learners to discuss questions in pairs, e.g.

What has happened?
What is she doing now?
What is the driver feeling and thinking?

3. Now tell learners to imagine they were in this situation and discuss what they would do. To make it more challenging tell them their phone has run out of battery.

4. Now get learners to discuss what they would do in other tricky imaginary situations, e.g.

What would you do if you …
… had all your money stolen in another country? (You don't speak the language)
… found a large number of newspaper reporters and photographers waiting outside your front door?

4 Topic Language Activities

Definitions (1)
Defining relative clauses with *who, which, that*
1. Show learners a list of 15-20 words related to the theme of your lesson. Choose words that you think learners will probably know, such as e.g.

Theme 1: Family
father, mother, son, daughter, husband, wife, brother, sister, uncle, aunt, grandfather, grandmother, nephew, niece, son-in-law, mother-in-law, brother-in-law, sister-in law, great grandfather …

Theme 2: Electrical devices
TV, radio, washing machine, dishwasher, laptop, tablet, lamp, fridge, CD player, printer, phone, desktop computer …

2. Learners work in pairs or small groups. They take turns to choose a word and define it for other learners to guess. For example
The person who / that is your mother's brother.
The thing which / that you use to keep things fresh.

3. Teach learners to use sentences like this to find out the word for something. Teach them to ask questions like this:
What's the thing that you rest your head on in bed called?

5 Topic Language Activities

Definitions (2)
Defining relative clauses with *who, which, that*
1. Ask learners to make up definitions which could be understood by a child for the following people:
an adult, a politician, a philosopher, a genius, an eccentric

2. Now ask them to think up definitions which could be understood by an older person for the following modern inventions
the internet, Amazon, eBay, YouTube, Wikipedia, WhatsApp, Facebook, Instagram, smartphone …

6 Topic Language Activities

Newspaper headlines
Non-defining relative clauses: *which, who*
1. Show learners a series of real or made-up newspaper headlines and ask them to convert them into "normal" sentences using non-defining relative clauses. Remind learners if they are writing, to add commas. If they are speaking, they could add small pauses round the relative clause.
Examples:

BILLIONNAIRE RONALD BUMP, 56, BUYS MEXICO

Ronald Bump, who is 56 and a billionaire, has bought Mexico.
Other examples could be:

CAT AS BIG AS TIGER ATTACKS 73-YEAR-OLD WOMAN

GRANDMOTHER, 90, SAVES GRANDCHILD FROM FROZEN LAKE

7 Topic Adding information
Language Defining and non-defining relative clauses with *which, who*
Activities Give learners an incomplete text and separate additional details to fit into the text. (If you want to make the task easier for learners, you can mark the places where the additional information can be added with gaps as in the example below.)

I first came across Moxie, …….., last year when they appeared on a TV programme, ……… I've always been a great fan of traditional Irish music, …….., but I found Moxie's music different and exciting. The group, …….., plays Irish music in a very modern way, ……… .
Cillian Doheny, …….., started playing music when he was 11. Ted and Jos, …….., play guitar and accordeon. Patrick Hazelton, …….., was born in Uganda, ……… .

Additional details
Being born in Uganda is unusual for an Irish musician.
Cillian Doheny is from a very musical family.
Cillian plays the banjo and the guitar.
I first heard traditional Irish music in my teens.
Moxie are a young Irish band.
Patrick Hazelton is the percussionist.
Ted and Jos are brothers.
The group has four members.
The TV programme was broadcast live from Sligo.
The way they play was completely new to me.

Key

I first came across Moxie, *who are a young Irish band / which is a young Irish band,* last year when they appeared on a TV programme *which was broadcast live from Sligo*. I've always been a great fan of traditional Irish music, *which I first heard in my teens*, but I found Moxie's music different and exciting. The group, *which has four members*, plays Irish music in a very modern way, *which was completely new to me.* Cillian Doheny, *who is from a very musical family,* started playing music when he was 11. Ted and Jos, *who are brothers*, play guitar and accordion. Patrick Hazelton, *who is the percussionist,* was born in Uganda, *which is unusual for an Irish musician.*

8 Topic Personal preferences
Language Defining relative clauses with *who, which, that*
Activities 1. Give learners a list of sentences like these:
I like / don't like talking to people who …
I enjoy / don't enjoy visiting places where …
I love meeting people who …
I like rooms that …
I can't stand dogs which …

2. Learners complete these sentences in their own way and then compare answers with a partner. This may lead to further discussion about likes and dislikes and reasons for these.

9 Topic Correcting errors
Language Relative clauses
Activities Give learners a text which contains mistakes in the relative clauses and

ask them to spot and correct the mistakes. Add or remove commas if necessary. For example:

I remember when I was young, we always went on holiday to Kingscliff, that is a small seaside town north of Sydney. We always went in September which it was quieter. We used to stay in a holiday cabin, who was right on the beach. There were five or six cabins in the complex which we stayed.
On the first weekend of September, we'd drive there in our old Ford, which always broke down on the way. My sister Anne which was always car sick used to sit in the front. Our dog, who was a German Shepherd called Honey, sat in the back between Mum and me. I remember we always stopped at a place that we could have a barbecue, to break the journey. I enjoyed those beach holidays.

Key
I remember when I was young, we always went on holiday to Kingscliff, *which (~~that~~)* is a small seaside town north of Sydney. We always went in September *when (~~which~~)* it was quieter. We used to stay in a holiday cabin, *which (~~who~~)* was right on the beach. There were five or six cabins in the complex *where (~~which~~)* we stayed.
On the first weekend of September, we'd drive there in our old Ford, which always broke down on the way. My sister Anne, *who (~~which~~)* was always car sick, used to sit in the front. Our dog, *which (~~who~~)* was a German Shepherd called Honey, sat in the back between Mum and me. I remember we always stopped at a place *where (~~that~~)* we could have a barbecue, to break the journey. I enjoyed those beach holidays.

10 Topic Language Activities

Longer sentences
Relative clauses and conjunctions
Explain that learners are going to work in groups to make up stories using long sentences. Give each group a short sentence and ask them to lengthen it by adding new made-up information. Suggest they use relative clauses and conjunctions (coordinating and subordinating).
Short sentence starters:
I could hear a dog barking.
We reached the top of the mountain.
The train left the station.
My foot was stuck.

Note: If you have an advanced group, you could show them an example of a genuine very long sentence, for example this single sentence of 92 words from the novel *Us* by David Nicholls:

We shape and sentimentalise these first encounters into creation myths to reassure ourselves and our offspring that it was somehow 'meant to be', and with that in mind perhaps it's best to pause there for the moment, and return to where we came in – specifically the night, a quarter-century later, when the same intelligent, amusing, attractive woman woke me to say that she thought she might be happier, that her future might be fuller, richer, that all things considered she might fell more 'alive' if she were no longer near me.

Lesson plan 10

Lesson profile

Description	Lesson based on a coursebook
Topic	Myths and facts
Grammar point	Conjunctions (e.g. *but, although* etc.) to contrast ideas.
Aims	To be able to identify the function of conjunctions in clauses and practise their use in contrasts.
Material	WS 10.1 (simulation of a coursebook unit)

WS 10.1

Unit 10 The earth is round. Right?

Task 1

a) Compare these two photos of earth. How is the photo on the right different?

b) People used to believe the earth was flat – some people still do. How do we know it is round not flat?

Task 2

Match these words with the right meaning.

ancient conspiracy curvature evidence fake lie prove sink

a) false
b) something spoken or written that is not true
c) proof or support
d) show something is right
e) go down lower
f) very old
g) plot or scheme to mislead
h) shape of being bent, not straight

Task 3

Read the text on the right and consider these questions:

a) Does the text mention any of the points you discussed?
b) Which do you think is the best explanation?

Task 4

Discuss these questions with a partner:

a) Can you think of any other things that most people would believe are facts?
b) Can you think of other lies which are repeated so often that many people believe them?
c) What do you understand by the post-truth era and fake news?
d) Do you know of any other common conspiracies?

Is the earth really round?

In today's world there are not many facts we can be absolutely sure about, but there are two we can all agree on: we will all die one day and the earth is round. However, recently the ancient belief that the earth is flat has been becoming popular again. Lies which are repeated often enough may become the new truth. This is an aspect of living in the "post-truth era" of fake news when we're unsure whether information we hear is true or false. Although scientists proved over 2000 years ago that the earth is round, it seems that their evidence is once again being questioned by people who say that because they cannot see the curvature of the earth themselves, it must be flat, not round.

In order to remind ourselves of the truth, here are some of the ways we can prove that the earth is round. If you climb a tree, you can see further from the top of the tree than you can from the ground. If the earth was flat, you would see the same distance however high you were. Similarly, if you stand on a beach and watch a ship sailing out to sea, its mast or funnel will sink lower and lower until the ship disappears completely. Perhaps the most convincing proof are the photos of the earth which were taken from space.

Despite the fact that these proofs are accepted by 99.999% of the population, the flat-earthers believe they are part of an international conspiracy to mislead the world.

ISBN 978-3-12-501628-6

176

WS 10.1

A contrast between 2 things is the difference between them!

Task 5

In these extracts from the text, underline words and phrases used to point out a contrast between two facts or ideas.

i. In today's world there are not many facts we can be absolutely sure about, but there are two we can all agree on: …
ii. we will all die one day and the earth is round. However, recently the ancient belief that the earth is flat has been becoming popular again.
iii. Although scientists proved over 2000 years ago that the earth is round, it seems that their evidence is once again being questioned.
iv. Despite the fact that these proofs are accepted by 99.999% of the population, the flat-earthers believe they are part of an international conspiracy to mislead the world.

Task 6

Discuss these questions in pairs.

a) Which words or phrases contrast ideas in a single sentence?
b) Of these, which word or phrase is placed between the two clauses?
c) Which word contrasts ideas or facts in separate sentences?
d) Which words or phrases could be used instead of ***Although*** *(sentence iii.) and* ***Despite the fact that*** *(sentence iv.)?*

Task 7

Complete the following sentences with one of these words or phrases.

although • but • however • despite the fact that

a) …………………… bulls are colour-blind, people think the colour red makes them angry.
b) Humans are said to have five senses …………………… in fact they have many more than that.
c) …………………… people think bats are blind, they can actually see very well.
d) People say that the Great Wall is visible from space …………………… a Chinese astronaut said this was not true.
e) Humans did not evolve from monkeys. …………………… it is true that we share a common ancestor.

Task 8

Match the images below with these common statements.

MYTH OR FACT?

- *Most of the body's heat is lost through the head.*
- *Lie detectors are not reliable.*
- *Carrots help you see in the dark.*
- *Too much sugar causes hyperactivity in children.*
- *Water goes down a drain clockwise in the southern hemisphere.*

A B C D E

LIES

Which of them are true? And which are myths? Discuss your ideas in pairs.

177

ISBN 978-3-12-501628-6

Pre-reading

Task 1 – Visual prompt

Before learners open their books

- Show one or more images of earth on your whiteboard if you have one. Alternatively use photographs or maps.
- Elicit answers to questions such as
  - *What is this?*
  - *Why does it look like this?*
  - *Is it really like this?*
  - *Does anyone believe it is like this?*

Ask learners to open their books and discuss questions 1a and b in pairs.
Elicit ideas.

Task 2 – Pre-teaching vocabulary

You think your learners can cope with the reading text without doing this exercise first. If need be, you can come back to this after they have read the text. Alternatively, you could set it for homework.

Key:
a) fake | b) lie | c) evidence | d) prove | e) sink | f) ancient | g) conspiracy | h) curvature

Reading

Task 3 – Reading for gist

Draw learners' attention to the while-reading questions 3a & b. They provide learners with a purpose for reading the text. Allow learners about 5 minutes to read the text (*Is the earth really round?*). If this turns out not to be enough, allow a minute or two longer. This is a gist reading exercise rather than one which demands a detailed understanding.
Ask learners for their answers to questions 3a & b. There are no right or wrong answers, so allow learners to express ideas and maybe disagree with each other.
Before moving on to the questions in Task 4, ask if there were any words in the text learners didn't understand. You might wish to set a time limit on this or the number of words you talk about. Try and elicit the meaning from other learners rather than simply giving the answer yourself every time.

Task 4 – Speaking activity

You may decide that you would prefer to leave this exercise until later because these are discussion questions rather than ordinary comprehension questions. Perhaps just check learners' understanding of the phrases *post-truth era* and *fake news*.

Grammar focus

Task 5 – Identifying the target language

Make sure learners understand what to do. You may need to explain the word "contrast" and/or give a very simple example:
Although I slept well, I'm still tired.
I'm still tired but I slept well.
Each of these sentences has two contrasting facts, the contrast being sign-posted by the words *Although* and *but*.
Ask learners to work through the sentences from the text, underlining the words or phrases which point this out.

Key
i. In today's world there are not many facts we can be absolutely sure about, <u>but</u> there are two we can all agree on: ...
ii. we will all die one day and the earth is round. <u>However</u>, recently the ancient belief that the earth is flat has been becoming popular again.
iii. <u>Although</u> scientists proved over 2000 years ago that the earth is round, it seems that their evidence is once again being questioned.
iv. <u>Despite the fact</u> that these proofs are accepted by 99.999% of the population, the flat-earthers believe they are part of an international conspiracy to mislead the world.

Task 6 – Pair discussion

Instead of a pair discussion you may prefer to discuss these questions as a whole class if you think some learners will find them too tricky. 6d may prove to be too difficult, so you may decide it is not worth spending too much time on it at this stage.
Check answers.

Key
a) but (i.) / although (iii.) / Despite the fact that (iv) | b) but (i.) | c) However (ii.) | d) Though / Even though (Although, iii.) / In spite of the fact that (Despite the fact that, iv.)
You may need to spend a little more time on this before moving on to Task 7.

Task 7 – Gap-fill

Ask learners to work through this exercise individually before checking answers with a partner. You could point out that although these items are primarily language practice, they also refer to other common myths rather than being random unrelated sentences.

Check answers. Resist the temptation to discuss the content at this stage.

Key
a) Although | b) but | c) Despite the fact that / Although | d) but | e) However

Note: Learners will need more practice in using these connecting words, so look for further exercises in other grammar practice books you are familiar with.

Points to discuss

Task 8 – Speaking activity

This is primarily a fluency activity and is not designed to provide more practice of conjunctions.

Make sure learners understand the idea of common myths before allowing them time to discuss the ideas in pairs.

If time allows, hand out the answers and allow learners time to read and discuss the ideas in pairs or as a whole class. If no time is left, hand out the answers for learners to read at home. Note that each answer includes at least one contrasting conjunction.

Answers

Most of the body's heat is lost through the head. (image E) → MYTH
We are often told to wear a hat when it's cold because 80 percent of our body heat escapes through our heads, but in fact, according to the British Medical Journal, you only lose between 7 and 10 percent of your body heat there (because the head only represents about 10% of the body's total surface area) – not much more than you would lose through any other exposed part of your body, whether hands, shoulders, or ankles.

Lie detectors are not reliable. (B) → TRUE
Polygraph tests do not measure deception or lying directly, although they may show that a person could be deceiving the interviewer.

Carrots help us see in the dark. (A) → MYTH
The myth that eating large quantities of carrots leads to excellent night vision arose from a rumour deliberately started by the Air Ministry during World War II to deceive the Germans. The story fooled not only them but also the British public and never really went away. In fact, the carrot became the first ever "superfood". Although the vegetables do contain carotene, a natural compound that is needed to construct the light receiving apparatus in the retina, they won't help your superpowers!

Too much sugar causes hyperactivity in children. (C) → MYTH
Even though some parents might believe that sugar causes hyperactivity, there is no proof that it is to blame for out of control children. There have been several controlled trials to examine how children react to diets containing different levels of sugar. However, none of these studies could detect any differences in behaviour between the children who had had sugar and those who had not.

Water goes down a drain clockwise in the southern hemisphere. (D) → MYTH
Water flows both counterclockwise and clockwise down drains in both hemispheres. Some people would like you to believe that the Coriolis force (caused by the earth's rotation and which e.g. affects the direction of wind) affects the flow of water down the drain in sinks and bathtubs, but don't believe them! The Coriolis force is simply too weak to affect such small bodies of water.

Note: You may at this stage want to go back to Task 2, the vocabulary matching activity.

Add your notes here!

Turn the page to find WS 10.1!

Unit 10 The earth is round. Right?

Task 1

a) Compare these two photos of earth. How is the photo on the right different?

b) People used to believe the earth was flat – some people still do. How do we know it is round not flat?

Task 2

Match these words with the right meaning.

ancient conspiracy curvature evidence fake lie prove sink

a) false

b) something spoken or written that is not true

c) proof or support

d) show something is right

e) go down lower

f) very old

g) plot or scheme to mislead

h) shape of being bent, not straight

Task 3

Read the text on the right and consider these questions:

a) Does the text mention any of the points you discussed?

b) Which do you think is the best explanation?

Task 4

Discuss these questions with a partner:

a) Can you think of any other things that most people would believe are facts?
b) Can you think of other lies which are repeated so often that many people believe them?
c) What do you understand by the post-truth era and fake news?
d) Do you know of any other common conspiracies?

Is the earth really round?

In today's world there are not many facts we can be absolutely sure about, but there are two we can all agree on: we will all die one day and the earth is round. However, recently the ancient belief that the earth is flat has been becoming popular again. Lies which are repeated often enough may become the new truth. This is an aspect of living in the "post-truth era" of fake news when we're unsure whether information we hear is true or false. Although scientists proved over 2000 years ago that the earth is round, it seems that their evidence is once again being questioned by people who say that because they cannot see the curvature of the earth themselves, it must be flat, not round.

In order to remind ourselves of the truth, here are some of the ways we can prove that the earth is round. If you climb a tree, you can see further from the top of the tree than you can from the ground. If the earth was flat, you would see the same distance however high you were. Similarly, if you stand on a beach and watch a ship sailing out to sea, its mast or funnel will sink lower and lower until the ship disappears completely. Perhaps the most convincing proof are the photos of the earth which were taken from space.

Despite the fact that these proofs are accepted by 99.999% of the population, the flat-earthers believe they are part of an international conspiracy to mislead the world.

ISBN 978-3-12-501628-6

A contrast between 2 things is the difference between them!

Task 5

In these extracts from the text, underline words and phrases used to point out a contrast between two facts or ideas.

i. In today's world there are not many facts we can be absolutely sure about, but there are two we can all agree on: …

ii. we will all die one day and the earth is round. However, recently the ancient belief that the earth is flat has been becoming popular again.

iii. Although scientists proved over 2000 years ago that the earth is round, it seems that their evidence is once again being questioned.

iv. Despite the fact that these proofs are accepted by 99.999% of the population, the flat-earthers believe they are part of an international conspiracy to mislead the world.

Task 6

Discuss these questions in pairs.

a) Which words or phrases contrast ideas in a single sentence?
b) Of these, which word or phrase is placed between the two clauses?
c) Which word contrasts ideas or facts in separate sentences?
d) Which words or phrases could be used instead of ***Although*** *(sentence iii.) and* ***Despite the fact*** *that (sentence iv.)?*

Task 7

Complete the following sentences with one of these words or phrases.

although • but • however • despite the fact that

a) …………………. bulls are colour-blind, people think the colour red makes them angry.

b) Humans are said to have five senses …………………. in fact they have many more than that.

c) …………………. people think bats are blind, they can actually see very well.

d) People say that the Great Wall is visible from space …………………. a Chinese astronaut said this was not true.

e) Humans did not evolve from monkeys. …………………. it is true that we share a common ancestor.

Task 8

Match the images below with these common statements.

MYTH OR FACT?

- *Most of the body's heat is lost through the head.*
- *Lie detectors are not reliable.*
- *Carrots help you see in the dark.*
- *Too much sugar causes hyperactivity in children.*
- *Water goes down a drain clockwise in the southern hemisphere.*

A

B

C

D

E

Which of them are true? And which are myths? Discuss your ideas in pairs.

ISBN 978-3-12-501628-6

Talking about now – Consolidation

There are two main verb forms used to refer to actions happening now or around now: the **present simple** (*I work for a small IT company in Ireland.*) and the **present continuous** (*I'm working on a new phone app.*). Both forms have a number of different uses.

1. Think about the differences in meaning between these pairs of sentences.

a	*1. I live in Madrid.*	*2. I'm living in Madrid.*
b	*1. Shh! I'm reading an important email about my application.*	*2. I'm reading War and Peace by Tolstoy – I'm up to page 372.*
c	*1. You always forget my name.*	*2. You're always forgetting my name.*

2. Sometimes these forms do not refer to now at all. What is the difference in meaning between these pairs of sentences?

a	*1. I'm just leaving work. I'll be home in about an hour.*	*2. I'm leaving work in about half an hour.*
b	*1. Normally, my flight leaves at 10.30 in the morning.*	*2. Tomorrow my flight leaves at midday.*

3. Look at examples of the two verb forms in these seven short texts. Underline all the present simple and present continuous verbs in the texts (don't forget negative and question forms!). Consider the following:

- Do the verbs refer to the past, the present or the future?
- Are the contexts spoken or written language?
- Where might you read or hear each extract?

Text 1

A rabbit goes into a shop and asks the assistant, "Do you have any carrots?" The assistant replies "Sorry, we don't sell carrots." The rabbit leaves.
The next day, the rabbit comes back and says, "Do you have any carrots?" The assistant replies "I told you yesterday we don't sell carrots." The rabbit leaves.
The next day, the rabbit returns again and says, "Do you have any carrots?" The assistant loses his temper and says "I told you yesterday we don't sell carrots. If you ask again, I'll nail your ears to the door!" The rabbit leaves.
The next day, the rabbit strolls into the shop and asks, "Do you have any nails?" The assistant replies politely "No, we don't sell nails."
The rabbit smiles and says. "Good, so do you have any carrots?"

Text 2

Trees absorb carbon dioxide as they grow and the carbon that they store in their wood helps slow the rate of global warming. They reduce wind speeds and cool the air as they lose moisture and reflect heat upwards from their leaves. Trees also help prevent flooding and soil erosion.
(© www.royalparks.org.uk)

Text 3

Hello?

Hi, is Pete there, please?

I'm afraid he's talking to a customer at the moment. Who's calling, please?

His brother. I'll call back.

ISBN 978-3-12-501628-6

Text 4

Haven't seen you for ages! What are you doing these days?

Well, I still live and work in town. I'm learning to drive.

That's great!

Text 5

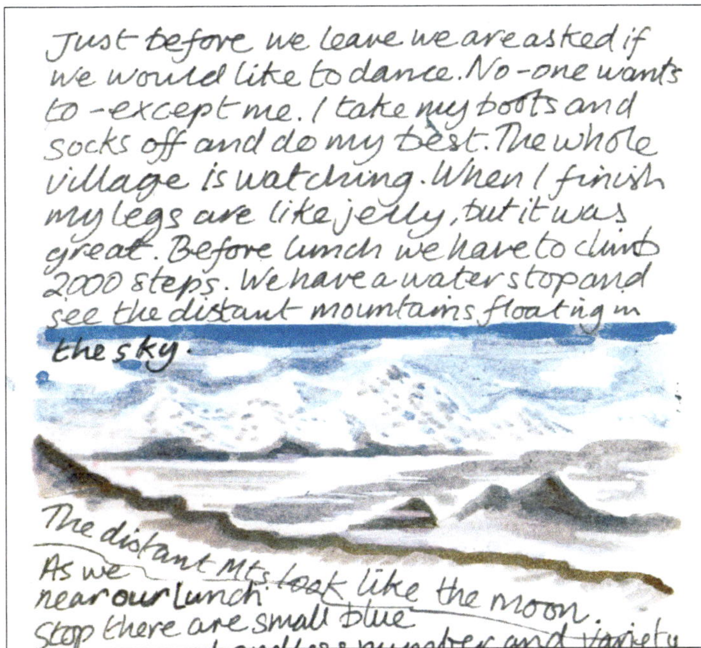

(© Glynn Thomas, *Nepal – An Illustrated Journey*)

Text 6

Here, these are for you.

Thanks, but you shouldn't have.

Why not?

You're always buying me presents. Are you feeling guilty about something?

Text 7

I get home between six and seven o'clock and I make my dinner. If it's been a busy day, and I'm feeling too tired to cook, I stick a ready-meal in the microwave. I usually eat on the sofa and catch up with any TV programmes I've missed. A couple of times a week, I phone my Dad – he always wants to know how my course is going. We often talk for over an hour, after which I'm tired and go to bed.

*4. Look through the **present simple** verbs you have underlined and find examples which are used to:*

a. refer to a scientific fact or a general truth.

b. describe a routine activity or a habit.

c. make a story sound more interesting, as if it's happening now.

*5. Now find examples of **present continuous** verbs in the texts which are used to:*

a. refer to a temporary activity happening right now.

b. refer to an ongoing action happening around now.

ISBN 978-3-12-501628-6

Talking about the past – Consolidation

Remember, there are four main verb forms and *used to* to choose from when we talk about something which happened in the past.

1. Match the tenses with their main uses.

Verb tense		Uses
a *past simple*		i *for actions that took place over a length of time in the past*
b *past continuous*		ii *to refer to an event that took place before an earlier past action*
c *past perfect simple*		iii *for habitual past actions that have now stopped*
d *past perfect continuous*		iv *for completed past actions which took place once or more than once*
e *used to*		v *to refer to an event that took place over a length of time before an earlier past action*

2. Write a microstory in 50-60 words using each of the four main forms listed in the table. Here's an example:

Jess and I were chatting about the day we met. We both remembered it well. I'd got to the party late because I'd been writing my letter of resignation. Jess had recently broken up with her boyfriend and was feeling fed up. As I arrived at the party Jess was putting her coat on to leave. Our eyes met and the rest is history.

....

....

....

....

....

3. Read the short texts overleaf.

a) Underline all the past verbs. Don't forget negative and question forms. Also, consider where you might read or hear each extract.

b) Find examples in the texts of past forms which

i. refer to a completed past action which took place once or more than once
ii. refer to past habits or routines which have stopped
iii. refer to an action that took place over a period of time in the past
iv. provide background information about an action in the more recent past
v. refer to a continuous action which happened prior to a past event.

ISBN 978-3-12-501628-6

Text 1

Billy Weaver had travelled down from London on the slow afternoon train, with a change at Swindon on the way and by the time he got to Bath it was about nine o'clock in the evening and the moon was coming out of a clear starry sky over the houses opposite the station entrance.

(© Roald Dahl, from *The Landlady in Roald Dahl Collected Short Stories)*

Text 2

I'm glad you like the photo. Did you take your driving test in that car?
I know we didn't get the VW until 2002, when you were 22.
Did you see that photo I sent of Dad on your motorbike. He used to drive it to the station, after you had stopped using it.
Talk to you again soon.

Text 3

Ben Thomas pulled a goal back for the Blues early in the second half, but Steve Johnson made sure the team got maximum points by scoring from a penalty in the 88th minute.
"The team really did a great job," said relieved manager Tom Edwards.

Text 4

(© Glen Baxter, *The Collected Blurtings of Baxter)*

Text 5

There's an old green Fordson tractor in the back of Grandpa's barn, always covered in cornsacks. When I was very little, I used to go in there, pull off the cornsacks, climb up and drive it all over the farm.

(© Michael Morpurgo, *The Farm Boy)*

Text 6

Skylar's voice sounded calm on my voice mail. Obviously, no calamity had occurred. It was like he'd been expecting to hear from me, but for some reason I just hadn't called … My heart was pounding when I dialled his number.

(© April Sinclair, *I Left My Back Door Open)*

ISBN 978-3-12-501628-6

Linking the past to the present – Consolidation

Remember present perfect verbs refer to a connection of some kind between the past and the present.

1. What is the connection between the present and the past in these sentences? What could you add to these sentences to make this connection completely clear?

a) She loves tennis, but unfortunately she's broken her arm.

....

b) They've worked in this office since it opened.

....

c) Ouch! I've pricked my finger.

....

d) He's travelled all over the world.

....

e) Breaking news: "There has been a serious accident on the motorway just outside Paris."

....

f) I've wanted to go to Australia for years.

....

g) The couple have lived in the same house since they got married.

....

h) The Eiffel Tower has dominated the Paris skyline for almost 130 years.

....

2. Some learners find it difficult to understand the difference in meaning between the simple and continuous forms of the present perfect. Compare these pairs of sentences and work out the difference in meanings between them.

NOTE: There isn't always a very clear difference.

i.	***I've been redecorating** my flat.*	***I've redecorated** my flat.*
ii.	***John's worked** for the same company for 15 years.*	***John's been working** for the same company for 15 years.*

i. ....

ii. ....

ISBN 978-3-12-501628-6

3. Find and underline present perfect simple and continuous verbs in the following texts. Consider these questions:

- *Are the contexts spoken or written language?*
- *Where might you read or hear each extract?*
- *Decide how each verb connects the present with the past.*

Text 1

Marine archaeologists believe they have located the remains of Captain James Cook's famed ship Endeavour after a centuries-long search.

Captain Cook used the vessel on a voyage of discovery to Australia and New Zealand in 1770 and it was later used by the British navy in the American War of Independence before it was scuttled off Newport, Rhode Island, in 1778.

The ship's final resting place has eluded archaeologists ever since, but now a team of Australian researchers believe they have pinpointed the vessel in Newport Harbour.

(news.sky.com, 19 September 2018)

Text 2

In his time, Frankie Gavin has played for four American presidents, starting, as a six-year old, when he played for John F. Kennedy on his 1962 visit to Ireland, then later for Presidents Clinton, Bush and Barack Obama.

Text 3

Thanks Phil,

I think their new album is superb. Although I haven't written the review yet, I've been playing it non-stop from the day I got it. I've also bought the book and have been learning some of the songs.

Cheers

Mike

Text 4

Hurray. Whole new positive perspective on birthday. [I] Have been talking to Jude about book she has been reading about festivals and rites of passage in primitive cultures and am feeling happy and serene.

(© Helen Fielding, Bridget Jones's Diary)

Text 5

The Japanese space agency has successfully landed two rovers on a large asteroid, and they have sent back images to Earth.

ISBN 978-3-12-501628-6

Looking forward – Consolidation

1. There are many different ways of referring to the future in English. What are the differences in meaning between these pairs of sentences?

a	i.	He's seeing his brother tomorrow.
	ii.	He'll probably see his brother tomorrow.
b	i.	I'm going to stop eating junk food.
	ii.	I'll stop eating junk food if you do.
c	i.	My train arrives at 5 o'clock tomorrow morning.
	ii.	My train will have arrived by 5 o'clock tomorrow morning.
d	i.	My sister's going to have a baby.
	ii.	I imagine my sister will have a baby in a couple of years.
e	i.	My next birthday's a big one. I'll be 20.
	ii.	I don't suppose I'll feel any different when I'm 20.
f	i.	He won't tell me where he's been.
	ii.	I hope he won't go anywhere without telling me.

2. Read these short texts which contain examples of future verb forms.

a) Underline all the future verbs in the texts.

b) Find the following uses:

- An intention
- An arrangement
- A scheduled event
- A refusal
- A promise or offer
- A prediction without evidence
- A prediction with evidence
- A future fact
- A decision made at the moment of speaking

Text 1

"Stand back," said the elephant,
"I'm going to sneeze!
I hate to alarm you,
But I don't wish to harm you.
My friends, I fear
It's clear …
Oh, dear.
You'd better stand back, I'm going to sneeze."

(© Patricia Thomas, "Stand back" said the elephant, "I'm going to sneeze")

Text 2

Is that that door?

Yes, I'll get it.

Do you know who it is?

It'll probably be the postman bringing something I ordered online.

ISBN 978-3-12-501628-6

Text 3

It's your lucky day. Someone you admire will pay you an unexpected compliment. By the end of the day you'll probably be wondering what the future holds for the two of you.

Text 4

In the filling station forecourt Arthur said. 'When did you last put oil in the car?'

'I don't remember.'

'Get in and open the bonnet.' He held the dipstick to the light. 'It's bone-dry. Something told me it was. I'll go and get a couple of litres.'

(© Alan Sillitoe, *Birthday)*

Text 5

ARSENAL TAKE ON TOTTENHAM IN THIS WEEKEND'S LONDON DERBY

Text 6

Hi,
Thanks for the invite. I'd love to catch up, but can't make next Tuesday evening – I'm working late again. Are you doing anything Thursday? I'm not working then.
I'll call you tomorrow.
Harry

Text 7

RenegadeMum 24/04/2020 15:33

My four-year-old daughter won't eat – and she's due to start school in three weeks' time!! It's got to the point, with me, where I just accept now that she won't eat or join in with family mealtimes.

Text 8

Two days ago I was 17, next year I'll be 20. (Only people born on December 31st can make this claim.)

Text 9

I am going to learn to play the guitar if it's the last thing I do!

ISBN 978-3-12-501628-6

Shades of meaning – Consolidation

1. Find the modal verbs in the four cartoons and decide how each of them is being used. Choose from this list of meanings associated with modal verbs:

- *speculation, probability, logical deduction*
- *necessity or obligation: request, suggestion, advice, moral or social responsibility*
- *permission or prohibition*
- *possibility or impossibility*
- *ability, inability or potential*

A

'Remember, son...money can't buy happiness, but it pays for a lot of anti-depressants."

B

C

"May I go home now?"

C

"Just because you *can* wear a sweatsuit all the time doesn't mean you *should.*"

2. With reference to the list of meanings in Task 1 above, what are the differences in the meaning between the modal verbs as they are used in the following sets of sentences. Remember, it is sometimes impossible to identify the precise meaning without knowing more about the context in which verbs are being used. Some of these sentences may be open to interpretation.

a)	i.	You **should drive** more slowly.	
	ii.	You **must drive** more slowly.	
b)	i.	I **could let** you know tomorrow.	
	ii.	I **might let** you know tomorrow.	
c)	i.	Q **Can** you **open** the window? A No, it's jammed.	
	ii.	Q **Can** you **open** the window? A Yes, of course. No problem.	
d)	i.	**May I use** your phone while you're away?	
	ii.	**I may use** your phone while you're away.	
e)	i.	I **don't have to wear** a suit for work.	
	ii.	I **mustn't wear** a suit for work.	
f)	i.	I **must phone** my parents this evening. I want to ask them something.	
	ii.	I **have to phone** my parents this evening. They'll worry if I don't.	

ISBN 978-3-12-501628-6

g)	i.	You **ought to take** responsibility for your actions.	
	ii.	You **must take** responsibility for your actions.	
	iii.	You **should take** responsibility for your actions.	

3. Read the following texts.

a) Underline the modal verbs in each text.

b) As you read the texts, consider the following:

- *Where might you read or hear each extract?*
- *Match each modal verb with one of the purposes in 1 above.*

Text 1

Can a vegan diet provide everything you need?

If you understand the basis of a healthy diet and plan effectively, you can get all the nutrients you need from a vegan diet. However, if you aren't careful enough in your planning, you could miss out on some essentials such as vitamin B12 and iron.

Text 2

So, when you fly east, such as from the Americas to Europe or Africa, you should go outside to get some bright light before people back home start to wake up. […] This should help you get up more easily the next day.

(© Sandra Aamodt & Sam Wang, Welcome to Your Brain: The Science of Jet Lag, Love and Other Curiosities of Life)

Text 3

I'd visited my mother and emerged into daylight once more. I lit a cigarette and contemplated the day ahead. "Excuse me," said an officious voice behind me. "You can't smoke here."

"Why not? I'm outside."

"You can't smoke anywhere on the hospital site."

"That's very odd. I could last time I was here."

Text 4

I am writing to let you know that unfortunately, I have to cancel the meeting that we had scheduled for 5.00 pm next Monday afternoon. Many apologies.

Text 5

And so I trudged along for hours, in a private little world of weariness and woe, up and over imposing hills through an endless cocktail of trees, all the time thinking: "I must have done seven miles by now, surely."

(© Bill Bryson, *A Walk in the Woods)*

Text 6

"I don't know what he'll say. You just can't tell with him."

"A year, we've never been apart so long – or so far apart."

"If only you could come."

"Some hope." Patsy laughs. Cassie can hear baby Katie grumbling in her arms.

(© Lesley Glaister, *As Far as You Can Go)*

Text 7

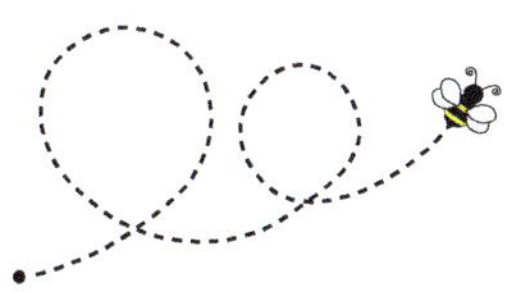

Fresh water must be available at all times: if there is no natural source of water close by, then one must be provided. […]

And finally, it goes without saying that if it wasn't already, your garden should now become an insecticide-free zone, for insecticides can also be blown towards hives by the wind.

(© Derek Hall, *Bees & Beekeeping)*

ISBN 978-3-12-501628-6

What if? – Consolidation

Remember, there are four conditional sentence types (the table below does not include mixed conditional sentences since these do not follow a set pattern of tenses). Each type uses a different set of verb tenses and is used for a different purpose.

1. Match the conditional sentence types with the verb forms it uses and its main use.

Type		***if* clause → main clause**		**Use**
Zero		a) if + past simple → *would* + infinitive		i. future possibilities that are quite likely
First		b) if + past perfect → *would have* + past participle		ii. past actions that did or didn't happen
Second		c) if + present simple → present simple		iii. future possibilities that are unlikely
Third		d) if + present simple → *will* + infinitive		iv. to describe actions that are always true

2. Look at these sentences. What verb tenses are used in each part?

a) If it'll make you feel any better, I'll phone him and tell him right now.

....

b) If you think he's a good candidate, vote for him.

....

c) He'd have been here by now if he was coming.

....

d) If she hadn't broken her arm, she'd be taking part in the competition tomorrow.

....

3. Consider the differences in meaning between these sets of conditional sentences.

a)	i.	*If I'm late, I apologize.*
	ii.	*If I'm late, I'll apologize.*
	iii.	*If I was late, I'd apologize.*
b)	i.	*If he passes his last exam, he'll go to Oxford University.*
	ii.	*If he passed his last exam, he'd go to Oxford University.*
	iii.	*If he had passed his last exam, he'd have gone to Oxford University.*
	iv.	*If he had passed his last exam, he'd be going to Oxford University next year.*

4. Rephrase these sentences using 'unless'.

a)	*If it doesn't rain, we'll go for a long walk tomorrow.*	....
b)	*They won't know if we don't tell them.*	....
c)	*If you don't work harder, you'll fail your exam.*	....
d)	*You can't go on holiday if you haven't saved enough money.*	....

ISBN 978-3-12-501628-6

5. Look at examples of conditional sentences in the following texts. Which of the actions mentioned took place in the future or are / were possible in these contexts? The actions in question are in ***bold type****.*

Text 1

I agree it was a mistake, Minister, in the light of events. I had reason to believe the man was at the hotel and intended to spend the night there. **If he had been motoring** in the vicinity, and **had been intercepted** by a motor-patrol man for driving a wanted car, he would almost certainly have shot the unsuspecting policeman, and thus forewarned made his escape.

"Which is precisely what he has done," said Saint-Xavier.

(© Frederick Forsyth, *Day of the Jackal*)

Text 2

If the sun were to stop burning and to form a black hole, it would measure about one and half kilometres in diameter.

(© Carlo Rovelli, *Seven Brief Lessons on Physics*)

Text 3

She really, really hated me. The way I looked. The way I sounded. My words. My pathetic jokes. My absurd attempts at melody. There was nothing that was happening on stage that she didn't absolutely loathe. **If I had stopped mid-song** and toppled over with a massive heart attack, I swear she would have stood up and punched the air with relief.

(from *The lady in the third row …* by Terence Blacker on www.mardles.org)

Text 4

If you were late for choir practice through having to wait for company before venturing into Dam-side, […] the organist would be furious and threaten to tell your Mum.

If you whispered or sniggered during service, you would get a clip on the ear from the leading tenor.

(© Fred Wilde, *The Clatter of Clogs in the Early Morning*)

Text 5

ISBN 978-3-12-501628-6

Who does what? – Consolidation

1. *Read these three sentences, then answer the questions below.*
   - *They have cancelled tonight's concert because of the weather.*
   - *Tonight's concert has been cancelled because of the weather.*
   - *Tonight's concert has been cancelled by the management because of the weather.*

a. Do the sentences have the same or similar meanings?

b. How are they different grammatically? Look at the verbs and the subjects of the verbs.

c. Which sentence tells us explicitly who cancelled the concert? Why don't the other two sentences give us this information?

2. *In passive sentences a – f below ...*
   - ▶ Who might have done the action?
   - ▶ Why doesn't the writer tell us who did the action?

   a) I think I'm being watched.

   b) English is spoken here.

   c) I wasn't invited to the party.

   d) Before 1933 beer was sold in bottles.

   e) The microwave was introduced as a consumer product in 1955.

   f) You could be forgiven for thinking that everyone has gone home.

3. *Read the following short texts.*

   a) Underline all the passive verbs in the texts.

   b) Consider the following questions:
   - ▶ Do the verbs refer to the past, the present or the future?
   - ▶ Are the contexts spoken or written lvanguage?
   - ▶ Where might you read or hear each extract?

ISBN 978-3-12-501628-6

Text 1

Morse code wasn't invented to help people in dire emergencies, but to send messages along a telegraph wire [...] Morse came up with a method of sending signals that could be received by a machine and marked on to paper as dots and dashes.

(© Richard Horne and Tracey Turner, *101 Things You Wish You'd Invented ... and Some You Wish No One Had*)

Text 3

I was brought up in a musical household so I started to learn by osmosis. As a youngster growing up in London, it was a remarkable period for high quality Irish music. When London was being rebuilt after the war, it was mainly by Irish labour from rural Ireland, and they brought their music with them. I also had uncles on my mother's side from Connemara who played. Also, I was lucky enough to be taught by one of the best Irish music teachers. The fact is I was given every possible chance you can imagine.

Text 2

In 1971 tax rates at the top were really high by today's standards, but had actually just been cut, from 90 per cent to 75 per cent. [...] They were raised again in 1974 to 83 per cent, but there was also a charge on unearnt income of 15 per cent, ...

(© Zoe Williams, *Get It Together*)

Text 4

All over the globe, crimes are committed, wars are started, women are being held back, and economies are disastrously distorted by men, because of their outdated version of masculinity.

(© Grayson Perry, *The Descent of Man*)

Text 5

"Okay, listen carefully. You'll be met at the airport by a driver from the embassy. He'll take you straight to the meeting where you will be welcomed by the other delegates."

"Can't I be taken to my hotel before the meeting? I'd like to shower and change."

"No, I'm sorry. There isn't time."

ISBN 978-3-12-501628-6

People, places, things – Consolidation

1. Find examples of the following types of nouns in the short text about fracking. You may find words or phrases going into more than one list.

singular countable nouns	plural countable nouns	uncountable nouns	compound nouns	proper nouns	noun phrases

Fracking

In the group I belong to we're very worried about fracking. A majority of the population in our area have voted against it but it's still going ahead. So much for democracy. We believe it would industrialize the wonderful countryside of England.

We believe that fracking should stop unless the company can clearly show that it would:

- not lead to serious damage to particular landscapes or to the countryside as a whole.
- be systematically controlled by strict rules and guidelines overseen by democratic planning. The whole process should be properly funded at both local and national levels.
- make sure there were significant reductions in carbon emissions that are needed to comply with planning policy and meet legally binding targets for climate change.

2. Some people consider four of the following sentences to be incorrect. Others see no problem with them. How would you explain this difference of opinion?

a) My daughter's class are going on a school trip next week.

b) The couple who live next door to me have had twins.

c) England are playing very well this season.

e) This evening's audience is smaller than last night's.

f) The government are spending more money on education this year.

**Which side of the argument are you on?
What other words might cause similar disagreement?**

ISBN 978-3-12-501628-6

3. What have the underlined nouns in these sentences got in common?

What difference does it make to the <u>dead</u>, the orphans and the <u>homeless</u>, whether the mad destruction is wrought under the name of totalitarianism or in the holy name of liberty or democracy?

(Mahatma Gandhi)

Kindness is a language which the <u>deaf</u> can hear and the <u>blind</u> can see.

(Mark Twain)

4. We rarely use words individually. And it certainly makes no sense to learn words on their own, for example as a list. In natural language words combine to create ***collocations*** *and* ***idioms****. Think about typical combinations for the word 'light' (as in brightness) and create a mindmap.*

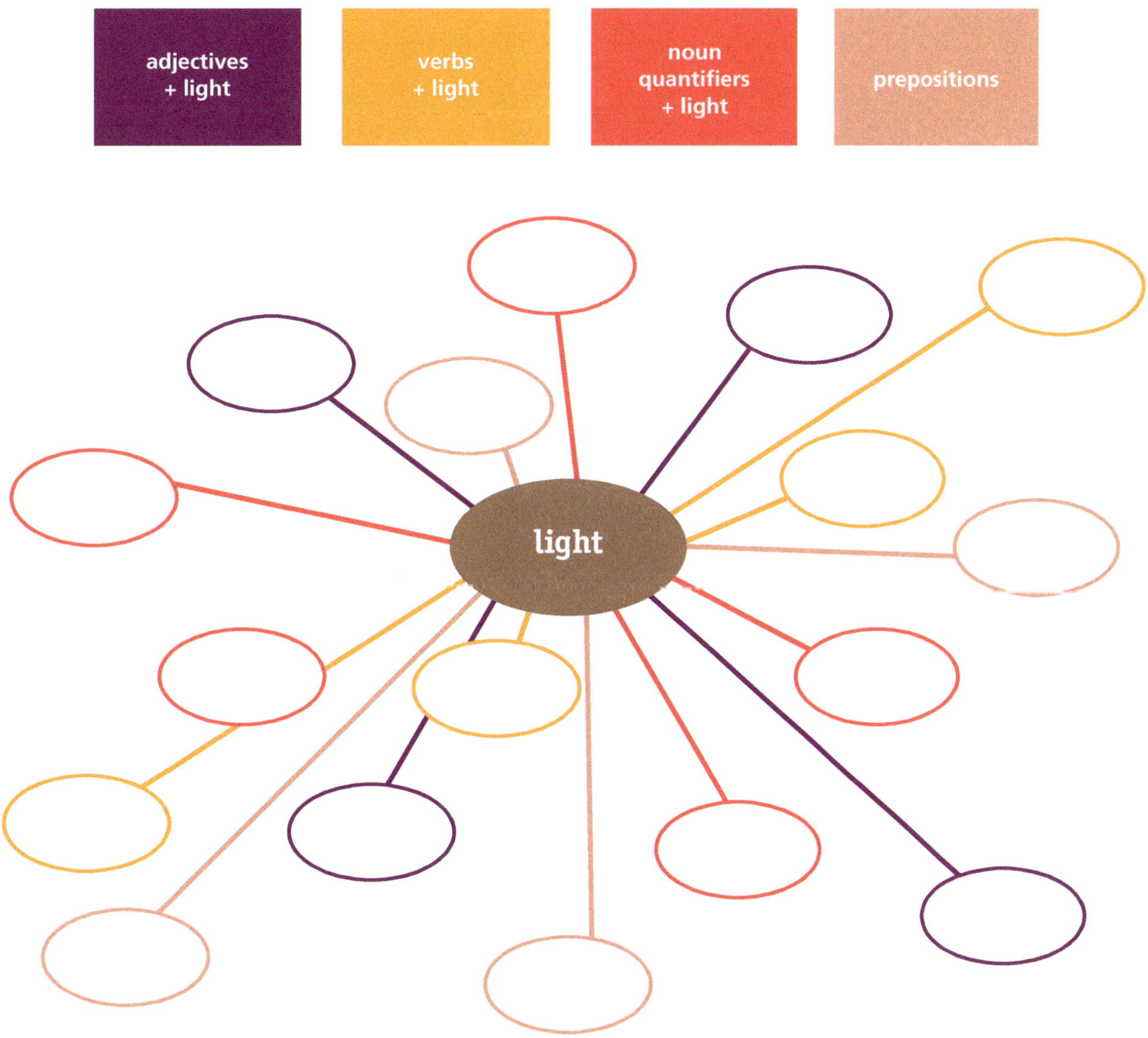

Describing people, places and things – Consolidation

1. Match each of these types of adjective with one of the words in the magnifying glass.

comparative • compound • gradable • possessive • superlative • ungradable

2. Now do the same for these types of adverb.

comment • degree • frequency • manner • place • time

ISBN 978-3-12-501628-6

3. In the five texts below:

a) underline the adjectives and adverbs.

b) find at least one of each of the types listed in 1 and 2 above.

Text 1

For the second time that night her blood froze to ice and she wanted to scream, but no sound came out. There at the window, with the curtains pushed aside, was the enormous long pale wrinkly face of the Giant Person staring in. The flashing black eyes were fixed on Sophie's bed.

(© Roald Dahl, *The BFG*)

Text 2

Text 3

According to many people, Robert Johnson is the greatest blues guitarist of all time and one of the founding fathers of rock 'n' roll. While his evocative and sometimes risqué lyrics have inspired singers of all kinds, it's his dazzling and innovative solo guitar playing that gives him a place in the history of popular music.

Text 4

It was a mild autumn night, the wind playing the occasional sharp sound of someone slamming a door or closing a window. He lay across the doorstep, trying to avoid the pavement. A man passed, singing a happy song to himself, noticing nothing. Arthur was half asleep, but opened his eyes now and again to make sure the street was still there, to convince himself that he was not in bed, because the hard stone step was as round and as soft as a pillow.

(© Alan Sillitoe, *Saturday Night and Sunday Morning*)

Text 5

If there is a common denominator in all Indian foods, it is, perhaps, the imaginative use of spices. Does this mean that Indian food is always spicy? Well, in a sense it does. It always uses spices, sometimes, just one spice.

(© Madhur Jaffrey, *Madhur Jaffrey's Indian Cookery*)

Text 6

Yesterday
All my troubles seemed so far away
Now it looks as though they're here to stay
Oh, I believe in yesterday

(© The Beatles, *Yesterday*)

ISBN 978-3-12-501628-6

Making connections – Consolidation

1. Join these sets of short sentences to form single sentences using the word or phrase in brackets.

a) The engineer's car broke down on the motorway. He was late for his appointment. (because)

b) I apologized profusely. The accident wasn't my fault. I'm English. (even though / although)

c) Many people believe that carrots help us see in the dark. There is no proof of this. (despite the fact that)

d) I can't find the address of an old school friend. I'd like to make contact with her. (but)

e) I was spending too much time playing games on my phone. That's why I leave it at home when I go to work. (so)

2. Rewrite these biographical notes in continuous prose using conjunctions, adverbs and relative clauses. (There are many possible ways of doing this.)

Pablo Picasso

- *Spanish painter, sculptor, printmaker / Son of an art teacher*
- *Born 1881 in Malaga / Died 1973 France*
- *Grew up in Spain / Spent most of adult life in France*
- *4 children*

Famous paintings

- *Les Demoiselles d'Avignon, 1907. New style, Cubism. This made Picasso famous.*
- *Guernica, 1937. Subject: the Spanish Civil War*

3. Read the following five short texts.

a) Find and underline words and phrases which make connections in the texts.

b) Where might you read or hear each extract?

Text 1

While I was in Melbourne, I twisted my foot and broke two bones. They x-rayed my foot but they didn't pick up the breaks and I walked on it for a month until I got back to Perth and saw my doctor. He sent me for a scan, which showed up the breaks. This has caused lots of complications and I'm still seeing an orthopaedic surgeon. It's a real drag as I still can't walk far or exercise, which means we've had to cancel a scheduled trip to Sydney.

ISBN 978-3-12-501628-6

Text 2

Bees are remarkable little insects that have been around for about 100 million years or so, going quietly and efficiently about their business of gathering their food from the nectar and pollen produced by flowers. In doing so, they provide a valuable and vital service to the plants they visit and ultimately to human beings and other animals, as they aid pollination through their foraging activities and thus ensure the spread and continuation of plant species.

(© Derek Hall, *Bees & Beekeeping*)

Text 3

There were only two items of furniture that went with the house. One was a vast carved oak sideboard that must surely have been built in the dining room, for it could never have been brought in through the door; …

(© Pat Barker, *The Ghost Road*)

Text 4

According to Thames Valley Police, the artwork, which is a fully-functioning 18-carat gold toilet called "America", was stolen from Blenheim Palace early on Saturday morning. It was installed near to the room in the palace where Winston Churchill was born. When the thieves removed it, there was serious flood damage because it had been connected to the water supply for visitors to use.

Text 5

Musicals aren't usually my cup of tea, but the whole family wanted to watch it so I reluctantly agreed. To my surprise, I was grabbed from the start, especially as it starred Hugh Jackman, an actor I've always admired. Even if you don't like musicals, watch this.

4. Look at the texts again.

a) Which of the relative clauses in the texts are defining and which are non-defining?

b) In which text is 'which' used to refer to a complete clause or idea rather than a noun?

c) In Text 2, where has a relative pronoun been omitted from a relative clause?

d) Which words are used to introduce a reason?

e) Which texts include coordinating conjunctions?

f) Which texts include subordinating conjunctions?

ISBN 978-3-12-501628-6

Glossaries

Grammar / Vocabulary

active / passive

page 108 ff.

An active sentence is one in which the subject of the sentence performs the action of the verb.

Subject	Active verb	Object
The dog	***attacked***	*my brother.*

By contrast, in a passive sentence, the subject is affected by the action of the verb. The person or thing which performs the action is the ***agent***.

Subject	Passive verb	Agent
My brother	***was attacked by***	*the dog.*

To form a passive verb, use the verb *be* in the tense you need and add the past participle of the main verb. Examples:

The roof ***is being repaired****.* — Present continuous passive
The road ***had been repaired.*** — Past perfect simple passive
My book ***will be published*** *next year.* — Future simple passive
Cars ***should be banned*** *from the city centre.* — Modal passive

adjective

page 142 ff.

An adjective is a word which describes a noun:
a ***long*** *sentence / a* ***windy*** *day / a* ***sore*** *thumb / a* ***clever*** *student*
There are different kinds of adjectives:

- **comparative / superlative** (for comparisons)

adjective	comparative form	superlative form
sharp / long	*sharper / longer*	*sharpest / longest*
nice / large	*nicer / larger*	*nicest / largest*
big / thin	*bigger / thinner*	*biggest / thinnest*
heavy / easy	*heavier / easier*	*heaviest / easiest*
important	*more important*	*most important*
expensive	*more expensive*	*most expensive*

- **gradable / ungradable**
  gradable: *(rather / very / extremely …) hungry, cold, angry …*
  ungradable: *ravenous, freezing, furious*
- **a compound adjective is** made up of more than one word
  slow-moving *car /* ***world-famous*** *singer /* ***handmade*** *furniture*

adjective order

page 143

If several adjectives are used in front of a noun, there is a generally accepted order:
Opinion → Fact → Noun
A ***beautiful old*** *house. / A* ***disappointing new*** *film.*
Order of fact adjectives: Size → Age → Colour → Origin → Made of → Noun
An ***enormous red German*** *car. / An* ***ancient Chinese woollen*** *coat.*
Note: It is unusual for more than three adjectives to be used with a noun.

adverb

page 142 ff.

A word or phrase which modifies the meaning of a verb, an adjective or another adverb. Many adverbs are formed by adding -ly to an adjective.
*She spoke **quickly**. / He's a **really** slow speaker. / They spoke **quite** slowly.*

Comparative / superlative:
*She spoke **more quickly**. / She interrupted **most frequently**.*
*He ran **faster** / **the fastest**.*

Adverbs can be grouped like this:
- *frequency adverbs: He **always** gets home late.*
- *manner adverbs: She works **hard**.*
- *degree adverbs: I found the test **extremely** difficult.*
- *attitude adverbs: **Hopefully**, I'll get the new job I've applied for.*
- *time adverbs: I saw him **yesterday**.*
- *place adverbs: As soon as we got **there** we went upstairs.*

affirmative

The affirmative form of a verb is positive rather than **negative**.
***I'm** a student. / **I'm learning** English. / **I've lived** in Moscow.*

agent

page 108 ff.

In a passive sentence the *actor* (the person or thing that does the action of the verb) is called *the agent*. Examples:
In the sentence *Macbeth was written by Shakespeare.* **Shakespeare** is the agent.
In the sentence *Trees were blown over by the wind.* **the wind** is the agent.

see also **active / passive**

article

page 127

- **definite article:** ***the***
  *When **the** judge came into **the** court, **the** jury stood up.*
- **indefinite article:** ***a / an***
  *A mouse took **a** stroll through **a** deep dark wood.*
  ***An** elephant ate **an** apple and **an** orange.*
- The term **zero article** is sometimes used to indicate that no article is used, e.g.
  *He is waiting for you **at home**.* *(not at ~~the~~ home)*
  *They go **to church** every Sunday.* *(not to ~~the~~ church)*

auxiliary verb

page(s) 19, 35, 72 ff.

A verb which is used in conjunction with **main** verbs. There are two kinds of auxiliary verbs:

primary auxiliary verbs
*She **is** playing tennis. / What **have** you done? / Why **didn't** you stop?*
playing, done, stop are main verbs

modal auxiliary verbs
*My brother **can't** swim. / You **shouldn't** eat too much. / We **must** hurry.*
Swim, eat, hurry are main verbs

bare infinitive, base form

see **infinitive**

causative verb

page 110 ff.

to have something done and ***to get something done*** are causative verbs. They indicate that the subject of the verb arranges for an action to take place, but does not do the action themselves. For example:
I'm having my eyes tested this afternoon.
He got his hair cut yesterday.
(Causative verbs can be thought of as a mid-way position between an active and passive verb.)

chunk

page 130

Formulaic language, groups of words which often occur together. Most chunks do not need to be analyzed grammatically or broken into their constituent parts. There are different types of chunks:
- Idiomatic expressions:
  the more the merrier / let's call it a day / few and far between
- conversational phrases:
  How're you doing? / See you later! / no worries / By the way, … / You must be joking!
- collocations:
  break a habit / keep a promise / crystal clear / moral obligation / evil grin
- binomial expressions
  pros and cons / safe and sound / peace and quiet / hustle and bustle
- phrasal verbs (2 or 3 part)
  put off / break in / look after / look forward to / run out of / put up with

clause

page(s) 90 ff., 162 ff.

A group of words which includes a subject and a verb, e.g.
We have breakfast at 8 o'clock.
Sentences can have more than one clause:
Before we go to work, we have breakfast. (2 clauses)
We have breakfast, before we go to work and we have lunch at midday. (3 clauses)

see also **main clause** and **subordinate clause**

conditional sentences

page 90 ff.

see **first conditional / second conditional / third conditional / zero conditional / mixed conditional**

conjunct

page(s) 163, 164

A word or phrase used to link two clauses, sentences or paragraphs.
Geoff cleared away the broken glass. ***Meanwhile****, I called the police.*
I don't agree with you. ***However****, I don't mind having a discussion.*
Conjuncts are also called adverbs.

conjunction

page(s) 92, 162 ff.

a word or phrase which links two parts of a sentence, such as *and, but, because, although.*
There are two types of conjunction
- **coordinating conjunctions** link words, phrases or clauses of equal value. For example:
I had fish ***and*** *chips for lunch. / We got home late* ***and*** *went to bed.*
- **subordinating conjunctions** link a dependent clause to a main clause. For example:
If *you get here early, we'll go swimming.*
He wore a thin T-shirt ***even though*** *it was freezing cold.*

contracted (verb) form

page(s) 20, 48, 63

Sometimes called a short form as opposed to **long or full form**.

short form	long/full form
I'm	*I am*
They're	*They are*
You'd	*You would*
We've	*We have* etc.

direct / indirect question

A **direct question** is the words used by a speaker who asks a question. For example:
What's the time? / Where's the toilet? / Can I use your phone?

An **indirect question** is a question contained in a sentence or another question.
***Can you tell me** what the time is? / **Do you know** where the toilet is?*
***I was wondering if** I could use your phone.*

dynamic (action) verb

page 20

A verb which refers to an action or an event:
*I **phoned** you twice this morning. / **He's singing** in the bath again.*
Dynamic verbs are used in all verb forms.

By contrast, **a stative verb** refers to a state or condition:
*I **want** to be a film star. / He doesn't **like** tea. / Do you **know** Paul?*
Stative verbs tend not to be used in the continuous form. So sentences such as the following sound strange:
*I **am wanting** to be a film star. / He **isn't liking** tea. / **Are you knowing** Paul?*

first conditional

page 90 ff.

The first conditional is used to refer to possible future situations or actions that we think are quite likely. The normal verb sequence is: ***If*** + present simple, → *will / may / might / could* + infinitive. For example:
*If **I see** him, **I'll remind** him to call you.*

full (verb) form

see **contracted (verb) form**

function

page(s) 4, 5, 11, 14

A function of language is a purpose for which language is used, for example: *apologizing, congratulating, expressing surprise, making suggestions, expressing an opinion*. In language teaching, functions are often linked to the grammatical forms used to express them, but there is no one-to-one link between grammar and function. For example, there are many grammatical forms which can be used to make suggestions, e.g.
Why don't you + infinitive
What about + -ing form
You could + infinitive

future continuous

page(s) 58, 63, 109

This verb form comprises *will* + *be* + the *-ing* form of the main verb. For example:
***We'll / We will be cruising** down the Irrawaddy this time next weekend.*

future perfect

page 59

This verb form comprises *will* + *have* + the past participle form of the main verb. For example:
*By this time next week **they'll / they will have moved** house.*

future simple

page(s) 58, 63, 109

This verb form comprises *will* + the infinitive form of the main verb. For example:
*I expect **he'll / he will phone** you tomorrow.*
Also called the *will* future.

gerund

see ***-ing*** form

***going to* future**

page 58 ff.

This verb form comprises *going to* + the infinitive form of the main verb. For example:
***I'm going to look for** a new job.*

indirect question

see **direct / indirect question**

infinitive

page(s) 19, 20, 72 ff., 90 ff.

Sometimes called the base form of a verb. People are sometimes taught that in English the infinitive is preceded by *to*, as in *I'd like* ***to tell*** *you a secret.* This is not always the case. The bare infinitive is used for example after modal verbs:
We might ***be*** *late. / You must* ***sign*** *your name here.*

-ing form

page(s) 16 ff., 32 ff.

The form of verbs which ends in -ing: *going, swimming, sleeping* etc.

It is sometimes referred to as the **gerund** or the **present participle.** The distinction between the two is not always made by teachers today.

- **gerund** – the *-ing* form used as a noun:
  Cycling *is good exercise, but* ***swimming*** *is better.*
- **present participle** – the *-ing* form used as a verb:
  Cycling *past the pool, I saw a lot of people* ***swimming****.*

intransitive verb

see **transitive verb**

irregular verb

page(s) 37, 48, 120

Any verb is irregular if it does not follow this regular pattern:

	How it's formed	**Examples**
Present simple	base form / infinitive *he/she/it* → base form + *-s*	*I / you / we / they smile / walk* *he / she smiles / walks*
Past simple & past participle	base form + *-d* or *-ed*	*he smiled / she walked* *we've smiled / they've walked*

Examples of **irregular** verbs

Present simple	**Past simple**	**Past participle**
give	*gave*	*given*
buy	*bought*	*bought*
put	*put*	*put*
go	*went*	*gone*

main clause

page(s) 90 ff., 163, 164

A clause which makes sense on its own and does not depend on another clause to complete its meaning. For example:
The leaves were shaking in the wind. / Where are you going?
Also called an **independent clause**.

main verb

page(s) 46, 109, 120, 198

A verb which has content or meaning and is not just a grammar word (e.g. an auxiliary verb):
He ***works*** *hard. / What are you* ***studying****? / I've never* ***eaten*** *meat.*
Main verbs are sometimes called **lexical verbs**.

mixed conditional

page 91

Unlike the other conditional forms, mixed conditional sentences do not have a specific sequence of tenses. For example they could be a mixture of third and second conditional forms, e.g. ***If** he **had followed*** (third) *my suggestion, **he wouldn't be*** (second) *stuck in New York.*

modal (auxiliary) verb

page 72 ff.

Often just called *modal verbs*. Modal verbs (*can, could, may, might, must, shall, should, will, would*) are a type of auxiliary verb that express ability, possibility, permission or obligation. For example:
*I **mustn't** forget my glasses. / We **should** hurry. / He **could** come later.*

negative form

The opposite of the affirmative form.
***I don't drink** tea. / **I'm not enjoying** this book. / I **didn't hear** a sound.*
Negative verb forms require auxiliary verbs (*don't* , *didn't* etc.).

noun

page 124 ff.

Nouns refer to people, places, things, abstract ideas. There are different types of nouns:
- **collective nouns** are singular nouns which refer to a group of individuals:
  crowd, team, committee, audience, staff
  Some collective nouns are formed from adjectives:
  the rich, the poor, the deaf, the unemployed
- **compound nouns** are nouns which comprise two or more parts, e.g.
  - 1 word: *bathroom, teapot, newspaper, grandmother*
  - 2+ words hyphenated: *son-in-law, runner-up, passer-by*
  - 2 words: *bus stop, washing machine, cheese sandwich*
- **countable nouns** are nouns which can be counted and have singular and plural forms, e.g.
  egg, ball, screwdriver, idea, thought, phone, sheep
- **uncountable nouns** are nouns which cannot be counted and have no plural form, e.g.
  information, furniture, food, water, air, light
  Note: some words can be countable and uncountable depending on their meaning. For example if *lamb* means meat, it is uncountable. If it refers to an animal it is countable.
- **proper nouns** are nouns which are names for people, places, months etc.: *April, Barry, Canada*. In English proper nouns start with a capital letter.

object

page(s) 110, 167, 207

The object of a verb is the thing or person that is influenced by the action of the verb. There are two types of object:
- **Direct object**: In the sentence *I met **my friend** in town*. *my friend* is the direct object.
- **Indirect object:** In the sentence *I gave **my friend** a book. my friend* is the indirect object and *a book* is the direct object.

passive

page 108 ff.

see **active / passive**

past continuous

page 32 ff., 109

The verb form or tense which comprises the past simple of the verb *be* followed by the *-ing form* of the main verb. Only the *be* part of the verb changes.
***We were running** fast. / **He wasn't doing** anything wrong. / What **were you looking at**?*

past participle

page(s) 33, 37, 44, 48, 59, 72, 91, 109, 110, 113

The verb form which is used to form the present perfect, the past perfect and the passive. For example:
*I've just **eaten**. / He'd completely **forgotten** where he was. / I've been **robbed**.*

past perfect page(s) 32 ff., 91, 109	The verb form which is used to refer to an event which took place before a more recent past event. It has simple and continuous forms: **Simple:** *Before we met,* ***I'd heard*** *a lot about you.* **Continuous:** *My father* ***had been working*** *at his firm for 25 years before he was made redundant.*
past simple page(s) 32 ff., 48, 91, 95, 109	The affirmative form is a single word, but the auxiliary verb *did* or *didn't* is needed to form the question and negative forms: ***They went*** *on holiday. /* ***We didn't meet*** *our friends./ What* ***did you see****?*
person	first person singular – ***I*** first person plural – *we* second person singular and plural – *you* third person singular – *he, she, it* third person plural – *they*
phrasal verb	A verb which comprises a verb plus one or two particles (prepositions or adverbs). The meaning of the phrasal verb is different from the original verb. Some examples: *I* ***grew up*** *in the north of England.* *She's* ***looking forward to*** *going to university.* *I don't like him – he always* ***looks down on*** *others.* *Will you* ***see to*** *it that he does his homework?*
possessive adjective page 143	Adjectives which refer to possession: *That's* ***my*** *phone. / Is this* ***your*** *coat? / Where's* ***her/his*** *car? / This is* ***our*** *classroom. /* ***Their*** *house has been burgled.*
possessive pronoun page 143	Pronouns which refer to possession (the item in question has already been mentioned): *That's* ***mine****. / Is this* ***yours****? / Where's* ***his/hers****? / This is* ***ours****. /* ***Theirs*** *had been burgled.*
preposition	Prepositions are words which link nouns, pronouns and phrases in sentences – they express a relation to another word or element in a sentence. There are different types: • place prepositions: *in, on, opposite, near* • time prepositions: *before, after, at* • direction prepositions: *down, into, through, along* Some adjectives and verbs are followed by particular prepositions: • Adjectives: *different* ***from*** */ similar* ***to*** */ afraid* ***of*** */ keen* ***on*** • Verbs: *apologize* ***for*** */ boast* ***about*** */ comply* ***with*** */ approve* ***of***
present continuous page(s) 16 ff., 48, 58, 61, 63, 109	The verb form or tense which comprises the verb *be* followed by the *-ing form* of the main verb. Only the *be* part of the verb changes. *We****'re having*** *a picnic. / The kids* ***are playing*** *with their toys. / What* ***are you doing****?*
present participle	see ***-ing*** form
present perfect page(s) 44 ff., 109, 156	The verb form or tense which comprises the present of the verb *have* + the past participle of the main verb. ***He has*** *just* ***come*** *home. /* ***They haven't had*** *any lunch. / Where* ***have you been****?*

present simple

page(s) 16 ff., 50, 61, 63, 91, 95, 109

Otherwise called the **present tense.** The affirmative form is a single word, but the auxiliary verbs *do / does / don't / doesn't* are needed to form the question and negative forms.
***They live** in Dublin. / **I don't speak** Chinese. / What **do you do**?*

question form

page 19

The form of the verb used to ask questions. Most question forms require auxiliary verbs.
***Did you go** there alone? / Where **have you been**? / Why **didn't you phone** me?*

regular verb

see **irregluar verb**

relative clause

page 162 ff.

A clause which adds information to a sentence and usually starts with a **relative pronoun**.
There are two types of relative clause:
- **A defining (identifying) relative clause** adds essential information and cannot be left out:
*People **who park their cars on the footpath** should be fined.*
*Food **which isn't eaten before its sell-by-date** should be thrown away.*
- **A non-defining (non-identifying) relative clause** simply adds extra information which is not essential to an understanding of the sentence:
*Paul, **who is a community police officer**, lives next door to us.*
*Colchester, **which is Britain's oldest town**, has a flourishing market.*

relative pronoun

page 162 ff.

Most relative clauses are introduced by one of these relative pronouns:
- *who* and *that* refer to people
- *which* and *that* refer to things
- *whose* refers to possession

These words can also be referred to as relative pronouns or relative adverbs: *where, when, why*.

relative adverb

see **relative pronoun**

reported speech

A way of reporting what someone says without using their actual words. For example:

Actual words (Direct speech)	Reported (indirect) speech
I'm feeling very tired	***He said he was feeling very tired.***
Where are we going?	***She asked where we were going.***
I used your phone yesterday.	***She said she had used my phone the day before.***

second conditional

page 90 ff.

The second conditional has two uses:
- to refer to possible future situations or actions that we think are unlikely, e.g.
*If **I saw** him, **I'd remind** him to call you.*
- to refer to impossible conditions, e.g.
*If **I were** you, **I'd ask** for a refund.*

The normal verb sequence is: ***If*** + past simple, → *would* + infinitive.

stative verb

see **dynamic verb**

structure	A grammatical pattern, e.g. article + adjective + noun — *the main road / a black dog* pronoun + modal verb + main verb — *I can't swim. / He may drown.*	
subject	The subject of a sentence is the *actor* (the person or thing) who does the action of the verb. For example: ***She** watched her friends play tennis.* (**She** is the subject of *watched)* ***Tennis** is her favourite sport.* (**Tennis** is the subject of *is)*	
subordinate clause page(s) 63, 95, 164, 166	A clause which does not make sense on its own without a connected main clause. For example: ***As soon as I get there**, I'll phone you.* *I'll tell Pete **if I see him**.* Also called a *dependent clause.*	
third conditional page 90 ff.	The third conditional is used to speculate about past situations or actions that didn't happen. The normal verb sequence is: ***If*** + past perfect, → would / could have + past participle *If **I had seen** him, **I'd have reminded** him to call you.*	
transitive / intransitive verb page 110	A **transitive verb** is one which can be followed by an *object*. For example: *build* — *They **built a house.*** (*a house* is the object) *eat* — *We all **ate falafel** for lunch*. (*falafel* is the object) An **intransitive verb** is one which cannot be followed by an object. For example: *come* — *They **came** to lunch.* *laugh* — *We **laughed** till we cried.*	
verb	A word which describes an action; sometimes called a *doing word*, e.g. *listen / am laughing / knew / might / should / didn't* Verbs can be: *simple* or *continuous*, *regular* or *irregular, transitive* or *intransitive*, *passive* or *active*, *stative* or *dynamic.*	
verb form page(s) 16 ff., 32 ff., 44 ff., 58 ff.	Another way of referring to the verb tenses.	
zero article	see **article**	
zero conditional page 90 ff.	The zero conditional describes general conditions or rules and is used to refer to situations where one action always follows another. The normal verb sequence is: ***If*** + present simple, → present simple / present continuous *If **I have** a headache, **I take** paracetamol.*	

Methodology

accuracy activity	see **fluency / accuracy**
activate	see **lesson structures (E-S-A)**
back-chaining page 95	A method of getting learners to improve their pronunciation of long sentences or structures. For example, if you want learners to practise the pronunciation of the sentence: *If I see him, I'll pass on your message.* with the correct intonation and stress, break it down like this: Teacher: *your message* – repeat Learners: *your message* Teacher: *pass on your message* – repeat Learners: *pass on your message* Teacher: *I'll pass on your message* – repeat Learners: *I'll pass on your message* Teacher: *see him, I'll pass on your message* – repeat Learners: *see him, I'll pass on your message* Teacher: *If I see him, I'll pass on your message* – repeat Learners: *If I see him, I'll pass on your message*
concept questions	Questions designed to check learners' understanding of a grammar point without the use of terminology. For example:

Structure	Concept question(s)
It's time we had lunch.	*Is this sentence about the past, or the present?* Answer: *Present*
I've had my hair cut.	*Did this person cut their own hair?* Answer: *No* *Did someone else cut it?* Answer: *Yes* *Did the person arrange the hair cut?* Answer: *Yes*

context	The situation in which language is used, for example *at breakfast / a job interview / on the phone / …*
controlled practice	see **practice activities**
coursebook	A book based on a **syllabus**, usually comprising chapters or units which provide lesson material for learners and teachers. A typical coursebook package includes a Student's Book, a Teacher's Book, a Workbook which provides further a practice, and audio recordings. Many coursebooks also have additional online components.

drill

Repetitive oral practice to reinforce a point of grammar. Drills which include an element of choice for learners are sometimes referred to as *meaningful drills*. Those which can be done without thought or choice may be called *meaningless drills*. The latter were a common feature of the audio-lingual / -visual approach. The communicative approach advocates that drills should be *meaningful*.
Drills can also be used to improve learners' pronunciation.

eliciting

A method of finding out what learners know or can work out about the target language (grammar) of a lesson. It is an alternative to giving learners information or explaining a language point. For example, if your lesson is about the difference in meaning between the first and second conditional forms, you might simply ask learners: What is the difference in meaning between
1. *If I get the job, I'll earn more money.*
and
2. *If I got the job, I'd earn more money.*

Learners might find this question too open, so you could lead them towards an answer with a **concept question** like this: *How optimistic is the speaker about getting the job?* You would hope to elicit the idea that the speaker of sentence 1 is more optimistic than the speaker of sentence 2.

Eliciting information has three purposes:
- It is a way of recognizing that learners have existing knowledge or an ability to work out meanings.
- It is a way of involving learners in the process of learning.
- It is a strategy for reducing teacher talking time.

fluency / accuracy

page(s) 10, 14, 21, 37, 50, 115, 158, 174

These words are often used to describe oral practice activities in the language classroom.
A **fluency activity** is one whose main purpose is to allow learners to practise speaking without worrying too much about grammatical accuracy. For example:
- *Discuss this question in pairs: If you could introduce a new law to control noise, what would it be? How would you enforce this law?*
- *Fast food will be the death of all. What is your view?*

An **accuracy activity** is one whose main aim is the correct grammar or pronunciation. For example:
- *Repeat these words making sure you stress the correct syllables*: *'humour / a'pologize / under'standing*
- *Turn these sentences into the past using 'have to':*
  - ▶ I must talk to Bill today. → *I had to talk to Bill yesterday.*
  - ▶ She must come and see me. → *She* ....
  - ▶ He doesn't have to work today. → *He* ....

free practice

see **practice activities**

gap-fill

A type of practice exercise which requires learners to add a word or phrase to a sentence or text (often from a list of choices). It is a simple straightforward way of checking whether a grammar point or vocabulary item is known.

group work

Tasks which involve three or more learners working together. Most group work involves oral tasks, such as exchanges of opinion or discussions but could also be a collaborative project.

ice-breaker / warmer	An activity, often at the beginning of a lesson, which introduces the topic of the lesson in an interesting way which involves learners in a non-threatening way.
input	*Input* is spoken or written language that learners are given. For example an audio recording or a written text which contains examples of target language counts as *input*.
language laboratory page 14	Language laboratories are rooms equipped with individual booths where learners can listen to language through headphones and can respond or record themselves using a microphone. They are used mainly for drills to practise pronunciation or grammar points. Teachers can monitor and talk to individual learners or communicate with the whole class. They were an important feature of the audio-lingual/-visual approach to language learning.

lesson structures

page(s) 9, 14 ff.

There are many recognized grammar lesson structures in common use in language classrooms. These are a few (see also page 14):

- **E → S → A (Engage → Study → Activate)**
  - **Engage** – This phase often involves a warmer or icebreaker and introduces the topic or theme of the lesson. It may also lead learners toward the target language, or the need to use that language.
  - **Study** – This phase presents the grammar structure and checks that learners understand how it is formed and used. It may involve the teacher asking concept questions, illustrating patterns or explaining rules.
  - **Activate** – This phase gives learners opportunities to make use of the grammar point they have been studying. To start with activities will be controlled and move on to freer or less controlled tasks.

- **P → P → P (Presentation → Practice → Production)**

  This structure has been established for many years and is still commonly followed by teachers and teaching materials.

  - **Presentation** – This phase presents several examples of the target language in a context which should make meaning clear. The teacher may ask questions to check learners' understanding.
  - **Practice** – In this phase learners practice the new target language to achieve accuracy of pronunciation and grammatical forms. The context will often be the same as that used in the presentation phase.
  - **Production** – In this phase, learners are given the opportunity to use the target language in new and sometimes personalized contexts. This phase is sometimes called *Transfer*, because it attempts to get learners to transfer knowledge and skills in new contexts.

- **T → T → T (Test → Teach → Test)**

  This lesson structure is often used to check how well learners already know the target language the teacher is about to teach. In many adult classes, there may be learners of different language levels. This method may help teachers to know which points of language most need to be taught.

  ▶ **Test** – In this first phase learners are asked to complete a task which involves the use of the target language. The teacher monitors to check the learners' level and to decide which particular points need teaching or reinforcing in the next phase.

  ▶ **Teach** – In this phase the teacher may teach a grammar point from scratch or revise those aspects that learners had difficulty with during the first phase of the lesson. This phase may involve concept questions, teacher explanations and controlled practice tasks.

  ▶ **Test** – In this final phase the learners are asked to do an activity which is similar to the initial *Test*. By monitoring learners' handling of the task the teacher will find out the extent of improvement made by learners.

- **A - R - C (Authentic, Restricted, Clarification)**

  Unlike the previous lesson structures described, this is not a linear structure. *Authentic*, *restricted* and *clarification* are words used to describe the nature and purpose of classroom activities.

  ▶ **Authentic** activities are those which are similar in kind to real life activities learners may be involved in outside the classroom. Examples might include: *asking for directions* or *exchanging opinions*.

  ▶ **Restricted** activities are those designed to get learners to practise language in a controlled way.

  ▶ **Clarification** activities are those designed to help learners to understand the form and use of the target language. These are often teacher-led.

L1

A learner's first language or mother tongue is often referred to as their L1. **L1 interference** is sometimes given as the reason for errors learners make in the language they are learning (L2).

mingle activity

An activity which involves learners moving around the classroom talking to other learners, to find out information. Examples might be:

- *Find other learners in the class whose birthdays are in the same month as yours.*
- *Find someone who enjoys the same kinds of food as you.*

model sentence

A correct sentence used by a teacher or a coursebook to illustrate a point of grammar, vocabulary or pronunciation. It should be a sentence which learners can use to produce similar sentences of their own, e.g.

The most unusual person I have ever met is …
If I won $1 million in the lottery, I would …

monitoring

When teachers set activities for learners to work on independently, they should go round the class checking that learners understand what they are doing and are on task. If the activity requires learners to produce correct language, monitoring might also involve correction by the teacher (or making a note of frequent errors to be addressed at a later point in the lesson).

pair work

Similar to **group work**, but involving two learners.

personalized practice
Activities in which learners can use their knowledge and experience or express their opinions.

practice activities
- **Controlled** grammar practice activities focus on getting learners to produce the target language accurately. Errors will be corrected by the teacher.
- **Free** practice activities are designed to allow learners to use the target language without being overly concerned with accuracy.

role play
A type of pair or group work in which learners each assume the role of a particular person. A pair of learners might be asked for example to act out a conversation between a shop assistant and a customer or an interviewer and a job applicant.

syllabus
The stage-by-stage content of a course of study. A language syllabus usually involves a sequence of units which include grammar, functions, vocabulary and skills.

target language
The unknown grammar which a lesson sets out to introduce and teach.

theme
The subject or topic used to present language – ideally something which will interest students, e.g. *Extreme sports / Families / Holidays / Food …*

timelines
page 36
Timelines are a visual representation of how verb forms relate to time and to each other. For example:

*As soon as I saw (**b**) him, I knew (**b**) we had met (**a**) before.*

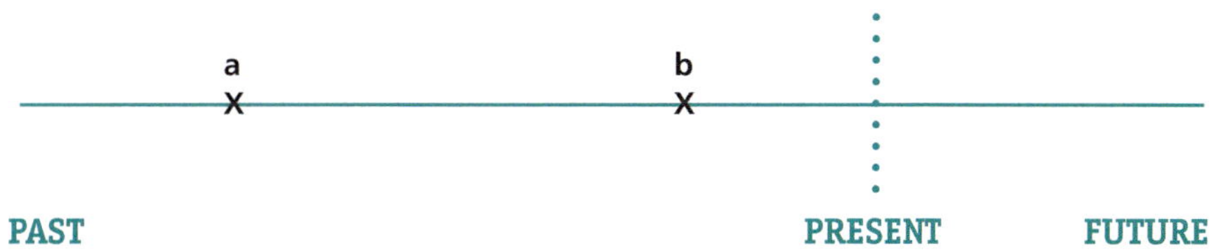

warmer
see **ice-breaker**

Key WS 1 C

1.

a 1. = it's a fact
2. = it's possibly only temporary

b 1. = I'm reading it this very moment
2. = I have been reading it recently and am not finished yet

c 1. = it's a fact, something you always do
2. = I'm hoping it's just a phase

2.

a 1. = I am actually leaving this very minute
2. = I'm still at work, but plan to leave then

b 1. = usually the flight I catch leaves at 10.30
2. = tomorrow (for some unspecified reason) I'm on a later flight / the flight is delayed

3.

Text 1

A rabbit goes into a shop and asks the assistant, "Do you have any carrots?" The assistant replies "Sorry, we don't sell carrots." The rabbit leaves.
The next day, the rabbit comes back and says, " Do you have any carrots?" The assistant replies "I told you yesterday we don't sell carrots."
The rabbit leaves.
The next day, the rabbit returns again and says, " Do you have any carrots?" The assistant gets very angry and says "I told you yesterday we don't sell carrots. If you ask once more, I'll nail your ears to the door!" The rabbit leaves.
The next day, the rabbit runs into the shop and asks, "Do you have any nails?" The assistant replies politely "Sorry, we don't sell nails."
The rabbit smiles and says. "Good, so do you have any carrots?"
→ spoken / joke

Text 2

Trees absorb carbon dioxide as they grow and the carbon that they store in their wood helps slow the rate of global warming. They reduce wind speeds and cool the air as they lose moisture and reflect heat upwards from their leaves. Trees also help prevent flooding and soil erosion.
→ written or spoken / website, documentary, factual book

Text 3

Hello?
Hi, is Pete there, please?
I'm afraid he's talking to a customer at the moment. Who's calling, please?
His brother. I'll call back.
→ spoken / phone call

Text 4

Haven't seen you for ages! What are you doing these days?
Well I still live and work in town. I'm learning to drive.
That's great!
→ spoken / chance meeting

Text 5

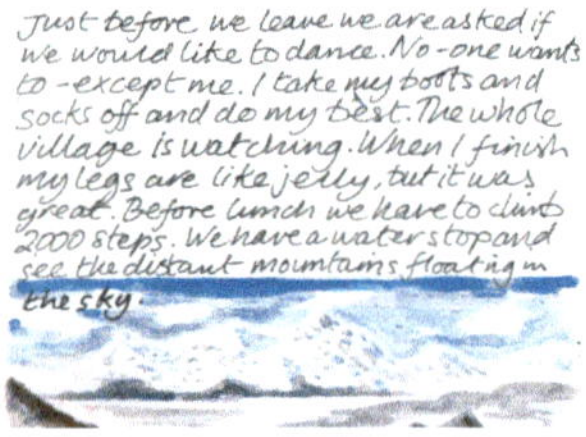

we leave / no-one wants / I take / do / is watching / I finish / my legs are / we have to / we have / see
→ written / diary, journal, travelogue

Text 6

Here – these are for you.
Thanks, but you shouldn't have.
Why not?
You're always buying me presents.
Are you feeling guilty about something?
→ spoken / conversation

Text 7

I get home between six and seven o'clock and I make my dinner. If it's been a busy day, and I'm feeling too tired to cook, I stick a ready-meal in the microwave. I usually eat on the sofa and catch up with any TV programmes I've missed. A couple of times week, I phone my Dad – he always wants to know how my course is going. We often talk for over an hour, after which I'm tired and go to bed.
→ spoken or written / conversation, email

4.

a. Trees absorb carbon dioxide (2)
b. I usually eat on the sofa and catch up with any TV programmes I've missed. (7)
c. A rabbit goes into a shop (1) / I take off my boots and socks and do my best (5)

5.

a. he's talking to a customer at the moment (3)
b. I'm learning to drive (4)

Key WS 2 C

Task 1

a) iv. | b) i. | c) ii. | d) v. | e) iii.

Task 3a

Text 1

Billy Weaver had travelled down from London on the slow afternoon train, with a change at Swindon on the way and by the time he got to Bath it was about nine o'clock in the evening and the moon was coming out of a clear starry sky over the houses opposite the station entrance.
→ narrative text, description

Text 2

I'm glad you like the photo. Did you take your driving test in that car?
I know we didn't get the VW until 1993, when you were 22.
Did you see that photo I sent of Dad on your motorbike. He used to drive it to the station, after you had stopped using it.
Talk to you again soon.
→ personal email

Text 3

Ben Thomas pulled a goal back for the Blues early in the second half, but Steve Johnson made sure the team got maximum points by scoring from a penalty in the 88th minute.
"The team really did a great job," said relieved manager Tom Edwards.
→ newspaper report, sports write-up

Text 4

had searched / she found
→ cartoon, joke

Text 5

There's an old green Fordson tractor in the back of Grandpa's barn, always covered in cornsacks. When I was very little, I used to go in there, pull off the cornsacks, climb up and drive it all over the farm.
Note: *pull off*, *climb up* and *drive* are all short for *used to pull off*, *used to climb up* and *used to drive*
→ novel, narrative text, memoir, biography

Text 6

Skylar's voice sounded calm on my voice mail. Obviously, no calamity had occurred. It was like he'd been expecting to hear from me, but for some reason I just hadn't called ... My heart was pounding when I dialled his number.
→ novel, narrative text

Task 3b

i. got / was (1) | Did you take / we didn't get / were / did you see / sent (2) | pulled / made / got / did / said (3) | found (4) | was (5) | sounded / dialed (6)
ii. used to drive (2) | used to go / pull off / climb up / drive (5)
iii. was coming (1) | was pounding (5)
iv. had travelled (1) | had stopped (2) | had searched (4) | had occurred /

hadn't called (6)
v. he'd been expecting (6)

Key WS 3 C

1.

a) She can't play tennis (for the foreseeable future).
b) They still work there now.
c) My finger's bleeding. It really hurts.
d) That's why his geographical knowledge is extensive.
e) Five vehicles were involved. Emergency services are at the scene. Five people are being taken to hospital.
f) I still want to go. / I'm finally going this year. It'll be a dream come true.
g) They still live there now. / They have never lived anywhere else.
h) And it still dominates the skyline.

2.

i. *I've been redecorating my flat.*
= The redecoration may not be finished
I've redecorated my flat.
= The redecoration is finished.
ii. *John's worked for the same company for 15 years.* =
This is a fact.
John's been working for the same company for 15 years.
= This is the same fact but the emphasis is on the duration of the activity.

3.

Text 1
Marine archaeologists believe they have located the remains of Captain James Cook's famed ship Endeavour after a centuries-long search. Captain Cook used the vessel on a voyage of discovery to Australia and New Zealand in 1770 and it was later used by the British navy in the American War of Independence before it was scuttled off Newport, Rhode Island, in 1778.
The ship's final resting place has eluded archaeologists ever since, but now a team of Australian researchers believe they have pinpointed the vessel in Newport Harbour.

Text 2
In his time, Frankie Gavin has played for four American presidents, starting, as a six-year old, when he played for John F. Kennedy on his 1962 visit to Ireland, then later for Presidents Clinton, Bush and Barack Obama.

Text 3
Thanks Phil,
I think their new album is superb. Although I haven't written the review yet, I've been playing it non-stop from the day I got it. I've also bought the book and have been learning some of the songs.
Cheers
Mike

Text 4
Hurray. Whole new positive perspective on birthday. [I] Have been talking to Jude about book she has been reading about festivals and rites of passage in primitive cultures and am feeling happy and serene.

Text 5
The Japanese space agency has successfully landed two rovers on a large asteroid, and they have sent back images to Earth.

Key WS 4 C

1.

a i. arrangement
ii. prediction
b i. intention / resolution
ii. promise
c i. scheduled event
ii. prediction
d i. prediction with evidence
ii. prediction (no evidence)
e i. future fact
ii. prediction
f i. refusal
ii. prediction

2a.

Text 1
"Stand back," said the elephant,
"I'm going to sneeze!
I hate to alarm you,
But I don't wish to harm you.
My friends, I fear
It's clear …
Oh, dear.
You'd better stand back, I'm going to sneeze."

Text 2
Is that the door?
Yes, I'll get it.
Do you know who it is?
It'll probably be the postman bringing something I ordered online.

Text 3
It's your lucky day. Someone you admire will pay you an unexpected compliment. By the end of the day you'll probably be wondering what the future holds for the two of you.

Text 4
In the filling station forecourt Arthur said. 'When did you last put oil in the car?'
'I don't remember.'
'Get in and open the bonnet.' He held the dipstick to the light. 'It's bone-dry. Something told me it was. I'll go and get a couple of litres.'

Text 5
Arsenal take on Tottenham in this weekend's London derby

Text 6
Hi,
Thanks for the invite. I'd love to catch up, but can't make next Tuesday evening – I'm working late again.
Are you doing anything Thursday?
I'm not working then.
I'll call you tomorrow.
Harry

Text 7
My four-year-old daughter won't eat – and she's due to start school in three weeks' time!! It's got to the point, with me, where I just accept now that she won't eat or join in with family mealtimes.

Text 8
Two days ago I was 17, next year I'll be 20.
(Only people born on December 31st can make this claim.)

Text 9
I am going to learn to play the guitar if it's the last thing I do.

2b.

intention (9) | arrangement (6) | scheduled event (5) | refusal (7) | promise or offer (4 / 6) | prediction without evidence (2 / 3) | prediction with evidence (1) | future fact (8) | decision made at the moment of speaking (2)

Key WS 5 C

1. A *can't buy* → impossibility | **B** *must be* → speculation / probability | **C** *may I go* → (asking for) permission | **D** *can wear* → possibility / permission and *should* → advice (the implication is *you shouldn't* or *it's is not advisable*)

2.

a) i. advice | ii. necessity
b) i. possibility | ii. less likely
c) i. ability | ii. request
d) i. polite request | ii. quite likely possibility
e) i. lack of necessity | ii. it's prohibited
f) i. strong personal obligation | ii. obligation imposed from outside
g) i. moral obligation | ii. strong obligation | iii. advice, recommendation

3

Text 1
a: Can a vegan diet provide everything you need?
If you understand the basis of a healthy diet and plan effectively, you can get all the nutrients you need from a vegan diet. However,

if you aren't careful enough in your planning, you could miss out on some essentials such as vitamin B12 and iron.

b: health leaflet / website | can get / could miss out → both possibility

Text 2

a: So, when you fly east, such as from the Americas to Europe or Africa, you should go outside to get some bright light before people back home start to wake up. … This should help you get up more easily the next day.

b: travel advice leaflet / website | should go → advice / suggestion | should help → probability

Text 3

a: I'd visited my mother and emerged into daylight once more. I lit a cigarette and contemplated the day ahead.

"Excuse me," said an officious voice behind me. "You can't smoke here."

"Why not? I'm outside."

"You can't smoke anywhere on the hospital site."

"That's very odd. I could last time I was here."

b: novel / story | can't smoke / could → all permission / prohibition

Text 4

a: I am writing to let you know that unfortunately, I have to cancel the meeting that we had scheduled for 5.00 pm next Monday afternoon. Many apologies.

b: email / text | have to cancel → obligation / necessity

Text 5

a: And so I trudged along for hours, in a private little world of weariness and woe, up and over imposing hills through an endless cocktail of trees, all the time thinking: "I must have done seven miles by now, surely."

b: travel story | must have done → speculation / logical deduction

Text 6

a: "I don't know what he'll say. You just can't tell with him."

"A year, We've never been apart so long – or so far apart."

"If only you could come."

"Some hope." Patsy laughs. Cassie can hear baby Katie grumbling in her arms.

b: novel | can't tell → impossibility / could → possibility / can → ability

Text 7

a: Fresh water must be available at all times: if there is no natural source of water close by, then one must be provided. …

And finally, it goes without saying that if it wasn't already, your garden should now become an insecticide-free zone, for insecticides can also be blown towards hives by the wind.

b: handbook / website concerned with wildlife, insects etc. | must be / must be provided → obligation / necessity | should become → obligation / social responsibility | can → possibility

Key WS 6 C

1

zero conditional = c) and iv. | first conditional = d) and i. | second conditional = a) and iii. | third conditional = b) and ii.

2

a. If it'll make you feel any better, I'll phone him and tell him right now. (3x will future)

b. If you think (present simple) he's a good candidate, vote (imperative) for him.

c. He'd have been (would have + past participle) here by now if he was coming. (past continuous)

d. If she hadn't broken (past perfect simple) her arm, she'd be taking part (would be +-ing form) in the competition tomorrow.

Main point: all these sentences are mixed conditionals. They don't follow the "normal" pattern of first, second or third conditionals.

3

a) i. Something I always do as a matter of course.

ii. Something I will do if it happens (I think this is quite possible, even likely).

iii. Something I would do if it happened (I think this is unlikely).

b) i. The speaker thinks this is quite likely.

ii. The speaker thinks this is less likely – even unlikely.

iii. He failed his exam so he didn't go to Oxford University.

iv. He failed his exam so he didn't go to Oxford University, but this was his plan for next year.

4

a) Unless it rains, we'll go for a long walk tomorrow.

b) Unless we tell them, they won't know.

c) Unless you work harder, you'll fail your exam.

d) You can't go on holiday unless you've saved enough money.

5

Text 1: Action did not take place. He wasn't motoring in the vicinity / he wasn't intercepted.

Text 2: Possible: It is possible (though of course extremely unlikely) that the sun will stop burning.

Text 3: Action did not take place: He didn't stop singing mid-song.

Text 4: Possible: the writer could be late and he could whisper or snigger.

Text 5: It did not happen: Pete did not ask Allison.

Key Worksheet 7 C

1. a) Yes | b) Sentence 1 has an active verb / Sentences 2 and 3 have passive verbs. / Sentence 3 includes mention of the agent (who did the cancelling) | c) Sentence 3 (by the management). Sentences 1 and 2 don't give us this information because it is unnecessary or obvious and because the most important information is the fact of and the reason for the cancellation.

2.

a) who? - an unknown person
why? - for the very reason that the watcher is unknown

b) who? - everyone you might meet why? - it is obvious, therefore unnecessary

c) who? - whoever hosted the party
why? - it is obvious or it is embarrassing to say

d) who? - beer companies
why? - it is obvious – beer companies decide what containers are used for their beer

e) who? - white goods dealers
why? - it is obvious, so unnecessary to say

f) who? - anyone | why? - *You could be forgiven* is a standard expression which never includes the person who does the forgiving

3

P = past | Pr = present | F = future

Text 1

Morse code wasn't invented (P) to help people in dire emergencies, but to send messages along a telegraph wire … Morse came up with a method of sending signals that could be received (P) by a machine and marked (P) on to paper as dots and dashes.

→ written | history book, factual book

Text 2

In 1971 tax rates at the top were really high by today's standards, but had actually just been cut (P), from 90 per cent to 75 per cent. … They were raised (P) again in 1974 to 83 per cent, but there was also a charge on unearnt income of 15 per cent, …

→ written | book about politics or finance

Text 3

I was brought up (P) in a musical household so I started to learn by osmosis. As a youngster growing up in London, it was a remarkable period for high quality Irish music. When London was being rebuilt (P) after the war, it was mainly by Irish labour from rural Ireland, and they brought their music with them. I also had uncles on my mother's side from Connemara who played. Also, I was lucky enough to be taught (P) by one of the best Irish music teachers. The fact is I was given (P) every possible chance you can imagine.

→ written or spoken | interview, biography

Text 4

All over the globe, crimes are committed (Pr), wars are started (Pr), women are being held back (Pr), and economies are disastrously distorted (Pr) by men, because of their outdated version of masculinity.

→ written | opinion column

Text 5

"Okay, listen carefully. You'll be met (F) at the airport by a driver from the embassy. He'll take you straight to the meeting where you will be welcomed (F) by the other delegates."
"Can't I be taken (F) to my hotel before the meeting? I'd like to shower and change."
"No, I'm sorry. There isn't time."
→ spoken | conversation (face to face or on the phone)

Key WS 8 C

1

singular countable nouns: group, majority, population, area, company, process, policy | **plural countable nouns:** landscapes, rules, guidelines, levels, reductions, emissions, targets | **uncountable nouns:** fracking, democracy, countryside, damage, planning | **compound nouns:** countryside, guidelines, carbon emissions, climate change | **proper nouns:** England | **noun phrases:** the group I belong to, a majority of the population of the area, the wonderful countryside of England, serious damage to particular landscapes, the countryside as a whole, strict rules and regulations, democratic planning, the whole process, local and national levels, significant reductions in carbon emissions, planning policy, legally binding climate change targets

2

In sentences a, b, c and e the subjects of the verbs are singular nouns (*class / couple / England / government*) which are followed by plural verbs (*are / live / are / are*).
In the past, strict grammarians insisted on singular nouns being followed by singular verbs, but common usage now regards nouns like *class, couple* etc. as collective nouns which represent a plural reality (e.g. England as a team made up of individual players). It has become quite normal to use plural verbs in such cases. Other examples might include: *crew, staff, team, congregation,* the name of any sports team.
Sentence d has a singular subject noun (*audience*), and a singular verb (*is*). This pattern is more natural when the collective noun is regarded as a single entity rather a collection of individuals.

3

The underlined words are all adjectival nouns.

Key WS 9 C

1

comparative → heavier | compound → low-hanging | gradable → warm | possessive → our | superlative → busiest | ungradable → ravenous

2

comment → interestingly | degree → extremely | frequency → rarely | manner → gently | place → here | time → soon

3a

Text 1

For the second time that night her blood froze to ice and she wanted to scream, but no sound came out. There at the window, with the curtains pushed aside, was the enormous long pale wrinkly face of the Giant Person staring in. The flashing black eyes were fixed on Sophie's bed.

Text 2

We were travelling slowly on an incredibly busy section of the M3. Our ancient Renault 4 was surrounded on both sides by massive lorries, all of them evidently in a frantic hurry to get to Southampton. For much of the time they were closer to us than felt comfortable. We couldn't travel any faster than about 60. But amazingly we arrived there with 10 minutes to spare.

Text 3

According to many people, Robert Johnson is the greatest blues guitarist of all time and one of the founding fathers of rock 'n' roll. While his evocative and sometimes risqué lyrics have inspired singers of all kinds, it's his dazzling and innovative solo guitar playing that gives him place in the history of popular music.

Text 4

It was a mild autumn night, the wind playing the occasional sharp sound of someone slamming a door or closing a window. He lay across the doorstep, trying to avoid the pavement. A man passed, singing a happy song to himself, noticing nothing. Arthur was half asleep, but opened his eyes now and again to make sure the street was still there, to convince himself that he was not in bed, because the hard stone step was as round and as soft as a pillow.

Text 5

If there is a common denominator in all Indian foods, it is, perhaps, the imaginative use of spices. Does this mean that Indian food is always spicy? Well, in a sense it does. It always uses spices, sometimes, just one spice.

Text 6

Yesterday
All my troubles seemed so far away
Now it looks as though they're here to stay
Oh, I believe in yesterday

3b

Adjectives

comparative: closer (2) | **compound**: half asleep (4), far away (6) | **gradable**: long (1), pale (1), wrinkly (1), flashing (1), busy (2), comfortable (2), evocative (3), risqué (3), innovative (3), popular (3), mild (4), occasional (4), sharp (4), happy (4), hard (4), round (4), soft (4), common (5), imaginative (5), spicy (5) | **possessive**: our (2), my (6) | **superlative**: greatest (3) | **ungradable**: black (1), ancient (2), massive (2), frantic (2), dazzling (3), Indian (5)

Adverbs

comment amazingly (2), evidently (2) | **degree**: incredibly (2) | **frequency**: sometimes (3), always (5), sometimes (5) | **manner**: slowly (2), faster (2) | **place**: there (2), here (6) | **time**: yesterday (6) / now (6)

Key WS 10 C

1

a) The engineer was late for his appointment because his car broke down on the motorway.
b) Even though the accident wasn't my fault, I apologized profusely because I'm English.
c) Despite the fact that there is no

proof, many people believe that carrots help us see in the dark.
d) I'd like to make contact with an old school friend, but I can't find her address.
e) I was spending too much time playing games on my phone so I leave it at home when I go to work.

2 e.g.

Pablo Picasso, who was born in Malaga in 1881, was the son of an art teacher. He grew up in Spain but spent most of his adult life in France. His painting *Les Demoiselles d'Avignon*, which appeared in 1907 was famous because it introduced a new style of painting: Cubism. *Guernica*, which shows the horrors of the Spanish Civil War, was painted in 1937. Picasso had four children and died in France in 1973.

3

Text 1

While I was in Melbourne, I twisted my foot and broke two bones. They x-rayed my foot but they didn't pick up the breaks and I walked on it for a month until I got back to Perth and saw my doctor. He sent me for a scan, which showed up the breaks. This has caused lots of complications and I'm still seeing an orthopaedic surgeon. It's a real drag as I still can't walk far or exercise, which means we've had to cancel a scheduled trip to Sydney.

→ email or letter / maybe part of conversation

Text 2

Bees are remarkable little insects that have been around for about 100 million years or so, going quietly and efficiently about their business of gathering their food from the nectar and pollen produced by flowers. In doing so, they provide a valuable and vital service to the plants *[No relative pronoun]* they visit and ultimately to human beings and other animals, as they aid pollination through their foraging activities and thus ensure the spread and continuation of plant species.

→ handbook / encyclopaedia / website

Text 3

There were only two items of furniture that went with the house. One was a vast carved oak sideboard that must surely have been built in the dining room, for it could never have been brought in through the door; …

→ Novel / short story

Text 4

According to Thames Valley Police, the artwork, which is a fully-functioning 18-carat gold toilet called "America", was stolen from Blenheim Palace early on Saturday morning. It was installed near to the room in the palace where Winston Churchill was born. When the thieves removed it, there was serious flood damage.

→ newspaper report

Text 5

Musicals aren't usually my cup of tea, but the whole family wanted to watch it so I reluctantly agreed. To my surprise, I was grabbed from the start especially as it starred Hugh Jackman, an actor *[No relative pronoun]* I've always admired. Even if you don't like musicals, watch this.

→ letter / email / online review

4

a)

Defining relative clauses

Bees are remarkable little insects that have been around for about 100 million years (Text 2)
vital service to the plants they visit (Text 2)
two items of furniture that went with the house. (Text 3)
a vast carved oak sideboard that must surely have been built in the dining room (Text 3)
It was installed near to the room in the palace where Winston Churchill was born (Text 4)
it starred Hugh Jackman, an actor I've always admired (Text 5)

Non-defining relative clauses

which showed up the breaks. (Text 1)
which means we've had to cancel a scheduled trip to Sydney. (Text 1)
the artwork, which is a fully-functioning 18-carat gold toilet called "America" (Text 4)
b) I still can't walk far or exercise, which means we've had to cancel a scheduled trip to Sydney. (Text 1)
c) a vital service to the plants [No relative pronoun] they visit
d) It's a real drag as I still can't walk (Text 1)
as they aid pollination through their foraging activities (Text 2)
for it could never have been brought in through the door (Text 3)
because it had been connected to the water supply for visitors to use (Text 4)
I was grabbed from the start especially as it starred Hugh Jackman (Text 5)
e) I twisted my foot and broke two bones. (Text 1)
They x-rayed my foot but they didn't pick up the breaks and I walked on it for a month (Text 1)
I got back to Perth and saw my doctor. (Text 1)
they aid pollination through their foraging activities and thus ensure the spread and continuation of plant species. (Text 2)
but the whole family wanted to watch it (Text 5)
f) until I got back to Perth (Text 1)
as they aid pollination through their foraging activities (Text 2)
When the thieves removed it (Text 4)
so I reluctantly agreed (Text 5)
as it starred Hugh Jackman (Text 5)
if you don't like musicals, watch this. (Text 5)